CABINET
300 Nevins Street
Brooklyn, NY 11217 USA
phone + 1 718 222-8434
fax + 1 718 222-3700
info@cabinetmagazine.org
www.cabinetmagazine.org

Issue 63, Spring 2017

Cover: Photo by Dan Wilcox, 2012. In December 2012, Wilcox spent two weeks as a member of a five-person crew that participated in a simulated Mars mission in the high desert near Hanksville, Utah. The site, known as the Mars Desert Research Station, is operated by the non-profit Mars Society, which has hosted more than 180 simulated missions involving over a thousand individuals since 2001. The station includes a small, two-story cylindrical habitat in which the crew lives and works. Crew members wear space suits while outside, use compression airlocks to enter and exit the habitat, monitor their resource usage, and cook with dehydrated food. There is a greenhouse and an observatory, and all-terrain vehicles are used as Mars rovers. Wilcox's time at the station as a member of Crew 119 formed part of his research for his astronaut rock opera *robotcowboy: Onward to Mars*.

Cabinet (ISSN 1531-1430, USPS # 020-348) is a quarterly magazine published by Immaterial Incorporated, 181 Wyckoff Street, Brooklyn, NY 11217. Periodicals Postage paid at Brooklyn, NY, and additional mailing offices.

POSTMASTER: Please send address changes to Cabinet, 300 Nevins Street, Brooklyn, NY 11217.

Printed in Belgium by Die Keure, an oasis in the desert of printing.

ADVERTISING
phone + 1 718 222-8434
advertising@cabinetmagazine.org

DISTRIBUTION
Cabinet is available in the US and Canada through Disticor, which distributes both using its own network and through Ingram, Ubiquity, Small Changes, Cowley Distribution, Kent News, MSolutions, the News Group, Chris Stadler, and Don Olson Distribution.

To carry Cabinet through one of these distributors, contact Melanie Raucci at Disticor: phone + 1 631 587-1160, mraucci@disticor.com

Cabinet is available in Europe and elsewhere through Central Books, London: orders@centralbooks.com

Cabinet is available worldwide as a book, with an ISBN, through DAP: phone + 1 212 627-1999, dap@dapinc.com

For further information, contact: circulation@cabinetmagazine.org

INDIVIDUAL SUBSCRIPTIONS

1 year (4 issues):	2 years (8 issues):
US $32	US $60
Canada $38	Canada $72
Western Europe $40	Western Europe $76
Elsewhere $50	Elsewhere $96

Please send a check in US dollars made out to "Cabinet," or mail, fax, or email us your Visa/MC/AmEx/Discover info to:

300 Nevins Street
Brooklyn, NY 11217 USA
phone + 1 718 222-8434
fax + 1 718 222-3700
subscriptions@cabinetmagazine.org
www.cabinetmagazine.org/subscribe

INSTITUTIONAL SUBSCRIPTIONS
Institutional subscriptions are available through library agencies such as EBSCO, or directly from Cabinet:
www.cabinetmagazine.org/subscribe

SUBMISSIONS
We only accept submissions via email. Guidelines available at:
www.cabinetmagazine.org/information/submissions.php

Cabinet is a non-profit 501(c)(3) magazine published by Immaterial Incorporated. Our survival depends on support from generous foundations and individuals. Please consider supporting us at whatever level you can. Donations are tax-deductible for those who deal with Uncle Sam. All gifts are acknowledged online. Contributions of $25 or more will be acknowledged in the next possible issue; those above $100 will be noted in four issues. Checks to "Cabinet" can be sent to our office; please write "Don't feel deserted!" on the envelope.

Cabinet wishes to thank the following visionary foundations and individuals for their support of our activities during 2017. Additionally, we will forever be indebted to the extraordinary contribution of the Flora Family Foundation from 1999 to 2004; without their support, this publication would not exist. We would also like to extend our enormous gratitude to the Orphiflamme Foundation and the Opaline Fund for their generous support.

$100,000
The Lambent Foundation

$50,000
The Warhol Foundation for Visual Arts

$15,000
The New York City Department of Cultural Affairs

$10,000
The National Endowment for the Arts

$6,000
Margaret Sundell & Reinaldo Laddaga

$3,000
The Danielson Foundation

$1,500–$2,500
Stina & Herant Katchadourian, Steven Rand & Nancy Wender, Terry Winters

$501–$1,000
Anonymous, Martha & Thomas G. Armstrong, Sara Clugage, Spencer Finch, Christian Scheidemann, Sandy Tait & Hal Foster, Edward C. Wilson and Hesu Coue Wilson Family Fund

$500 or under
Pamela Cederquist, David Hariton & Tod Lippy, Steven Igou, Lenore & Richard Niles, Debra Singer & Jay Worthington

$250 or under
Tauba Auerbach, Jeff Beall, Mia Enell & Nicholas Fries, George Ganat, Alex Goodfriend, Cynthia Hansen, Peter Hapstak, Peter Jaszi, Craig Kalpakjian, James Katzenberger, Carin Kuoni & John Oakes, Scott LeBouef, Deborah Lovely, Meredith Martin & Joshua Siegel, Paul McConnell, Helen Mirra, Jason Olin, Andrew Pederson, Jocelyn Price & Christopher Leone, John Sargent, Eric Schmid, Pooja Shah & Rebecca Ward, John Sherburne, James Siena, Jude Tallichet & Matt Freedman, Volker Welter, Margaret Wertheim

$100 or under
Randi Cardia, Nelson Fitch, Susan Harris, Thomas Schmatzhagen, Ian Scott, David Skorton, Brad Threatt

CONTRIBUTORS

Leonard Barkan teaches comparative literature, as well as the history of art, at Princeton University. His most recent book is *Berlin for Jews: A Twenty-First Century Companion* (University of Chicago Press, 2016), and his current scholarly project, about eating and drinking from antiquity to the Renaissance, is entitled *Reading for the Food: Art, Literature, and the Hungry Eye.*

D. Graham Burnett is an editor of Cabinet and teaches at Princeton University. He is part of "The Year of the TransHistorical" at Mildred's Lane. Burnett is affiliated with the collective ESTAR(SER); for more information, see <www.estarser.net>.

Brian Dillon is UK editor of *Cabinet*, and teaches critical writing at the Royal College of Art, London. His books include Essayism (Fitzcarraldo Editions, 2017), *The Great Explosion* (Penguin, 2015), *Objects in This Mirror: Essays* (Sternberg Press, 2014), *I Am Sitting in a Room* (Cabinet Books, 2011), and *Sanctuary* (Sternberg Press, 2011). His writing has appeared in the *Guardian*, the *London Review of Books*, the *New York Times*, *Artforum*, and *frieze*. He is working on a book about Michael Powell and Emeric Pressburger's 1944 film *A Canterbury Tale*.

Emilio Distretti holds a PhD from the School of Art and Design at the University of Portsmouth, where his work focused on the aesthetics and politics of representation. A research fellow at the Council for British Research in the Levant's Kenyon Institute in East Jerusalem, he teaches urban studies and spatial practices at Al-Quds Bard College for Arts and Sciences in Abu Dis in the Occupied Palestinian Territories.

Chris Domenick is a multidisciplinary artist based in New York. His recent site-specific project *5 O D A Y S* was shown at MASS MoCA in North Adams, Massachusetts, and his exhibition "After the Sun" (in collaboration with Em Rooney) at the Vanity East in Los Angeles.

Yevgeniy Fiks is a New York–based artist. His books include *Lenin for Your Library?* (Ante Projects, 2007), *Communist Guide to New York City* (Common Books, 2008), *Moscow* (Ugly Duckling Presse, 2013), and *Soviet Moscow's Yiddish-Gay Dictionary* (Cicada Press, 2016).

Maria Golia is an American author who has been a longtime resident of Egypt. Her latest non-fiction book is *Meteorite: Nature and Culture* (Reaktion Books, 2015) and she is currently working on a book about musician and composer Ornette Coleman.

Elizabeth Knafo is a filmmaker, researcher, and graphic designer who lives in San Francisco. In 2016, she co-published *The Rare Earth Catalog: Tools for Reckoning with the Anthropocene* with Jesse Goldstein. For more information on her 2014 film *Rare Earth*, see <rareearthfilm.net>. For more information on her work, see <noctilucae.net>.

Michael Marder is Ikerbasque Professor of Philosophy at the University of the Basque Country in Spain and professor-at-large at the Humanities Institute, Diego Portales University, in Santiago, Chile. Among his most recent books are *Pyropolitics* (Rowman & Littlefield, 2015), *Dust* (Bloomsbury, 2016), and *Energy Dreams* (Columbia University Press, 2017).

Reed McConnell is a writer interested in environmental contamination and the American Southwest. She studies cultural history and theory at Humboldt University in Berlin.

David Scher is an artist living in New York City. He is represented by Pierogi in New York, Galerie Jean Brolly in Paris, and Galerie Ute Parduhn in Dusseldorf. In 1969, he cofounded o.n.e.m., a performance and music group that has persisted.

Tif Sigfrids is a gallerist based in Los Angeles. She is the recent recipient of the NADA Member Norwegian Residency, offered in collaboration with Unge Kunstneres Samfund.

Volker M. Welter teaches architectural history at the University of California, Santa Barbara. His books include *Biopolis: Patrick Geddes and the City of Life* (The MIT Press, 2002), *Ernst L. Freud, Architect: The Case of the Modern Bourgeois Home* (Berghahn, 2011), *Walter S. White: Inventions in Mid-Century Architecture* (Art, Design, and Architecture Museum, University of California, Santa Barbara, 2015), and *Tremaine Houses: Private Patronage of Mid-Century Domestic Architecture* (forthcoming).

Cecilia Sjöholm is professor of aesthetics at Södertörn University, Sweden. Her latest books include *Regionality/Mondiality: Perspectives on Art, Aesthetics and Globalization*, edited with Charlotte Bydler (Södertörn University Press, 2014), and *Doing Aesthetics with Arendt: How to See Things* (Columbia University Press, 2015).

COLUMNS

MAIN

THE DESERT

AND

COLUMNS

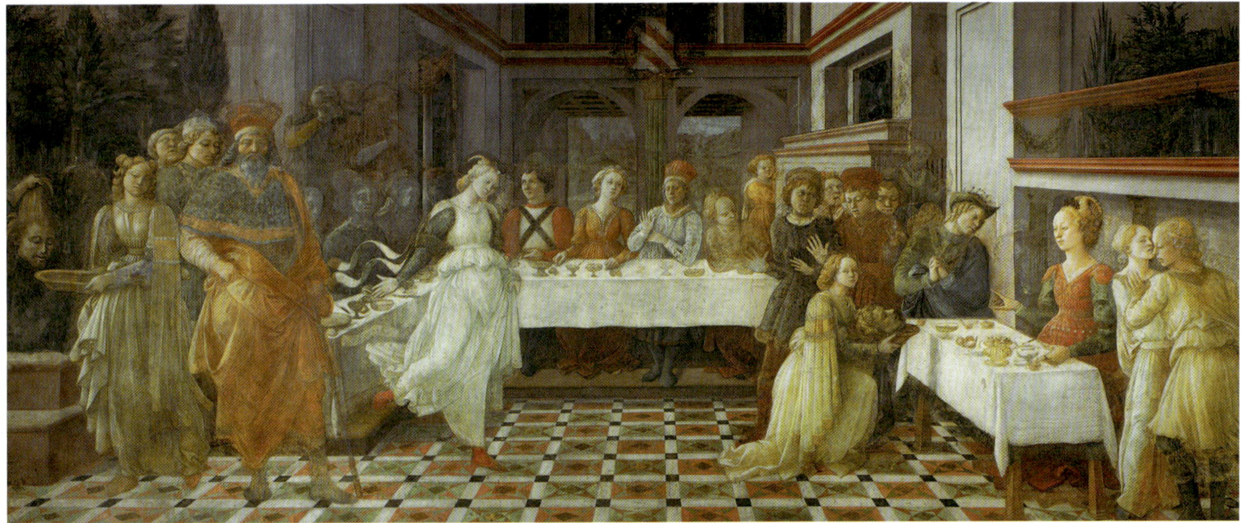

Filippo Lippi, "Herod's Feast," from *Scenes from the Life of Saint John the Baptist*, 1452–1466.

INGESTION / WHAT'S FOR DINNER?

Leonard Barkan

Suppose that you were a lonely analphabetic with no religious education—the year could be 2017 or 1617, it doesn't matter—and at the same time zealous for initiation into the narratives that the New Testament offers by way of instituting the Christian faith. You are fortunate enough to have access, whether by magic carpet or internet, to the world's treasury of sacred paintings. And from this rich sampling you set yourself to deduce the leading features of a creed that, from humble beginnings in Galilee, managed to spread its good news throughout the world.

You might well conclude that it was all about the lure of dinner parties.

If Jesus is sitting with two other guys and staring meaningfully at the bread, it's the Supper at Emmaus. If He is seated at a heavily laden banquet table in a big crowd and a woman is washing his feet, it's Christ in the House of Simon the Pharisee. If He is seated at a similar table but no woman is washing his feet, it's Christ in the House of Levi. If He is part of a domestic scene with one woman at his feet and another woman cooking, it's Christ in the House of Mary and Martha. If He is surrounded by a bunch of his man friends and there is bread and wine on the table, it's the Last Supper. If He is holding out loaves with one hand and fishes with the other, it's the Feeding of the Five Thousand, or it might be the Feeding of the Four Thousand. The bottom line is that He did a lot of feeding.

All of which suggests that we ought to pardon our hypothetical novice in matters Christian if she comes to believe that this is some kind of gastronomical eating club. She'd be quite mistaken, of course. The truth is that it's not Matthew, Mark, Luke, and John who have proclaimed this culinary sect; it's the painters following in their textual footsteps. For visual artists, whether medieval, Renaissance, or working in any other age, the project of depicting, say, the virgin birth, one God in three persons, or transubstantiation versus consubstantiation, is something of an uphill struggle, and not always easy on the spectators either. On the other hand, who doesn't like a dinner party? And so it comes to pass that Christianity on the walls of museums and even of churches may appear out of all proportion an affair of the dinner table.

These same cuisine-happy artists, as it turns out, were not content with merely depicting the consumption of meals as the Bible specified them; they insisted on pushing the envelope. Bread and wine are hardly sufficient for many a painter of the Last Supper, so their Holy Tables groan under the weight of what we in Manhattan used to refer to as a Great Neck bar mitzvah. Dozens of Madonna and Child paintings are decorated with a quite extraneous piece of fruit, whose variety—apples, grapes, pomegranates, cherries—suggests that it doesn't amount to a piece of sacred allegory so much as a means to enable viewers contemplating the Holy Mother and Child to fix their minds on something juicy at the same time.

Then there is the case of Herod and his feast. The biblical account—as sketchy as Bible history tends to be—needs some decoding. Herod Antipas (not Herod the Great of the Slaughter of the Innocents fame, but his son), hearing for the first time about Jesus's ministry, imagines that the new itinerant prophet is in fact the old one, John the Baptist, who has

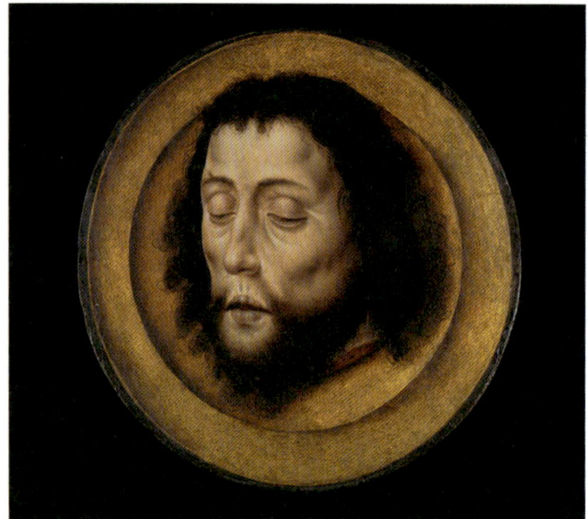

Aelbert Bouts, *Head of Saint John the Baptist on a Charger* (detail), ca. 1500.

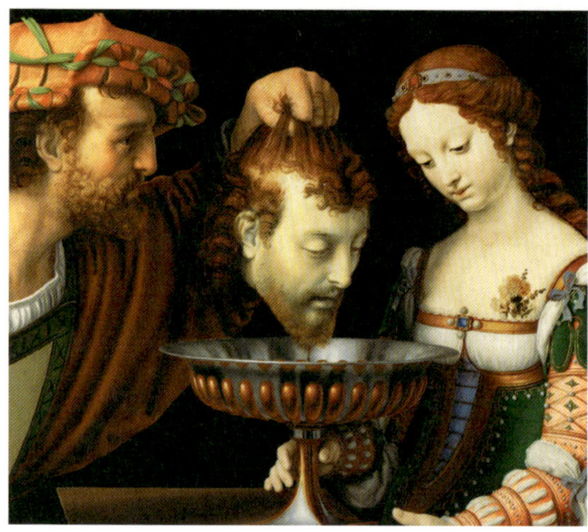

Andrea Solario, *Salome with the Head of Saint John the Baptist* (detail), ca. 1520–1524.

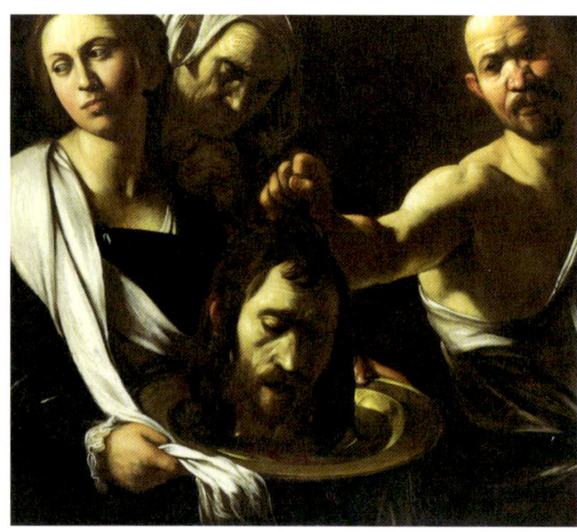

Caravaggio, *Salome Receives the Head of John the Baptist* (detail), 1607–1610.

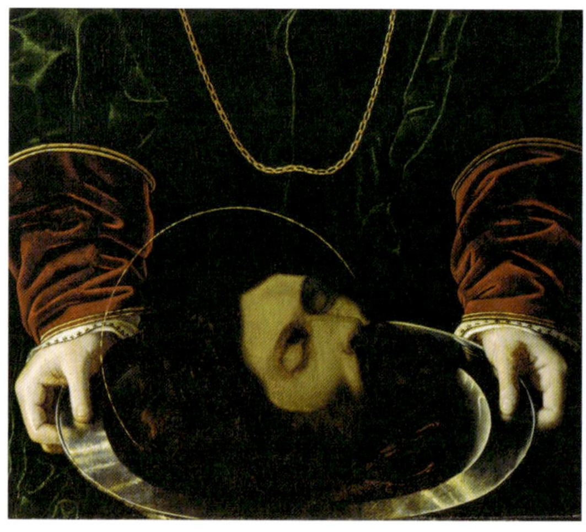

Bartolomeo Veneto, *Salome with the Head of Saint John the Baptist* (detail), early sixteenth century.

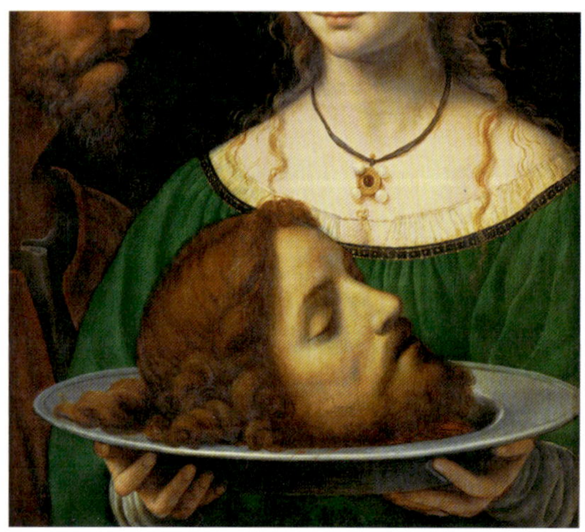

Bernardino Luini, *Salome with the Head of Saint John the Baptist* (detail), ca. 1525–1530.

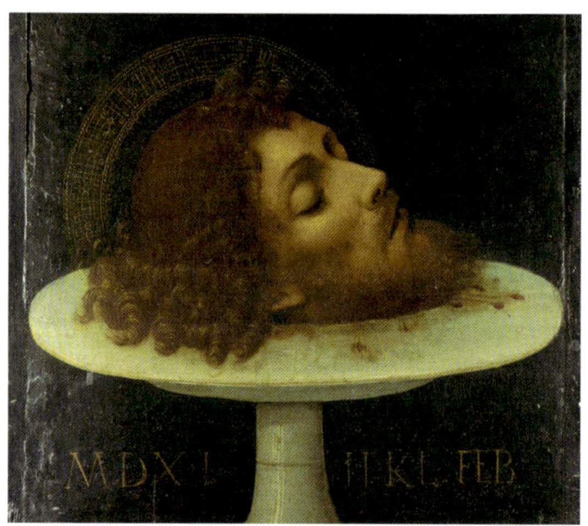

The Head of Saint John the Baptist (detail), 1511. Unknown Italian artist.

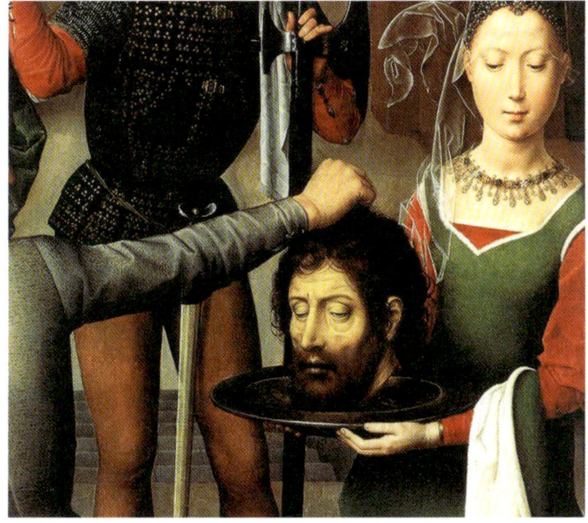

Hans Memling, *St. John Altarpiece* (detail), ca. 1474–1479.

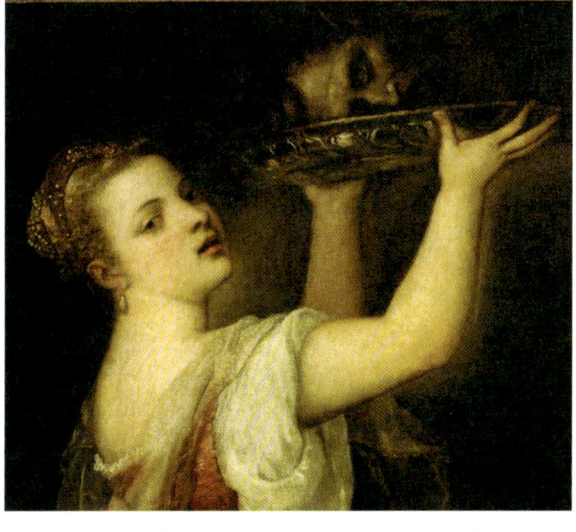

Titian, *Salome with the Head of John the Baptist* (detail), 1549.

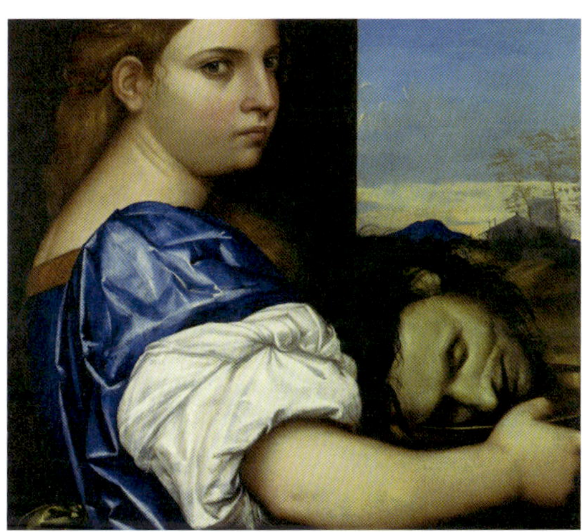

Sebastiano del Piombo, *The Daughter of Herodias* (detail), 1510.

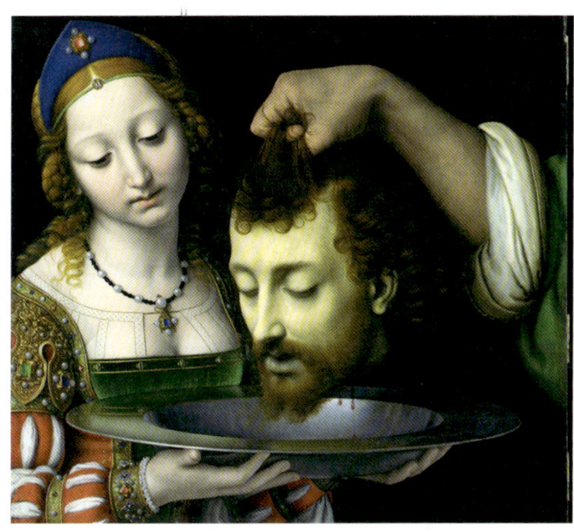

Andrea Solario, *Salome with the Head of Saint John the Baptist* (detail), undated.

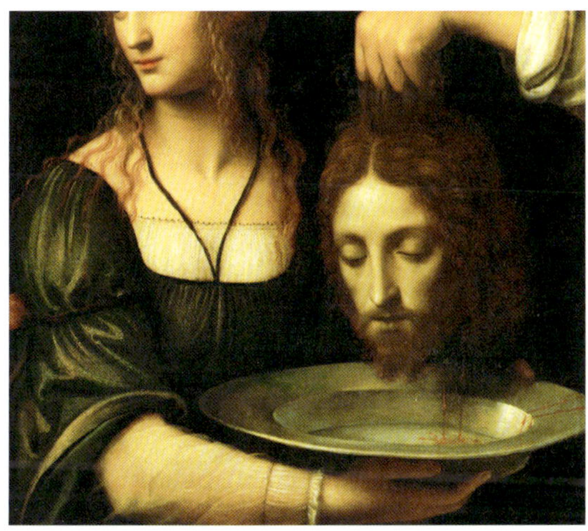

Bernardino Luini, *Salome Receives the Head of Saint John the Baptist* (detail), 1525–1530.

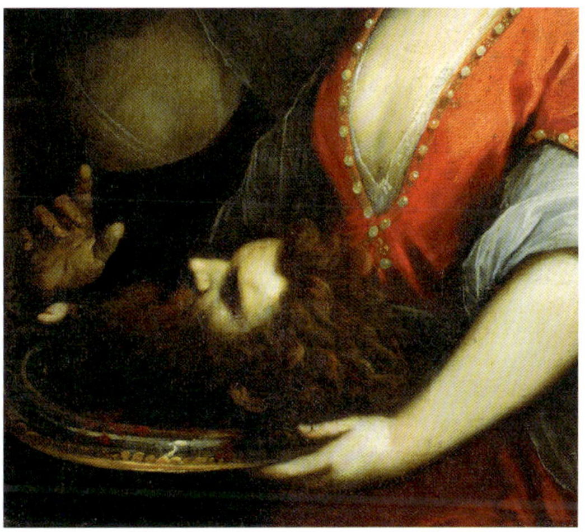

Jacopo Palma the Younger, *Salome with the Head of Saint John the Baptist* (detail), ca. 1599.

come back from the dead. At which point the whole story about Salome and the severed head gets introduced as a flashback informing us how John came to be dead. The scene in the biblical text is not a meal at all but rather a birthday party, which Herod has thrown for himself. This is the occasion when his stepdaughter provides the fatal entertainment.

On the premise of this celebration, gastronomic extravaganza erupts among the painters. As early as Giotto in the beginning of the fourteenth century, Herod's party becomes a grand occasion for banqueting. The biblical dance is taking place, but the largest share of picture space is devoted to a richly appointed dining room, at the center of which, on a pedestal, we see the table decorated with dishes and napery. An out-of-scale viola da gamba player is presumably on the scene in order to accompany Salome, but his placement is such that he could just as easily be construed as providing background music for the feast.

By the time of the High Renaissance a hundred and fifty years later, banqueting has all but swallowed up the story. Both Ghirlandaio and Filippo Lippi seize the occasion for the display of the most grandiose *all'antica* architecture, appropriate to Herod's status as a dependent of the Roman empire and designed along sharply perspectival lines. No expense has been spared on these two occasions of feasting: gleaming linens, elegant service pieces, the diners themselves in their finest attire. Ghirlandaio goes so far as to include a wall of gleaming gold and silver chargers, not being used for service, an act of conspicuous consumption along the lines of the advice given to Renaissance Italian princes that, while some dinnerware should be both beautiful and useful, other pieces should be used "for ornament and elegance alone." In both these late quattrocento frescoes, then, the principal business of the biblical story is overshadowed by the wish to present the latest and grandest fashions of banqueting.

Yet considering the outcome, there is bound to be something strange at this particular dinner. More of the backstory: back in the long-ago days when the Baptist was stirring up trouble in Judaea, Herod had been something of a protector, finding the prophet to be "a righteous and holy man" (Mark 6:20). But now—or rather in the more proximate past—John, with his tendency toward religious fundamentalism, has been declaring that Herod's marriage to his own brother's wife (the brother not yet being dead) is illegitimate. The wife, Herodias, has taken that judgment very ill. And she is one to carry a grudge.

Back to the bare-bones biblical narrative, then: Herod has a birthday; Salome dances. There is no banquet, no china, no silver, but there is something quite unexpected. Salome dances so alluringly that Herod offers to grant any imaginable wish, even, he says, half his kingdom. The girl herself shows no signs of having any wish in mind, but defers to her mother. Herodias, in no state of uncertainty at all, seizes her moment of vengeance and demands the head of John the Baptist. In Matthew, we hear this only in Salome's voice; in Mark, Herodias says it and Salome repeats it with a difference. In either case, it is Salome who frames the crucial form of the demand: the head of John the Baptist on a platter. Why *on a platter*? This curious supplement to the request for beheading has, so far as I can tell, excited rather little commentary, though it would seem to beg for exegesis. It does not appear to be a linguistic problem: the phrase itself, ἐπὶ πίνακι (in the Vulgate, *in disco*), is straightforward and gets translated variously as on a trencher, a charger, a platter, or a plate. In short, the kind of flat disk on which food is served.

What kind of intensification, whether arising from Herodias or magnified in Salome's transmission of the demand, is this? Not just dead, but decapitated, the head not just severed but on display, not just on display but subject to the formalities of a social occasion—indeed, the sort of occasion at which Salome has performed the dance that has set the whole chain of events in motion. Now that the head is to be presented on a platter, it may be less of a surprise that the occasion tips from a dance recital to a dinner. And, through the magic of narrative prolepsis, propelled by Salome's further specification that it be done *at once* (ἐξαυτῆς, *protinus* in the Vulgate), it turns into the kind of fiction where everything can happen simultaneously. Before the evening's festivities are over, the Baptist can be located in his prison cell, beheaded, and, as it were, served. Perfect for a medium like painting, in which long stories have to be displayed as though they took place in a single moment.

Though the artists may have imposed dinner upon a foodless biblical birthday party, scripture nonetheless was handing them a piece of narrative that cried out for the imagery of the feast, albeit of a perverse kind. Whatever the extent of dining paraphernalia in the visual production of artists from Giotto to the Renaissance, the Baptist's head becomes the evening's culinary *pièce de resistance*. The figure of the inclining servant, in banquet array, offering up the grisly platter in full view becomes quite canonical. It is exactly the posture for displaying to princely diners some highly confected piece of culinary art. Indeed, it fulfills the traditional Renaissance demand for elaborate visual presentation at grand dinners, more important even than the flavor once the food was tasted. The motif makes an appearance as early as Giotto and gets frequently replicated thereafter. Ghirlandaio places the kneeling servant discreetly at some distance from the diners, but Filippo Lippi erases that distance

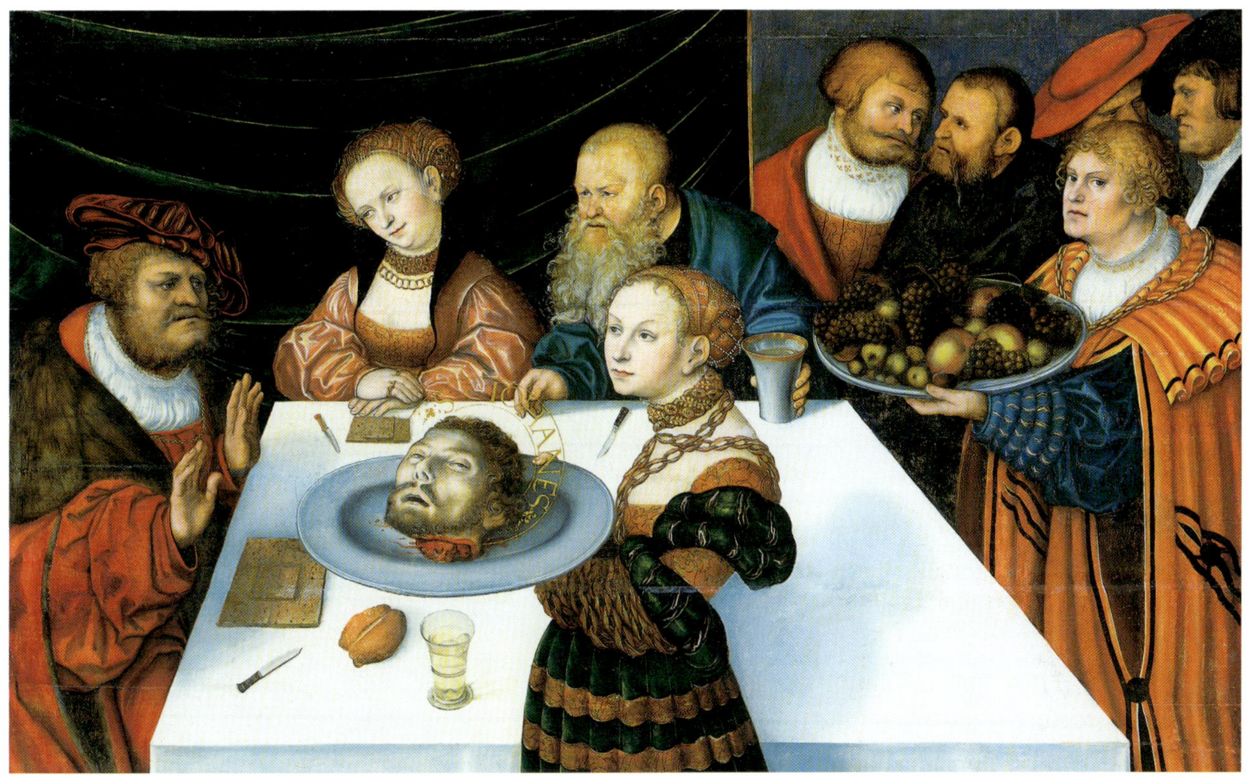

Lucas Cranach the Elder, *Herod's Banquet* (detail), 1533.

and has a female figure—not, I think, Salome, who is dancing off to the left—delivering the macabre menu item directly in front of the banquet table.

Is it, as I suggested in enumerating the representation of all of Jesus's feasts, that the painterly lure of the banquet extends so far as to make John the Baptist a cannibal sacrifice? Or was the Bible itself, with that fatal phrase "on a platter," indulging in the gruesome business of conflating dinner with decapitation, leaving the artists merely to realize in paint what lay implicit in words? Or am I just being a modern revisionist with his mind on the bizarre and the gastronomical?

One artist, transalpine and a few decades later into the Renaissance, may suggest some consciousness of what is at stake in this piece of startling visuality. Lucas Cranach was a painter of very considerable versatility, as comfortable with nude Venuses as with portraits of Luther, a maker of serious altarpieces but also capable of pictorial play, like his *Fountain of Youth*, where old women are transported via wheelbarrow to a swimming pool and emerge young and beautiful on the other side. Whether it was part of his piety or his love for the bizarre, he seems to have had a special taste for sacred beheading, as witness his numerous versions of Judith and Holofernes as well as his several Salomes. Indeed, the beautiful young woman holding the head of a decapitated greybeard is almost a Cranach signature piece.

Cranach's full-scale *Feast of Herod* is a bit different, though. As with many of his works, we have multiple versions, some of which may be even posthumous studio work undertaken by his son. The painting in Frankfurt is widely, and I think correctly, held to be autograph. As one might expect from its northern origins, the painting's subject here is not grand princely dining but more like a family affair among the well-heeled bourgeoisie. The linen is simple, the table appointments minimal. No curtsying liveried servant presents the severed head but, one presumes, Salome herself. There is no question, nevertheless, that this offering is (as it is with the Italians) to be understood in the category of dinner. Cranach in fact makes the point quite unmistakably. To the right of the dining scene, in perfect parallel to Salome with her platter, is another well-dressed figure who carries another platter. One is left to assume that he is part of a mealtime service sequence. On this second platter is a handsome array of apples, pears, and grapes. There is no missing the joke: John the Baptist is the main course; afterwards, there is fruit for dessert. Or in case we *do* miss the joke, we have the fruit server himself gazing outside the scene and making direct eye contact with us, as if to say, "Get it?"

COLORS / SIENNA

Tif Sigfrids

According to a favored website for parents, the name Sienna ranks 182nd in popularity among its members, up six positions this year from its standing in 2016. The meaning of the name, according to the website, is "reddish brown." Now, if these hordes of modern parents naming their daughters Sienna were being true to the defining characteristics of the color, they would either name their kids Burnt Sienna or request that babycenter.com change its definition to "yellow brown," but who is really keeping track of these Lilliputian shades of difference. Aside from a parental predilection for earthy, ocher tones, it is otherwise possible that scores of daughters across the world are being conceived on romantic Italian vacations or in Toyota minivans throughout America. When taking into account the origins of sienna, the color derived from an earth pigment and named after the city-state in Tuscany—whose own name may or may not be derived from the Latin word *senex*, meaning old—a fashionable level of baby-naming irony is achieved.

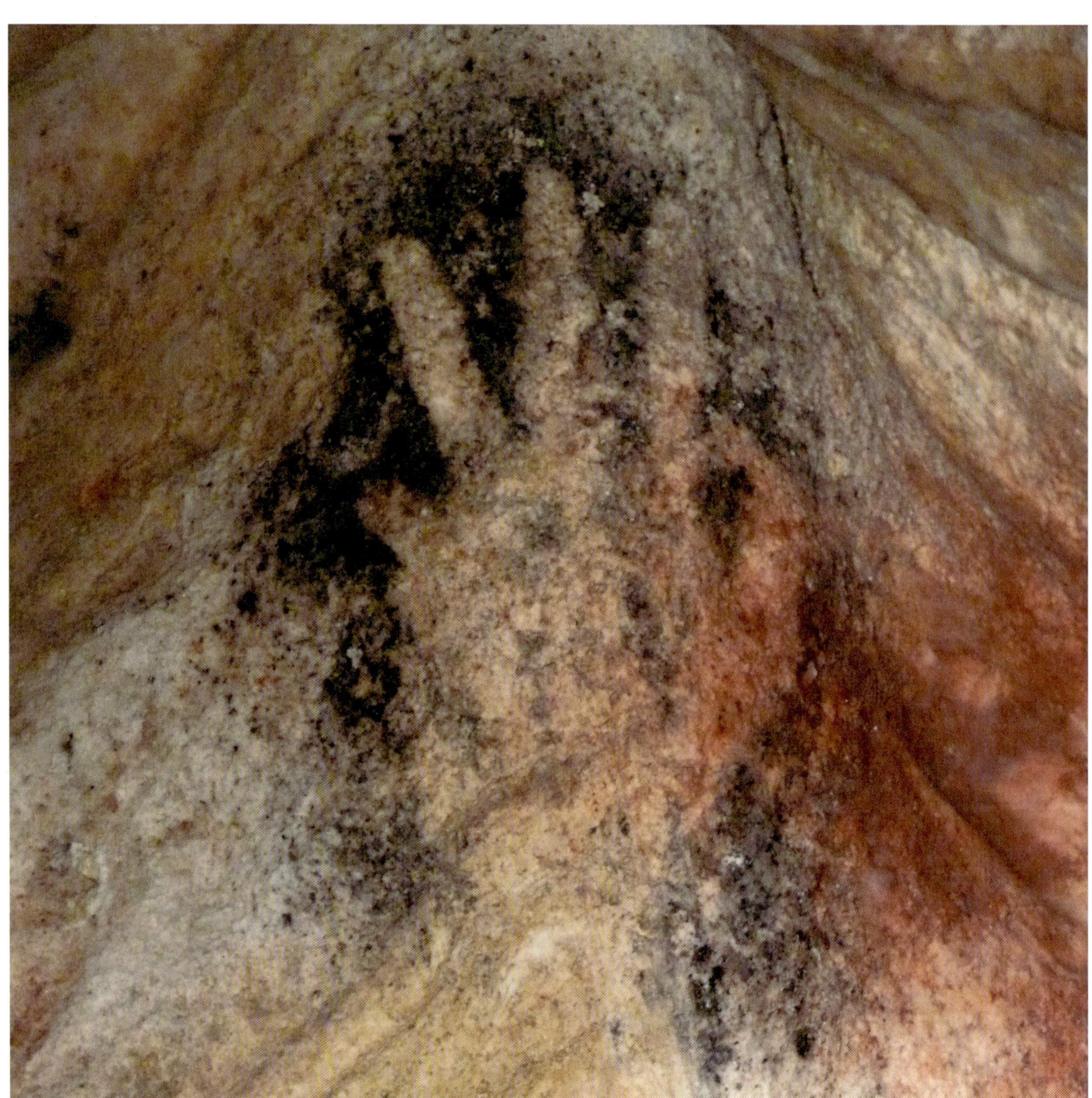

But truly, sienna is old. So old that we might, in fact, call it the first color—a color that has been around since the latter part of the Reindeer Age and a material for art making since the miracle of art making began. Within the interiors of tucked-away caves around the world, tools gained a more playful and delicate purpose as humans began using them to grind pigments into powder form. In his "Lascaux, or the Birth of Art," Georges Bataille breaks down the lineage of tool technology and its role in the development of humankind into two essential categories. The first are tools for labor, which in the early times of the Neanderthals would have meant those used to provide sustenance—tools for digging, hunting, cutting, and so on. The second category resulted from the eventual sublimation of work-oriented devices into art- and object-making devices—tools that incite the slightly more frivolous activities of play. *Homo faber* is joined in the fire-lit cavern by *homo sapiens*, who brought along an illustrative presence, and perhaps, a little bit of idle time to reminisce and replay the events of the day gone by.

Not unlike the room of a prodigious tobacco smoker where the yellow-brown stains of nicotine tint the atmosphere and furniture, the early dwellings and artistic grottos of early humans were colored with sienna. With tools freed from utilitarian tasks, powders of various colors were blown through hollowed-out bones onto dark, cavernous surfaces, tracing imprints of hands that waved to say hello for the first time. Depictions of wildlife in red, yellow brown, and charcoal leapt across these hidden stone walls spanning six continents. According to Bataille, the Aurignacian artists behind the paintings "were probably no less gay, no less merry, no less sensual than the Tibetans. We know almost nothing about them. True. Buy why attribute our own grave seriousness to them? Human laughter began somewhere. Perhaps not with Neanderthal Man; but Lascaux Man laughed."

And so, with its distinguished beginnings alongside the advent of man, art, and comedy, sienna's prominence proceeded into heavier times. Certainly, it is fair to say that laughter, gaiety, and the desire to draw out experience did not supplant toil, but it is our bit of fortune at least that this addition to our creative quiver in life has enriched experience. Or, one might say, the ability to accompany the necessities of toil, and its effects, with the visual articulation of representation and hindsight propelled humankind to a degree of self-reflection and examination that ultimately makes us more human.

Not to dissuade any would-be givers of the name, or even more so, not to offend anyone who proudly wears the title (however it was conceived), but sienna, and its fellow hues in the overarching brown spectrum, are characterized by some as "the least glamorous of pigments." Unlike its primary neighbors in the color wheel—think the loudness of red or the searing brightness of yellow—it has no vibrant pop. Rather, it's more somber, thoughtful, and subdued in tone. During the Renaissance, this color and its generally autumnal palette figured greatly into the golden glows and shadowy renderings of what are now deemed masterpieces. But perhaps the best-known agent for the ground pigment—comprised of iron oxide and manganese oxide—was Rembrandt, who loaded his canvases with every variety of earth color to create those bright lights and bulky shadows. The seventeenth-century painter worked with the earthy tone to great economical effect, and happily for conservators and, really, any art viewer these days, the pigment has proved to be stable, not losing its nature or integrity over time. As Morris Louis once said, "Materials influence form," and such was the case with sienna, with all its potential for complexity in both its raw and burnt forms. Sienna maintained its popularity from the beginnings of man right through the Renaissance, and its continued presence in the art that we view on the walls of both caves and museums results from its lasting qualities as a pigment. For some reason, it's one of those colors that ages really well. Both Rembrandt and early man had good intuition here.

But to return to the laughing man, of Lascaux or otherwise—if there has ever been an artist to have absorbed the story of sienna and reflected its symbolic representation of art's potential to free man from a tedious life of drudgery, it can only be Marcel Duchamp, who once famously said, "I like living, breathing, better then working." Looking at his *Chocolate Grinder* or *The Large Glass*, one can detect the hues of sienna in the yellows and browns of mechanical lines as they curiously merge with suggestive bodily forms. *The Large Glass*—or *The Bride Stripped Bare by Her Bachelors, Even*, to give the official name—details the process of grinding oneself, one's own chocolate sienna pigment, into the generative substance essential to a few different creative processes. And perhaps not coincidentally, it was around the same time that the sienna mines throughout Italy were depleted that Duchamp took an early retirement from art making and took up the game of chess.

Opposite: Paleolithic man says hello. These cave paintings from approximately 25,000 BC are located near the town of Gargas in the Luberon area of France, which is also home to a number of mines that produce sienna.

SENTENCES / A RITUAL FEAT

Brian Dillon

"This was the universe about which we have read so much and never before felt: the universe as a clockwork of loose spheres flung at stupefying, unauthorized speeds."
—Annie Dillard

On February 26, 1979, the shadow of the moon passed over Greenland, parts of Canada, and the states of North Dakota, Washington, Oregon, Idaho, and Montana. Elsewhere in North America, the skies merely dimmed appreciably and portions of varying size—from nail clipping to rocker knife or *mezzaluna*—were seen (do not look directly!) to be excised from the solar disc. But at the pencil point where the moon's cone of darkness met the earth's surface, all went black. It was the last total eclipse to be seen in the United States in the twentieth century, and TV anchormen counted the hours, minutes, and seconds to totality as if awaiting a moonshot or election result. A certain portentousness entered their language: an ABC announcer spoke of the "ritual feat" by which crowds sought the best vantage points, and addressed himself to viewers of the next total eclipse visible in the United States, on August 21, 2017: "May the shadow of the moon fall on a world in peace."

Annie Dillard published her essay "Total Eclipse" in the Spring/Summer 1982 issue of the literary quarterly *Antaeus*, and again later that year in her book *Teaching a Stone to Talk*. "It had been like dying, that sliding down the mountain pass"—the piece begins with the first of several descents, the first inkling that looking at the spectacle in the sky might also demand a glimpse within, a journey down "into the region of dread." The writer and her husband, Gary, are in a hotel near Yakima, Washington, and some unease about the very act of seeing is already in the air. Dillard lies in bed and tries not to look at a picture on the hotel-room wall: "It was a print of a detailed and lifelike painting of a smiling clown's head, made out of vegetables." In the two years that have passed between the eclipse and the writing of the essay, Dillard has forgotten many things, but not it seems this face, this Arcimboldo *manqué*, "or its lunatic setting in the old hotel."

The question is, in "Total Eclipse": Does Dillard know what she's looking at? A gulf opens, long before the moment of totality, between seeing and understanding: a void into which the author is pitched and must come up clutching—what? Images that might be real or might be metaphors, pictures composed of odd comparisons, efforts in prose not to end up missing the event, botching its description and placing on the page the written equivalent of a clown face made of vegetables. Attaining the top of a hill from which she'll view the eclipse, Dillard remarks that the valley below looks "like a thickness or sediment at the bottom of the sky." The air darkens without warning, like a race with no starter gun. The grass on the hill turns to platinum. The scene starts to resemble a photograph from the nineteenth century. Gary is in the photograph, and he seems to be speeding away, "down a chute of time." The moon heaves into position—"It did not look like the moon. It was enormous and black." People start to scream.

The sentence comes later, following totality and the shining miracle of an accompanying corona, in the aftermath of those deathly seconds, when the stone has been rolled away again. Everybody leaves quickly. Dillard and her husband find a restaurant full of other watchers, where they come back to life and start straight away to forget what they have just seen: after all, the "clamoring mind will hush if you give it an egg." Dillard struggles to recall the screaming and the speed of it all. Then the sentence: "This was the universe about which we have read so much and never before felt: the universe as a clockwork of loose spheres flung at stupefying, unauthorized speeds." There are small oddities and excellences of technique to admire in this sentence. The absence of a comma after "universe," which half implies there might be another one. The slight shift of tense, from "this was" to "have read." The combination of "stupefying" and "unauthorized," as if the universe were some ramshackle fairground ride that a delinquent carny boy has set going full pelt while his boss is not looking. The sentence, with its central colon, feels balanced but loose, centrifugal and strange.

But the sentence's more exacting thrills are in the nature of the image that it asks us to conjure. All along Dillard has had trouble *seeing*, but really seeing, the landscape and the appalling event—"appalling," that is, in the sense of casting a pall, shrouding itself at the moment it actually happens. It's the eye as much as mind that is "stupefied." She has to force herself—she who has hardly any knowledge of or feeling for physics, so she says—to picture otherwise what is going on: the music of the spheres gone manically out of tune, the stately orrery of the solar system running ragged. "How could anything moving so fast not crash, not veer from its orbit amok like a car out of control on a turn?" This amazing sight—just once in most lifetimes, so the ABC man says—is also a demand, or a test, as if an importuning divine voice had started up in the moment of totality: *Put you paltry language to work on* this, *mortal.*

To the alert and troubled essayist, a total eclipse is both a descriptive challenge and an opportunity to point, in description itself, to the limits of description: the lapses and

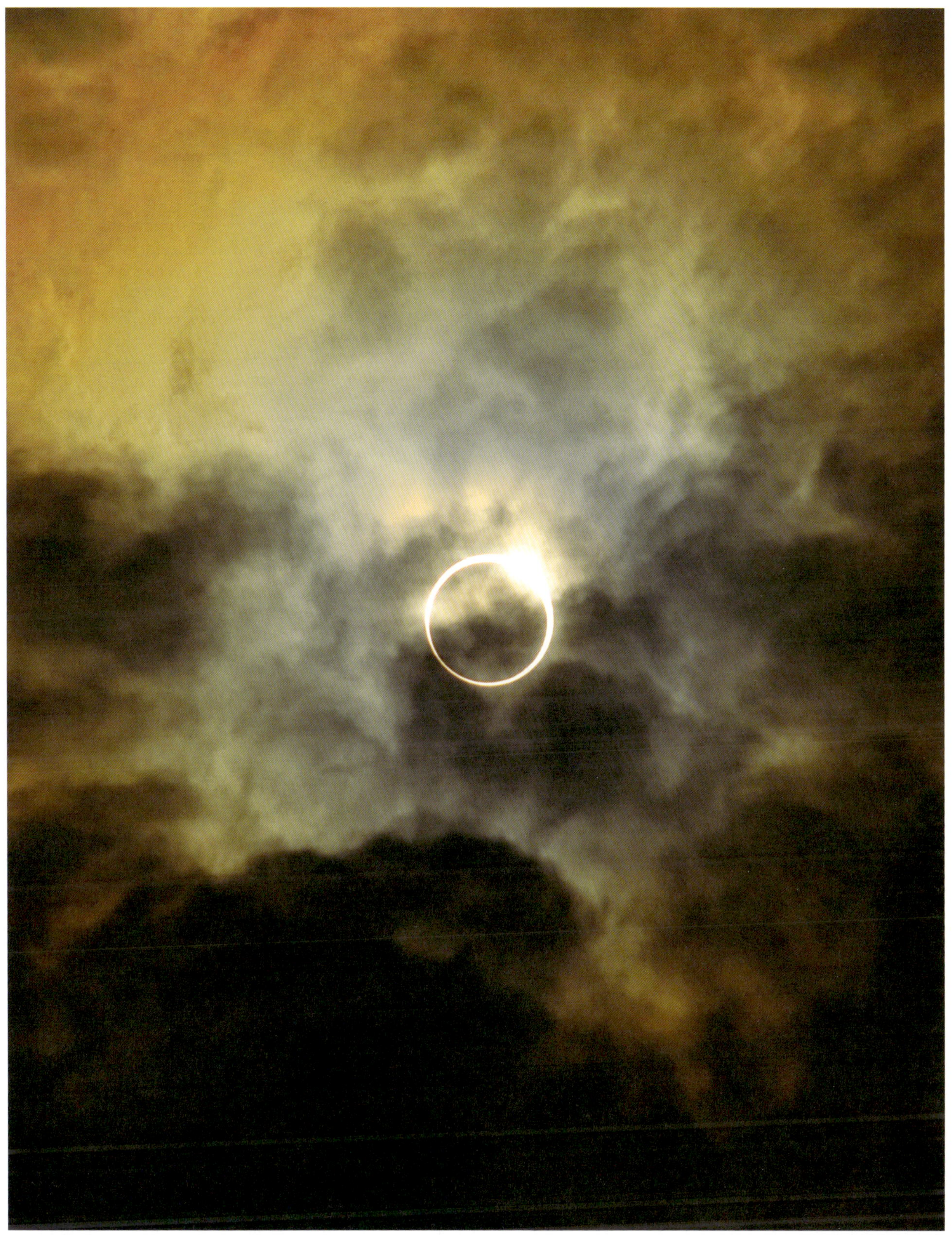

Solar eclipse over Tokyo, 21 May 2012. Photo Ken Okazaki.

pratfalls to which the writer's figural powers may succumb. In "The Sun and the Fish," her 1928 essay on viewing an eclipse in Yorkshire, Virginia Woolf prefaces the main event with a passage about her own variable facility for making word and image match in the mind. "When one says Queen Victoria, one draws up the most heterogeneous collection of objects, which it will take a week at least to sort." But when she says "Mont Blanc" or "Taj Mahal"—nothing, her mind is blank. Images marry emotions, and hope to thrive, but sometimes they do not. "Let us see that strange spectacle again"—the eclipse promises much when recalled by the writer. And sure enough, the images and metaphors proliferate: the sun is defeated in a race with the moon, the eclipse is like "the heeling over of a boat," the earth is skeletal and dead: "It hung beneath us, like a cage, like a hoop, like a globe of glass." But these images are swiftly overtaken by the memory of lizards and fish at London Zoo, and the way a bubble rises in an aquarium: "The silver drop bores its way up a spiral staircase."

What if Dillard's sentence is also a reflection on descriptive and figural language, on the fragile machinery of words and sentences and paragraphs, on the adventures (and consolations) this equipment makes possible? Early on in "Total Eclipse," she notes the presence in the hotel lobby of an aquarium with one large fish, and nearby a canary in its cage: "Beneath the cage, among spilled millet seeds on the carpet, were a decorated child's sand bucket and matching sand shovel." The bucket and shovel return, following the eclipse, when Dillard is sitting in the restaurant and hears a college student exclaim of the corona: "Did you see that little white ring? It looked like a Life Saver. It looked like a Life Saver up in the sky." And so it did, says Dillard. The young man has retained a power of image making, however modest, that the essayist has temporarily lost. "The mind—the culture—has two little tools, grammar and lexicon: a decorated sand bucket and a matching shovel. With these we bluster about the continents and do all the world's work. With these we try to save our very lives."

In the hotel lobby too, at six in the morning, are six bald old men stupefied in front of the television. Most of them are awake, but it seems they might miss the eclipse: "You might drown in your own spittle, God knows, at any time; you might wake up dead in a small hotel, a cabbage head watching TV while snows pile up in the passes, watching TV while the chili peppers smile and the moon passes over the sun and nothing changes and nothing is learned because you have lost your bucket and shovel and no longer care." It's not clear to Dillard, who has come with the tools (or are they just a child's toys?) of word and syntax, that she will fare any better than these men when it comes to capturing the miracle. But in the meantime, it is hard not to see that they are part of the sentence too, that they compose their own lazy little universe, that their hairless old heads are loose spheres orbiting the vacancy of the TV, hoping some image will resolve itself.

INVENTORY / BY ANY OTHER NAME
Cabinet

During a recent spring cleaning of our digital files, we discovered an unusual "historical" document from 1999 hiding in a disused folder named "magazine descriptions/ names." The file contains all the names considered, in moments of greater and lesser sobriety, while planning the first issue of this publication. It will be immediately clear why some of these names were rejected; what will be less clear is why some of them were ever there. So, dear readers, we hope you enjoy this issue of *Chalk and Cheese*. If not, try a subscription to *The Relentless Friend*, or any of the other stellar publications you might care to imagine into being from the following list.

Dit Dah
n
x
And…
Dotted Line
Appendix
Datum
i.e.
Fraction
Matter
Matters
Whetstone
The Wrench
Oven
Thermometer
Gauge
Grist
Mill
Coil
Rope
Immaterial
Locus
Parallax
The Wedge
The Fork
Omnivore
Mixer
Impurities
Alloy
Alloy: A Magazine for the Impurities of Mind and Matter
Collisions: A Magazine
for Impure Cultural
Phenomena
CROP, or C.R.O.P.
The Ostrich
Out of Joint
Compound
Chalk and Cheese
Betwixt (and Between)
Intermodal
Collisions
Strange Bedfellows
The Friend
The Relentless Friend
Dummy
Unq
Lead
Lead Balloon
Might
Rough Draft
Falls, The Falls
Suitcase
Baggage
Trunk
Silo
Information Van
Fill, Landfill, Page-Fill
Draft
Floss
Patch
The Pill
The Pharmacy
March
Spur
Trampoline
Bandwidth
Blink
Vein
In the Head
Plot
Soggy
Fin

MAIN

REAMBIGUATION

D. Graham Burnett

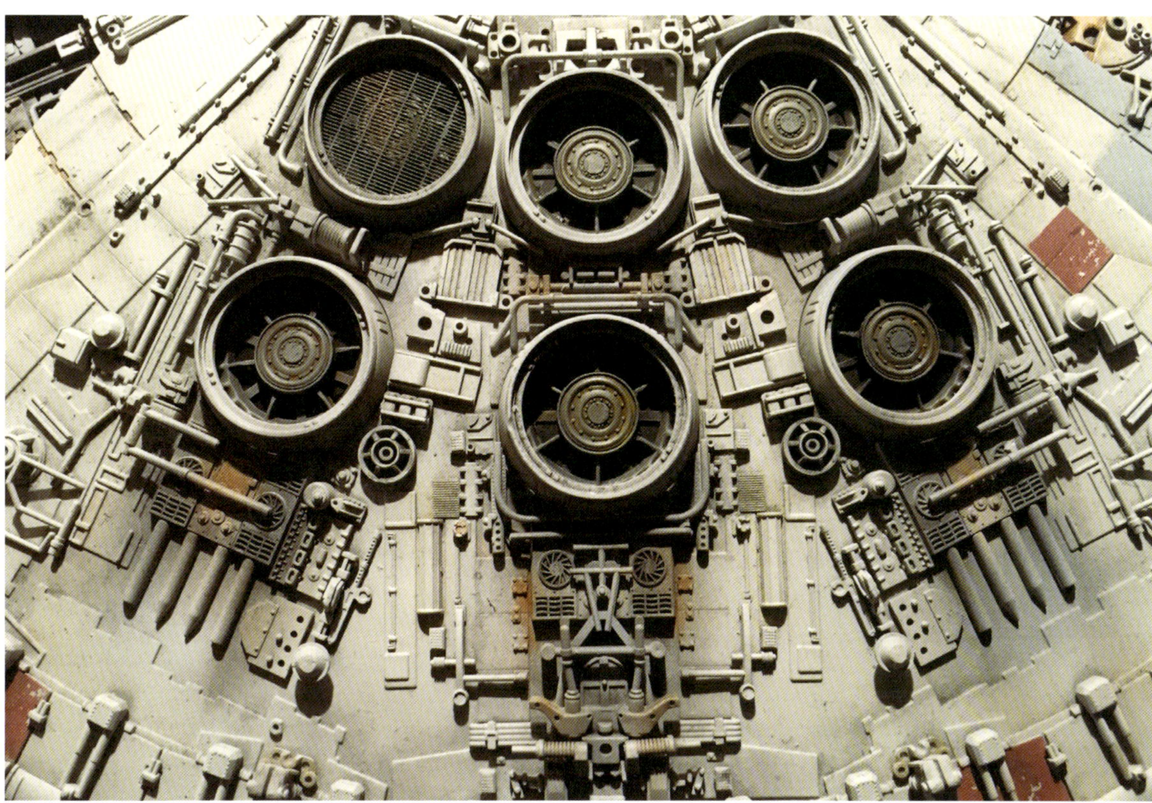

By 1996, the term "greeble"—an English neologism of uncertain origin—had come to designate two suggestively cognate entities. On the East Coast of the United States, a small group of psychologists and cognitive scientists (centered on Yale University) were, by that year, using the word to denominate a set of digitally rendered anthropomorphic forms developed for use as visual stimuli in facial recognition experiments. On the West Coast, among an elite coterie of Hollywood-oriented special-effects gurus and model-makers, the same term had been used for some time to refer to small, texturing forms that, when appliquéd to the surface of larger structures, convey an illusionistic sense of grandeur and intricacy.

It is the intention of this research note first, briefly to introduce and contextualize both these greeble-kinds; and then, speculatively to elaborate and weigh potential philological, genealogical, and conceptual links between the homonymous usages.

Our results will be inconclusive. But conclusions should, as a rule, be treated with suspicion.

THE WEST COAST GREEBLE

There remains a great deal of uncertainty as to the first usages of "greeble" to designate an individual element within the encrusting techno-textures that became a standard technique of science fiction cinematics in the wake of Stanley Kubrick's *2001: A Space Odyssey* (1968). Some have claimed that the term was already in use in Los Angeles–area art schools in the second half of the 1960s, where it reportedly meant something like fussy detail in sculptural or graphic work—the suggestion then being that the word wandered across to the garage-world of the *Star Trek* wizard-geeks then beginning to imageer intergalactic infrastructures for the major studios. But no definitive textual evidence has yet been brought forward to support this proposition.

Above: Close-up of the *Millennium Falcon*, showing the intricate analogue greebling of its exterior. The designers of the *Star Wars* spaceship employed a number of repurposed elements from World War II tank and aircraft model kits to achieve the effect.

Others have asserted that the origin of the term lies later, in the mid-1970s, with George Lucas himself, who, it is said, christened as "greeblies" (the "i" may or may not have been in there originally, and it eventually falls away) the meticulous elements that gave the surface of the *Millennium Falcon* and other *Star Wars* spacecraft their distinctive, even revolutionary, visual qualities—what might be described as an air of sublimely remote gigantism crossed with a finicky, mechanico-mysterious realism.[1]

What can be said with certainty is that these early "greebling" processes (the term regularly serves as a predicate in this setting) involved intensive manual labor with actual, physical model-making. "Kit-bashing," the reappropriation of parts from commercial plastic hobbyist models, served as the dominant shop practice.[2] The skunk-works team that would eventually become Industrial Light & Magic excelled in this repurposing of the myriad microcomponents of conventional airplane, car, and locomotive model kits—which bits, suitably reconfigured and strategically superglued all over the hulls of the larger spaceship forms, created exquisite tessellations of panel and circuit, hose and portal. Considerable artistry was involved, in that even a modestly mechanical eye reads the "plausibility" of such arrays quite intuitively—pipes must go somewhere and gears need to meet other gears. All such detailing is handcraft. You cannot, as the saying goes, just "dip the model in glue, and roll it in junk." In addition, distinctive parts with high recognition value among modeling buffs (automobile air filters, the air intake of a MIG fighter, the side panels of a train caboose) either had to be omitted or détourned with sufficient skill so as to pass unnoticed in a close-up shot.

This era of artisanal greebling in the material world mostly passed with the emergence of the powerful digital rendering tools that now dominate the special-effects industry.[3] A full account of this upheaval is well beyond our scope, but the transition occurred gradually across the 1990s. Initially, of course, the same visual effect had to be achieved with the new 3-D graphics tools by the programmer's equivalent of kit-bashing (i.e., borrowing, rescaling, and/or repurposing the virtual armature of various polygonal forms originally elaborated for other purposes), but this sort of "bespoke" CGI greebling is now relatively rare in that a host of "greeble plugins" are widely available for use with all the major rendering platforms. These dedicated greebling applications use recursive fractal algorithms and other clever mathematico-geometrical techniques to evolve huge libraries of greeble options. Countless elaborately greebled skins and scapes now populate these tools, which thereby secrete a vast, infinitely variable and combinable technological imaginary—a kind of pull-down palette for the pixel painters of our hyperworlds.

THE EAST COAST GREEBLE

We have more concrete information concerning the precise origin of the psychologists' greebles—both in name and form. In the early 1990s, graduate students in the Yale laboratory of Michael J. Tarr were working on different aspects of human vision. One of them, Isabel Gauthier, was specifically focused on facial recognition, and interested in understanding exactly how "special" this mode of object identification is in *Homo sapiens*.[4] Canonical work in the 1960s and 1970s appeared to establish that we see faces "differently" than we see other objects. Not only are brain-healthy persons very good at recognizing individuals by means of a glance at their faces (we do this a lot better than we recognize specific *leaves*, say—which, like human faces, are each visually particular but also all look a lot alike), cognitively normal people are also pretty sensitive to certain kinds of disruption in visual information about faces. (If you mix up face-bits, or flip things around, or displace the primary symmetries, it affects our recognition abilities more than similar reconfigurations in other objects.) All this, together with the existence of a number of pathological conditions that seem disproportionately to affect face recognition, suggests a distinctive cognitive mechanism for processing visual information about faces.

Gauthier was one of a number of young vision researchers at this time working to refine the extent and character of these face-seeing capacities. A basic way to do this? Test to what degree the apparently "special" features of face recognition could be discerned in an experimental subject working with various non-face stimuli.

What's a non-face? Well, in a basic way, everything that is "not a face" can be thought of, at least *in potentia*,

---

Opposite: An digitally greebled "sci-fi pipe," available for download for $29.

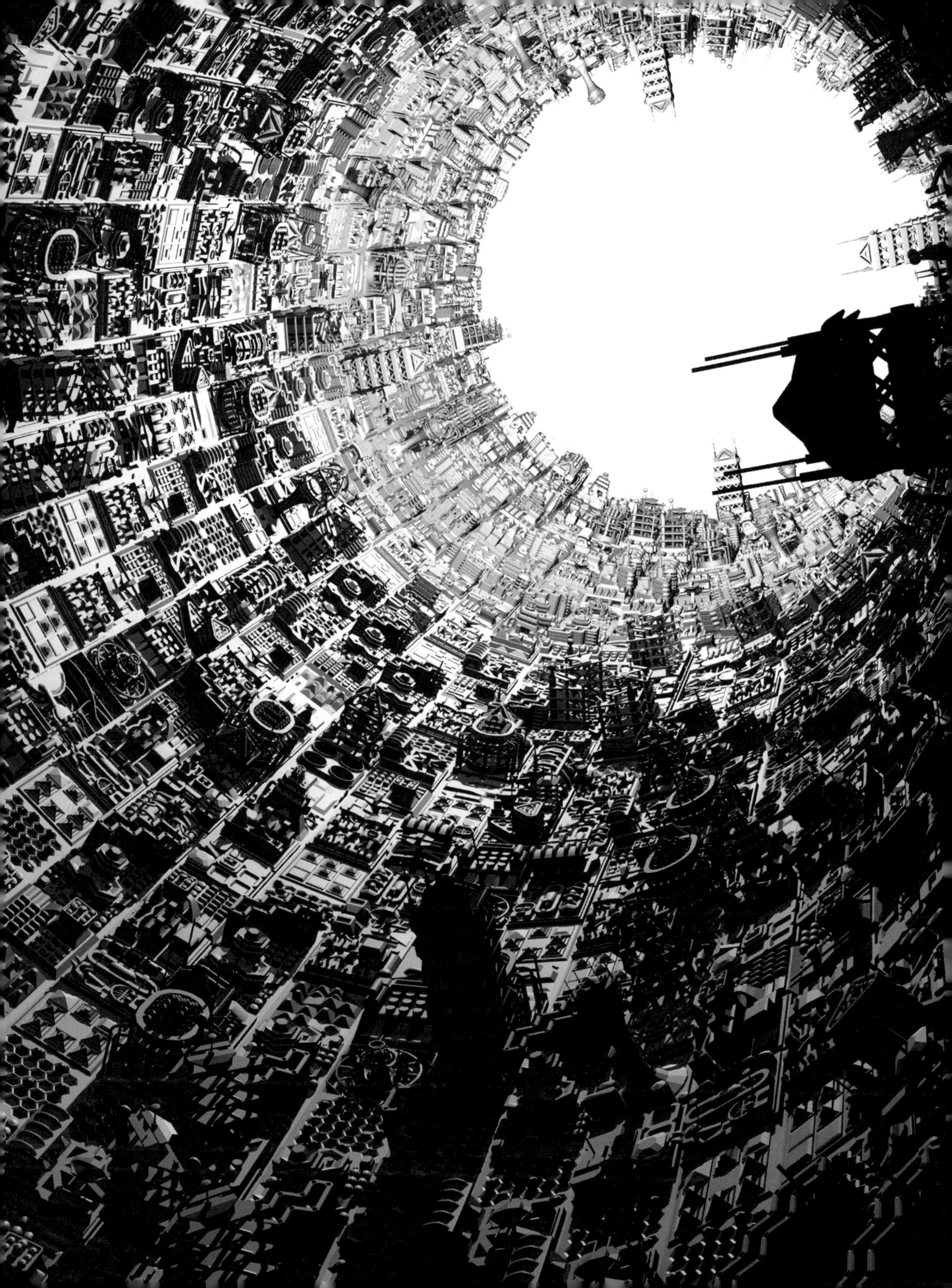

as a "non-face visual stimulus" for the purposes of a cognitive psychology experiment. You can take a picture of a fire hydrant or the paw pads of a miniature schnauzer and display either on the screen of a test monitor; you can manipulate them; you can place one or both in an array of similars; and you can show all or some of this to an undergraduate being paid minimum wage in the basement of a university building under experimental conditions that monitor response times, etc. You can train said undergraduate to recognize specific hydrants, then rotate them and flash them upside down and measure if identification requires more time in this orientation—and in this way, you might potentially compare, eventually in a statistically significant way, if inversion messes with hydrant recognition to the same extent that it messes with face recognition under otherwise identical circumstances.

And, sure enough, lots of this sort of experimentation was indeed being done in the era. But, pushing around the data, Gauthier and Tarr (and others) began to dream about a better non-face stimulus. The ideal non-face would be *face-like enough* to afford tightly targeted comparisons with actual faces: it would be available in a relatively large set (like humans); each exemplar would have a discrete number of "components" that varied in form and position, but that retained a relatively robust general configuration (like faces); and the set as a whole would offer opportunities for *individuation* ("hey, that's Jerry Lewis!"), and higher-level differentiation by kinds (in analogy to the various categorizations that are possible when working with human faces—e.g., male and female).

Enter Scott Yu. At the time Yu was a Yale undergraduate in his sophomore year—a self-described "lab rat" and video game addict (Street Fighter II, Mortal Kombat) who had found a congenial nest in the environs of Dr. Tarr's lab. A tinkerer with some aptitude for programming, Yu availed himself of the research toys stashed about the Tarr lab, including one of the just-released Wacom UD tablet inputs, as well as some primitive 2-D graphics tools on the desktop machines. Before long, he and Tarr had secured a copy of Form*Z, the new 3-D rendering tool developed for architects and designers (it had been released in 1991).[5] Yu, tinkering, became sufficiently adept with this software that he could soon use (the still relatively novel, in personal computing) NURBS curves ("Non-Uniform Rational B-Spline") to generate, shade, and rotate novel 3-D forms. The resulting glyphomorphs were horrible colors and weird shapes. But they got the attention of Gauthier and Tarr: could this new technology be used to *make a set of experimentally optimized non-faces?*

Yu (who went on to have an international career in video game design) took up the task, and along the way, began taking his newfound identity as a visual artist more seriously—signing up for figure-drawing classes in New Haven, and spending his evenings bent over sheets of newsprint, charcoal in hand. Before the screen of Form*Z, still later at night, he gradually evolved a strange little family of homuncular gremlins—a faceless army of non-faces. It was Gauthier, however, who was Xeroxing a page of renderings of these critters in the psychology office when the distinguished Yale political scientist (and quantitative psychologist) Robert Abelson shuffled into the room. Looking over her shoulder, he inquired with avuncular gruff, "What are those little *greebles* you are copying?" The name stuck. And the psychologists' greebles were born. They proved useful to their designed purpose, and beyond. Gauthier is today a well-respected neuroscientist, much of whose reputation can be traced back to her original greeble papers, and Yu's little non-faces have now been referenced in more than seven hundred scientific articles. They have become a familiar tool for a wide range of research programs, including the study of learning, sight, haptics, memory, and even language use.

DISCUSSION

A number of questions come to the fore immediately: Why did "greebling" in the West Coast sense emerge to prominence in science fiction imagery when it did? And relatedly, why had previous futuristic imagery (*Metropolis* to *Buck Rogers*) tended to privilege smooth, as opposed to techno-textured, forms? More generally, why does the judicious application of greebles to a surface produce such an uncanny illusion of scale

---

Opposite: Examples of both genders—plok and glip—of each of the five greeble families created at Yale University: Galli, Osmit, Radok, Samar, and Tasio. Each greeble is assigned to a family based on its basic body shape, which has appendages known as the "boges" (the two hornlike protrusions), the "quiff" (the nose), and the "dunth" (the penile proboscis on the lower body). The genders are identified according to the orientation of these appendages, which are always all either pointing down (plok) or up (glip). Courtesy Isabel Gauthier.

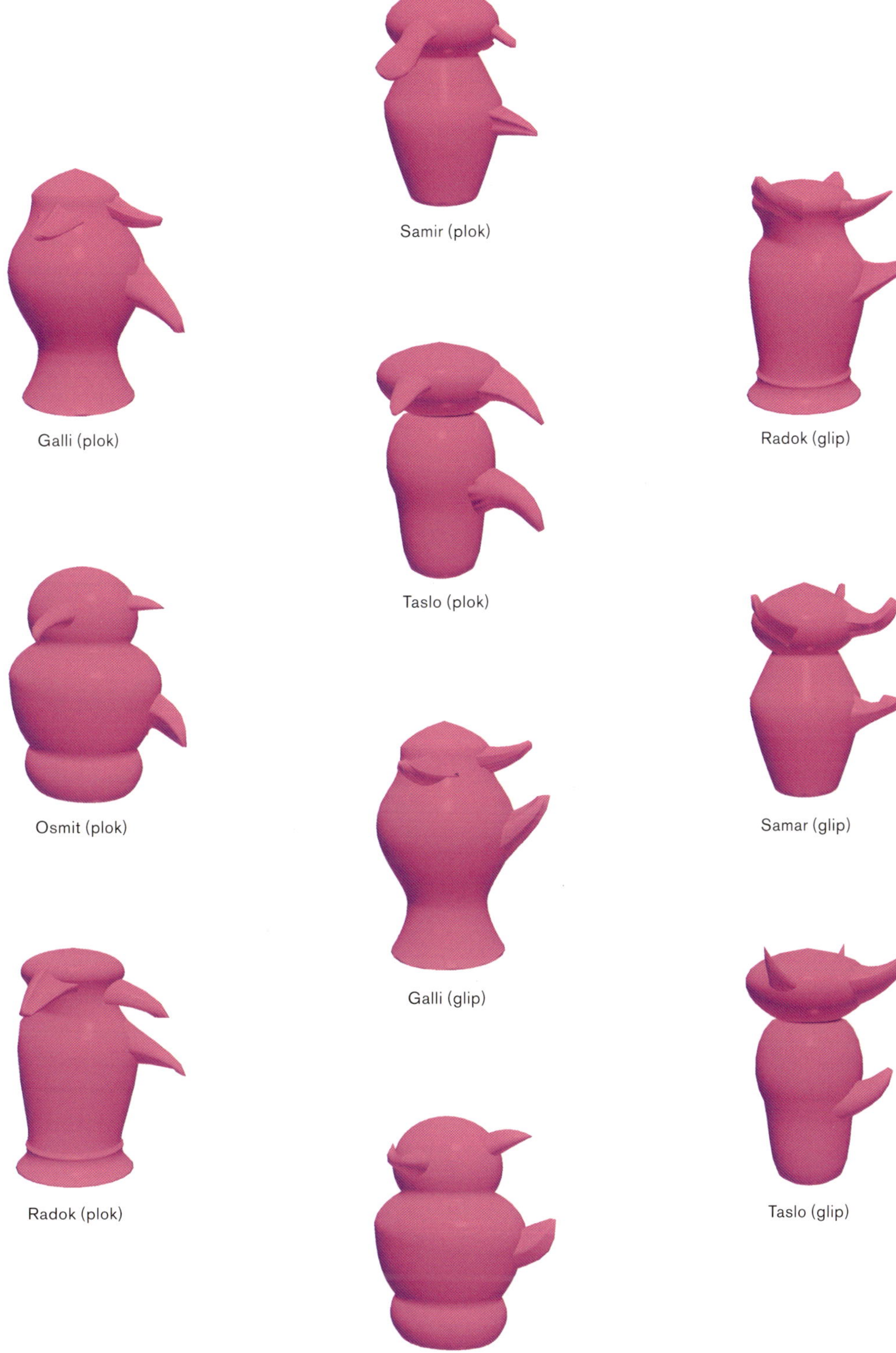

Samir (plok)

Galli (plok)

Radok (glip)

Taslo (plok)

Osmit (plok)

Samar (glip)

Galli (glip)

Radok (plok)

Taslo (glip)

Osmit (glip)

and distance? And, finally, furthering this observation: Can the aesthetic analysis of the sublime be stretched to accommodate or illuminate the visual experience of cinematic greeblescapes? If anything, the psychologists' greebles are even more puzzling. Why did a set of putatively non-face virtual entities end up looking for all the world like small (faceless?) homunculi? This question feels especially urgent, in that, their notional non-faceness aside, greebles seem very much to have "faces," if notably blank ones, and it is therefore immensely difficult to understand how, with the whole *universe* of non-face image forms to choose from, Yu and the Tarr lab researchers so closely re-evolved legibly "facial" pseudomorphs. Has this had implications for the results of research spooling out from the original greeble publications?[6] And even if we choose to leave that question to the scientists themselves, we could still turn to several significant concerns that arise upon any critical confrontation with Yu's greebles. For instance: In what ways can Yu's primary visual cultures of the mid-1990s (nude figure drawing and video games) be discerned in the forms he evolved at that time? What sublated psychosexual dynamics generated the phallic (non-?) face feature known as the "dunth"? And how did the taxonomic architecture of the greeble set as a whole immediately reproduce not only an archetypal dyadic bifurcation by gender but also the historically dominant pentamerous classification of racial difference?[7]

Tempting as each of these inquires is, I propose in what follows largely to bracket further specific reflection on the (different) things called greebles, and move instead to a subtending linguistic problem: Why are (all) these things called "greebles"?

Turning to this matter, then, I think we must begin by dismissing the notion that the self-consciously old-Ivy-League Bob Abelson had somehow acquainted himself with an obscure bit of argot then *au courant* among West Coast creative types in the ambit of Lucas et al. And if this is admitted, we would seem to find ourselves confronting parallel and, at least as best as can be made out, genealogically "unrelated" coinages. We are thus saddled with an unenviable mitosis in our etymological problem: not one but *two* emergent usages of the same hitherto unattested term.

But are they *completely* unrelated? Again, no plausible direct or lineal greeble-greeble link is, at present, in evidence. And yet, it must be conceded that the conceptual terrains at issue are at least adjacent, if not swampily conjoined. In each of our two usage-cases, the term "greeble" comes to designate a small, simulacral visual stimulus—a set of entities that draw attention to themselves only by being "in relation" to other (real) entities that they simultaneously evoke and disavow. The East Coast greeble is a face-ish antiface; West Coast greebling relied on the strategic misuses of pieces from ordinary (car, boat, or plane) models to pull the imagination to futuristic, rather than quotidian, technologies. In both situations, we confront intimacies that produce a kind of alienation, details that generate a sense of distance and disorientation. In both situations, we confront a new class of human-wrought "things made to be seen" that emerged within the nexus of the disruptive virtualities of screen-life in the last quarter of the twentieth century.

In all this, the West Coast and East Coast greebles seem not unrelated. Or at least not *unrelatable*. Nevertheless, all evidence points to our dealing, here, with a case of convergent *linguistic* evolution, rather than any common etymological *stemma*. In this context, putative hybridities (for instance, one can find, online, a graphically greebled image of a psychologists' greeble) must be understood as nervous expressions of the queer propinquity at issue, rather than historical reconstructions of some common ancestor or sudden reversion to wild type.

All of which is to say, onomastics can be spooky. But we must be brave. So it is to onomastics that I will, in conclusion, turn.

Whence, then, the actual word "greeble"—which does not appear in the *Oxford English Dictionary*, and has no obvious etymological provenance in the domains at play? Let us entertain several hypotheses. Many readers will, by this time, have reflected—perhaps fleetingly, and possibly unconsciously—on the cognate English term "grebe," referring to the various species of diving bird grouped in the order *Podicipediformes*, many fossil instances of which are known. While the intricacies of their fossilized bone patterns in shale or limestone matrix do bear a striking resemblance to certain early greebled surfaces, no more direct line to the West Coast greeble can readily be discerned. Approaching the problem from the other side, it is interesting to look at an upright grebe (particularly the great crested, least, or black-necked species) while thinking about one of the East Coast greebles.

The least grebe, I have come to feel, looks uncannily like a greeble of the Osmit family, and the great crested and horned varieties, when on their mating platforms, often strike strikingly Galli-esque poses.

But all this *similitudo* appears to remain precariously perched in the realm of mere form, leaving the philologist at the lip of the abyss, attending to the faint and diminishing echoes sounding from the depths of a chasm of unknowing.

Not greatly more satisfying, in the end, is the initially exciting realization that the term "greeble" itself does in fact make a handful of appearances in English in the nineteenth and twentieth centuries. In each case, the word is employed as an idiosyncratic orthographic effort to capture a colloquial and folkish articulation of the familiar adjective "agreeable." While both East and West Coast greebles are, I think, in their way, highly agreeable (in the sense of "producing pleasing effects"), one is again without any solid evidentiary links out of which to forge a chain capable of supporting the weight of a properly causal argument.

Also of interest, however, is a spate of possibly unrelated misspellings of "Gleeble" (the *r*/*l* transposition being well attested in historical linguistics), which similarly give rise to a smattering of published pre-"greeble-as-such" appearances of the word "greeble"— and, suggestively, the phrase "Greeble test" as well. But the testing at issue in these references is indeed "Gleeble testing," a standard engineering analysis of the hot ductility of metals, an assay of particular importance in rating construction materials. The large console of a Gleeble test station could certainly be said to be "greebled," in the West Coast sense, and the molten ingot that results from the "fail" of a Gleeble test *can* look a bit like a greeble in the East Coast sense, but pushing this line of reasoning too hard strains credulity, which can itself fail under adverse conditions of pressure and temperature.

And this brings us to the small, orbicular figurines known as "Weebles," developed by the Hasbro company of Pawtucket, Rhode Island. Released initially in 1971, these ovoid plastic dolls featured a non-homogenous body composition that located the center of mass of any given Weeble below the pivot point of said Weeble (oriented vertically). Combining this arrangement with a smoothly curved base (and ensuring only a single mechanical equilibrium), it became possible to guarantee what became the trademark of the brand: "Weebles wobble, but they don't fall down." While it is difficult to discern a link (other than chronological synchrony) between the sudden market domination of Weebles in the early 1970s and the advent of the West Coast greebles, the prominence of the "Weebles wobble" jingle certainly placed the "-eeble" vocalization in broad circulation in this period, and this must be understood as a component of the phonic preconditioning of the emergence of the term "greeble" in both settings. Morphological consonances between Weebles and greebles (in the East Coast sense) should also be acknowledged.

None of this can be described as settling the problem at issue, and it is possible that the totality of these insights and observations will be adjudged to have cast but a feeble light on the question as a whole. Pending new discoveries, we are left to ponder a troubling notion: What is new may, on occasion, actually come from no place at all. May be "unprecedented" and without cause. Spontaneous. *Sui generis*. Even "random."

Historical inquiry, under such circumstances, runs up against what may well be definitive methodological limitations.

1 The claim that Lucas coined the term is made, for example, by the notable special-effects expert Roger Christian in his recent memoir of those years, *Cinema Alchemist* (New York: Titan Books, 2016).

2 I am indebted, in this discussion, to a pair of articles in *Den of Geek* by Ryan Lambie, who has excavated some oral history of early Hollywood greebling. See both his "Greebles: How Tiny Details Make a Huge Star Wars Universe" (7 August 2015), and the interview with special effects artist Fon Davis (14 August 2015).

3 Though it should be noted that the advent of widely available 3-D printing has led to a new back-and-forth between physical models and digitally rendered greeble forms.

4 This is a classic problem in experimental psychology, and has been a subject of research interest going back to the second half of the nineteenth century. For a discussion, see Robert K. Yin, "Face Perception: A Review of Experiments with Infants, Adults, and Brain-Injured Persons," in *Perception*, ed. Richard Held, Herschel W. Leibowitz, and Hans-Lukas Teuber (Berlin: Springer-Verlag, 1978), pp. 593–610.

5 Pierluigi Serraino, *The History of Form*Z* (New York: Birkhauser, 2002).

6 The original paper was: Isabel Gauthier and Michael J. Tarr, "Becoming a 'Greeble' Expert: Exploring Mechanisms for Face Recognition," *Vision Research*, vol. 37, no. 12 (June 1997).

7 The influential German race-theorist Johann Friedrich Blumenbach (1752–1840) notoriously identified five fundamental racial types (Caucasian, Mongolian, Ethiopian, American, and Malay) out of his craniometrical studies—a paradigm that informed Anglo-European and American race thinking well into the twentieth century.

ARTIST PROJECT / PLESHKA-BIROBIDZHAN

Yevgeniy Fiks

"Pleshka-Birobidzhan" engages the relationship between identity, fiction, and history through imagining how a number of gay men—some from the Soviet Union and some leftists from abroad—formed a group in 1934 to travel from Moscow to Birobidzhan, capital of the Jewish Autonomous Region of the USSR.

Shortly after the 1917 revolution, homosexuality in the Soviet Union was decriminalized, and for the next sixteen years, no criminal punishment for "same-sex offenses" existed. This period, however, cannot be considered an era of true gay liberation. Instead, it was a time of liberalization, a moment that could have become the basis for greater liberation had it not been abruptly terminated in 1934 when Stalin once again made homosexuality (and abortion) illegal as part of a broad conservative turn to strengthen the nuclear family and return to petit bourgeois values.

In that same year, Stalin established the Jewish Autonomous Region, known mostly by the name of its capital city of Birobidzhan on the Trans-Siberian Railroad close to the border with China. Birobidzhan was supposed to become the home for Soviet Jews, where they would develop their own cultural autonomy, with Yiddish as the official language. In the long run, the Birobidzhan project turned out to be unsuccessful because very few Jews moved there of their own volition, and the government neither pressured them nor created incentives for them to do so. Birobidzhan is widely considered a failed Soviet utopian project.

The story told by the collages that constitute "Pleshka-Birobidzhan" begins in Moscow in the summer of 1934. The first group of images depicts an imaginary meeting at a *pleshka*—a Soviet urban gay cruising site—in front of the Bolshoi Theater. The attendees include historically significant gay figures such as writers Mikhail Kuzmin, Robert Duncan, Yevgeny Kharitonov, and André Gide, and activists Nikolai Alekseev, Bayard Rustin, and Harry Hay. The men meet to discuss the recriminalization of homosexuality as a failure of the October Revolution, the creation of the Jewish Autonomous Region, and their dream of a gay Soviet utopia.

The next set of collages depicts the journey of these men, who, disillusioned and fearing persecution, travel from Moscow to Birobidzhan. Upon their arrival, they find themselves in the middle of the Gay and Lesbian Autonomous Region, which appears to exist alongside, and at times overlaps with, the Soviet Jewish utopia.

אפֿן פּלעשקע

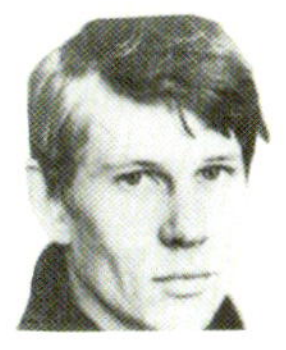

E.Kh. – an apolitical late-Soviet homosexual, avant-garde writer

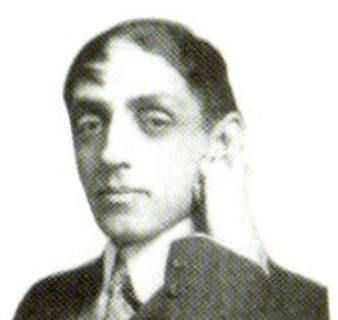

The Countess – an upper-class homosexual from the pre-Revolutionary "Silver Century" circles

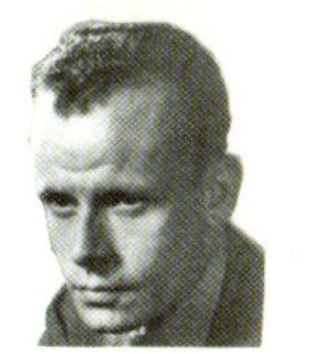

The New Homosexual – a post-Revolutionary queer communist who believes in the creation of a Gay and Lesbian Autonomous Socialist Republic in USSR.

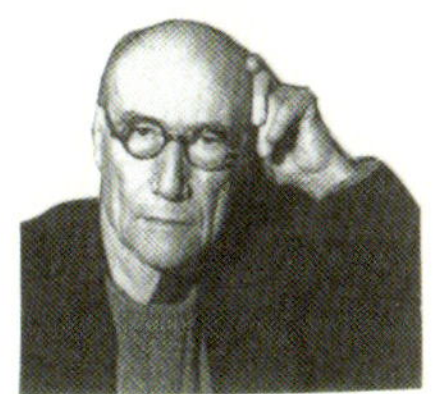

Old Gide – a middle-aged French homosexual *fellow traveler*

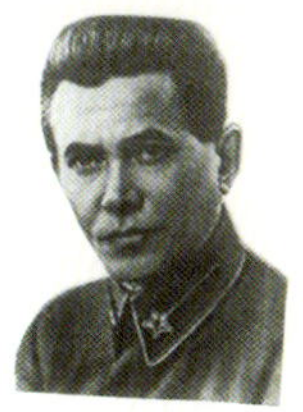

Nikolai 1 – the former head of the NKVD (People's Commissariat for Internal Affairs), a bisexual enemy of the people

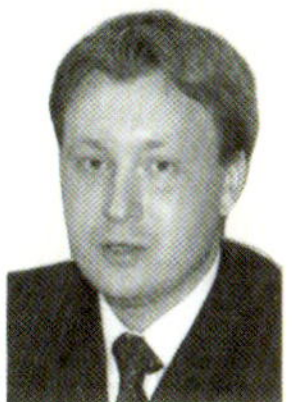

Nikolai 2 – a patriotically-minded LGBT leader of the first decade of the 21st century

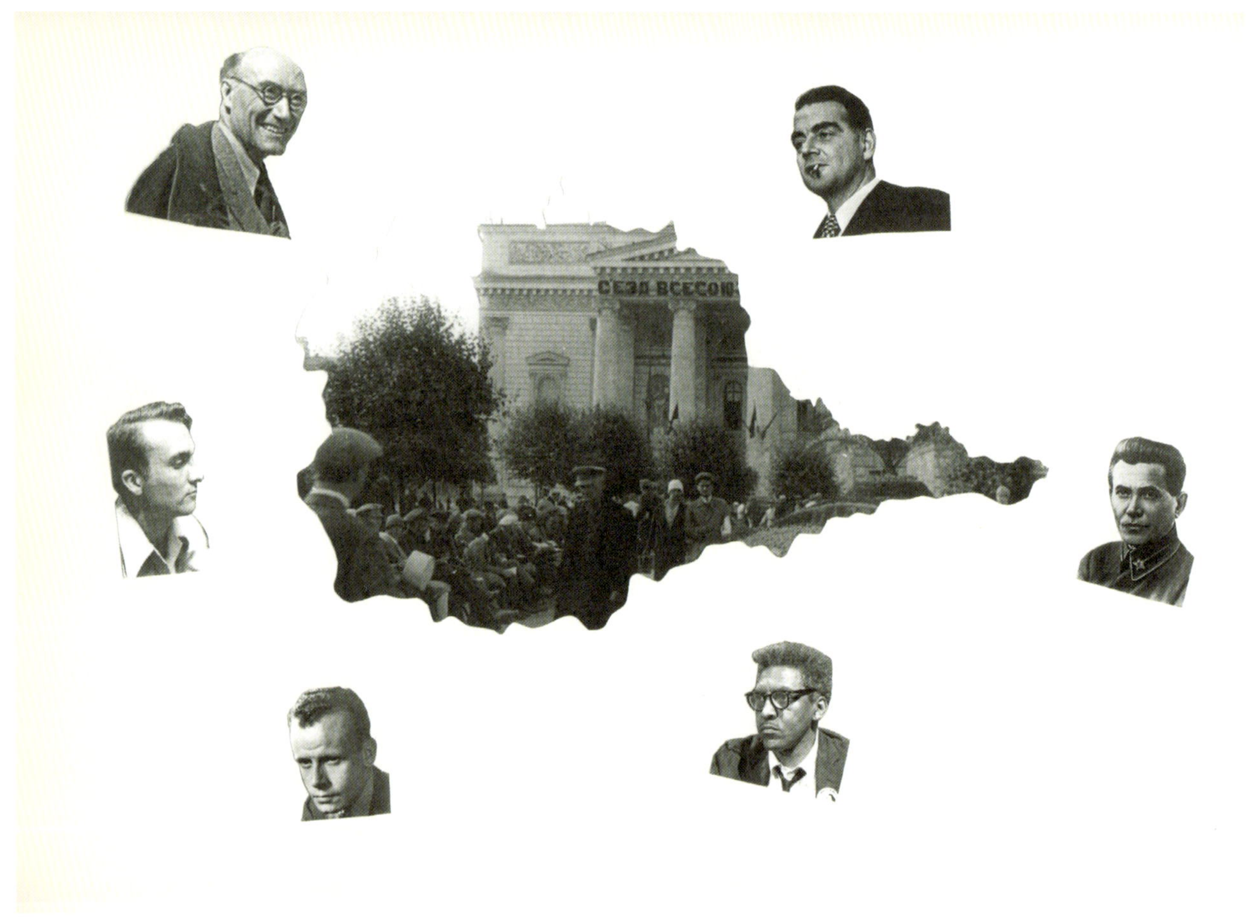
СЕЗД ВСЕСОЮ

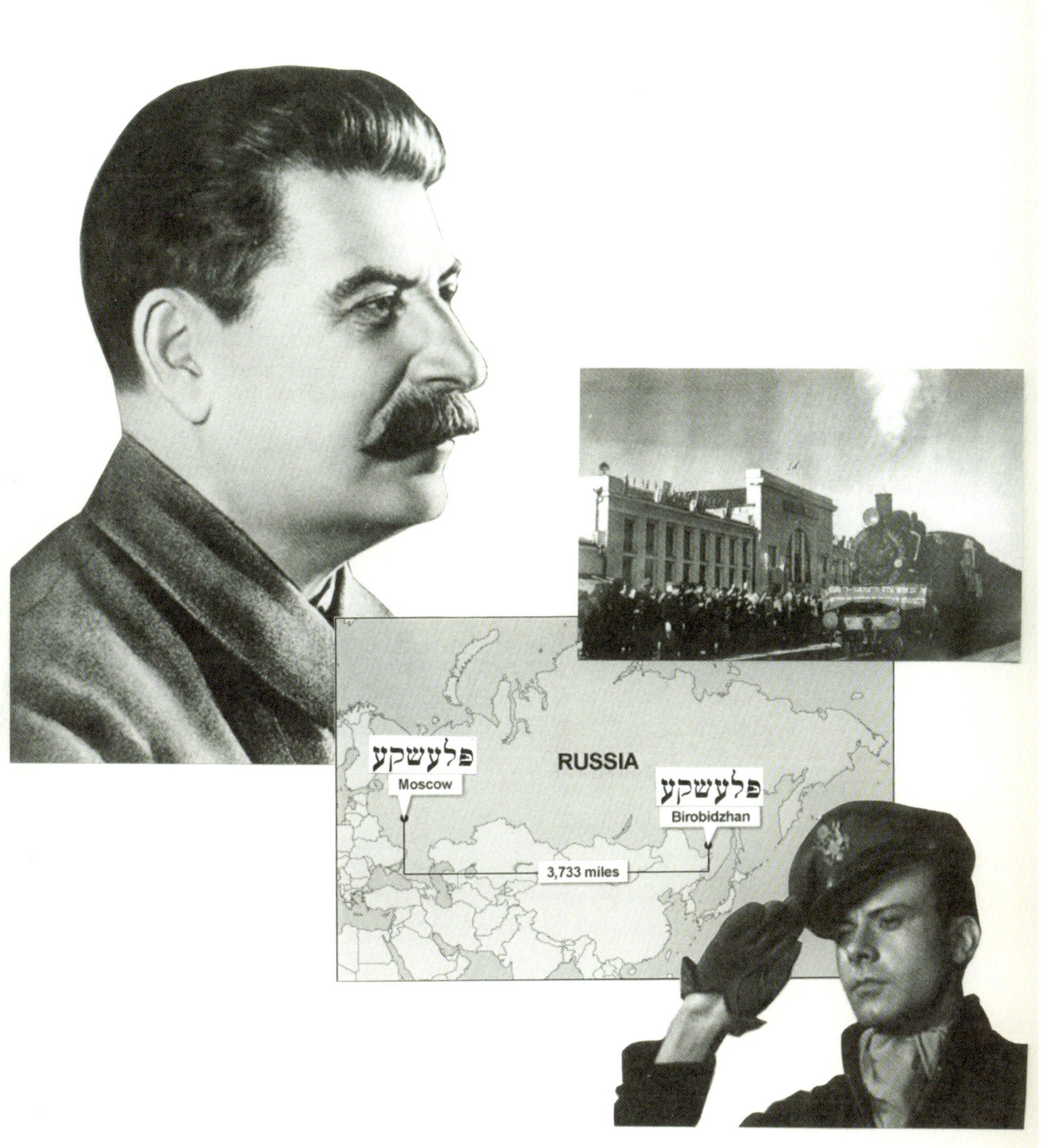

The New Homosexual

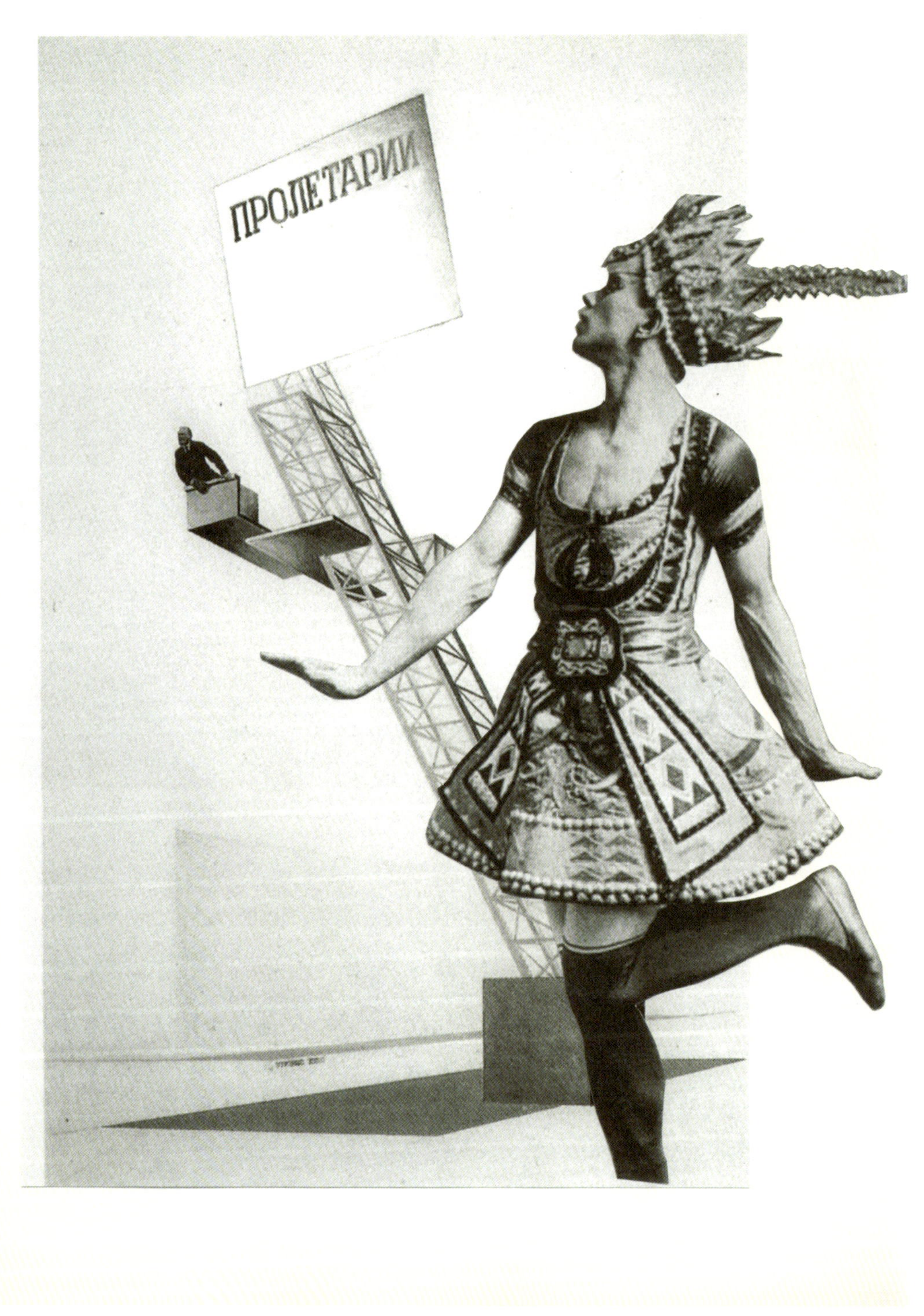
ПРОЛЕТАРИИ

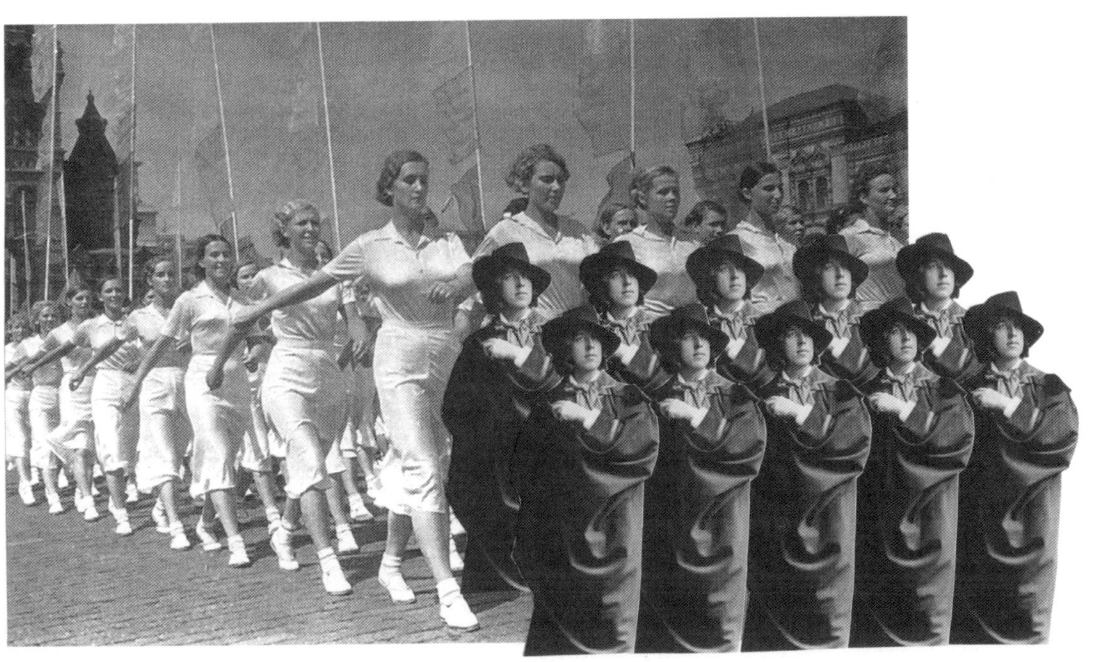

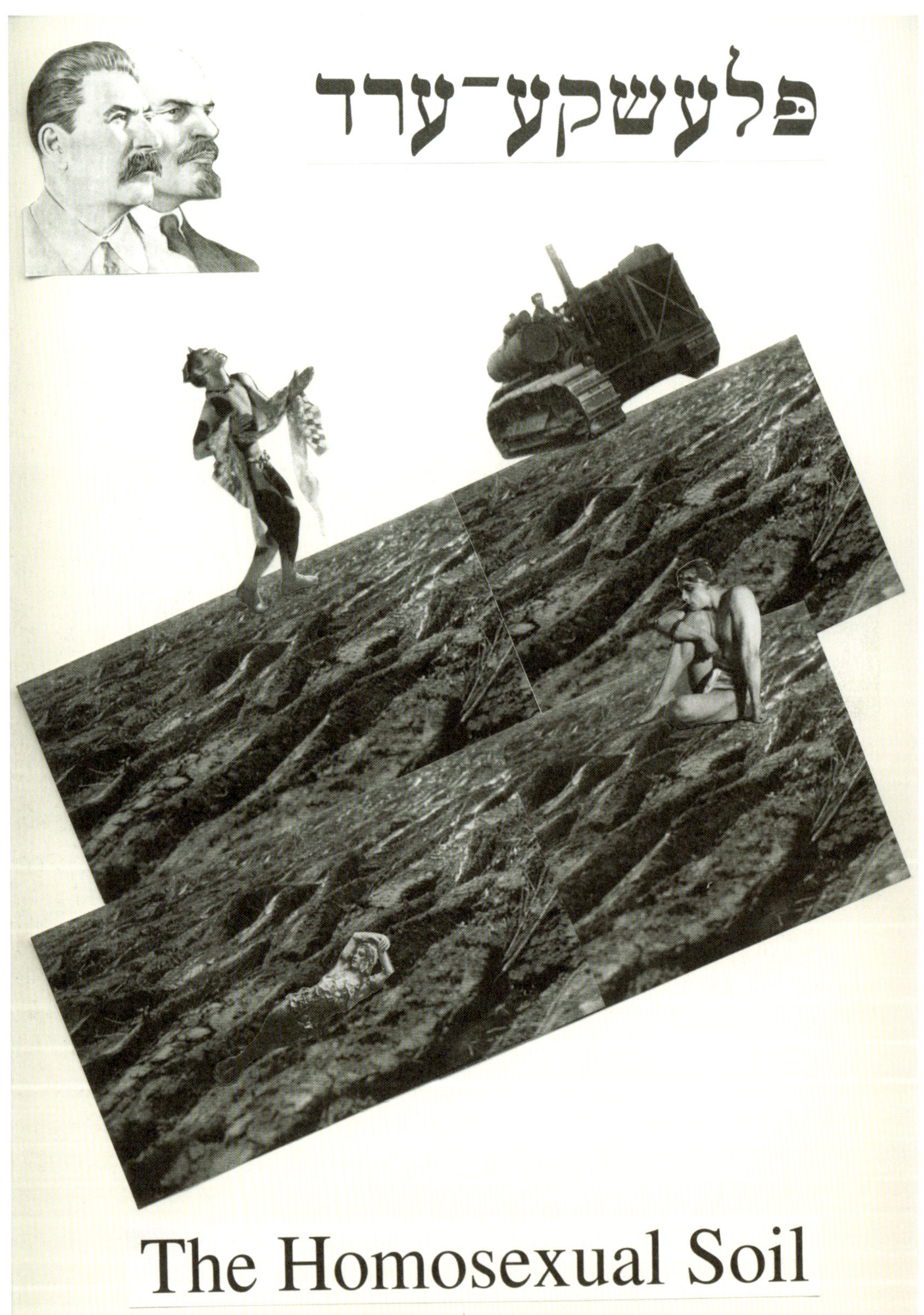
פֿלעשקע־ערד
The Homosexual Soil

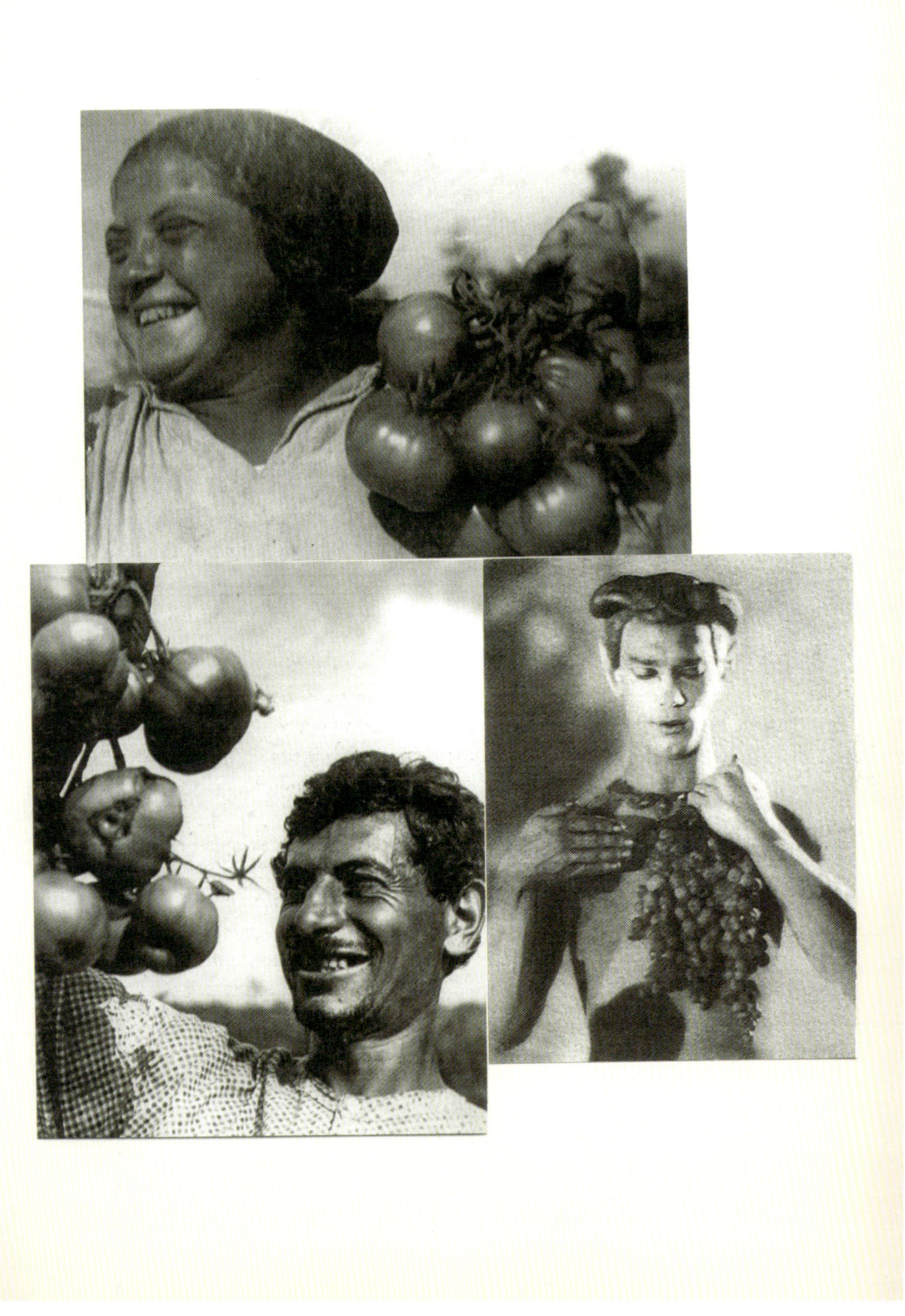

THE FIRE OF LITERATURE

Cecilia Sjöholm

WHY MUST BOOKS BURN?

"*Verbrennung* in Berlin," Freud wrote in his diary on 11 May 1933. Which means, "It is burning in Berlin." But also, "I am burning in Berlin." This echoes Heinrich Heine's saying, "Where they burn books, they burn people," or the claim made by John Milton in the turbulent seventeenth century that book burnings are a "kind of homicide."[1] The books that are burned may signify the "heretic," "Jew," "Muslim," or "homosexual." They can also signify the colonized, the forbidden, the taboo. Or a revolt against those in power: sometimes books are burned by revolutionaries. Each case has its own contingent historical significance. Why did churches all over the US throw Harry Potter in the fire? Why must the libraries of Mosul burn?

Book burnings have a ritual side: sometimes they are performed as magic rites in which society is being cleared of filthy objects. In France, the manuscript of the Marquis de Sade's *Les Journées de Flourbelle* disappeared in flames, at the initiative of the police and the author's own son, both intent on protecting the family honor.[2] In the early 1920s, the US postal service—dedicated to the country's "clean books" campaign—felt the need to obliterate James Joyce's *Ulysses*, torching several hundred copies in response to the book's obscenities, such as intercourse and toilet visits.[3] Book burnings may also establish ritual relationships. Harry Potter books were burned by church groups in a number of American towns in 2001 and 2003 as a rite that affirmed their members' allegiance to Christ even as it rebuked the books' occultism.[4]

Freud's anxiety at being burned was compensated only by a sense that he had been chosen for all the right reasons. The list of authors that burned in Berlin in 1933 was not arbitrary but set in motion by Goebbels as an "act of cleansing," of ridding Germany of Jewish, Marxist, and pacifist authors. "At least I am in great company," Freud said.[5] Albert Einstein, André Gide, Maxim Gorki, Ernest Hemingway, Erich Kästner, Helen Keller, Jack London, Thomas Mann, Marcel Proust, H. G. Wells: the list goes on. The principles for the "Cleansing of Public Libraries" campaign, drafted by librarian Wolfgang Herrmann, concluded that the cleansing was to be done in one of two ways. With some books, all copies were to be destroyed in an *auto-da-fé*. With others, a single copy (surprisingly, Lenin, for instance) was to be preserved in a so-called poison cabinet to be established at large city and university libraries. Herrmann determined that a third category should be created for books whose ultimate fate (fire or poison cabinet) remained to be determined. To the first group belonged writings that, among other criteria, served "the egocentric pleasure of the individual."[6] In other words: sexuality.

This aspect of the Nazi program did not just restage the American "clean books" campaign; it also looked back to even more archaic examples. Sappho's works were burned twice by Christians—first in 380 and then again in 1073. The poet, whose collected works filled nine volumes at the library in Alexandria before its destruction, was burned not only because she was a pagan, but also, as Page du Bois has shown, because of the "luxuriousness" of her writing and its sexual connotations.[7]

Erich Kästner saw his own books thrown into the flames in 1933 and wrote an account of it after making a narrow escape from the scene. Kästner tells how, after the Institut für Sexualwissenschaft was ransacked and closed down, the statue of its founder, the pioneering Jewish sexologist Magnus Hirschfeld, was symbolically decapitated and its head was paraded through town. But Kästner also movingly recounted how some of the students who had been called in to carry out the destruction attempted to rescue works from the fire. They hid them under their feet and in their jackets. These moments of tenderness, in which students acted against the orders not of the SS but of their university teachers and librarians, attest to the extent of the confusion in that historical moment. Kästner's conclusion is that the destruction, which was orchestrated by individuals at the university, was not targeted primarily at the other—Jews or Communists. It was, above all, an expression of self-hatred, and a kind of suicide. Here Kästner quotes Martin Heidegger, who gave his so-called inaugural address as vice-chancellor of Freiburg University, and therefore as a state official under the Nazi regime, that same year. Rather than refusing to represent, affirm, and distribute the symbolic order of a fascist regime, a rejection that philosophy, as well as literature, must perform,

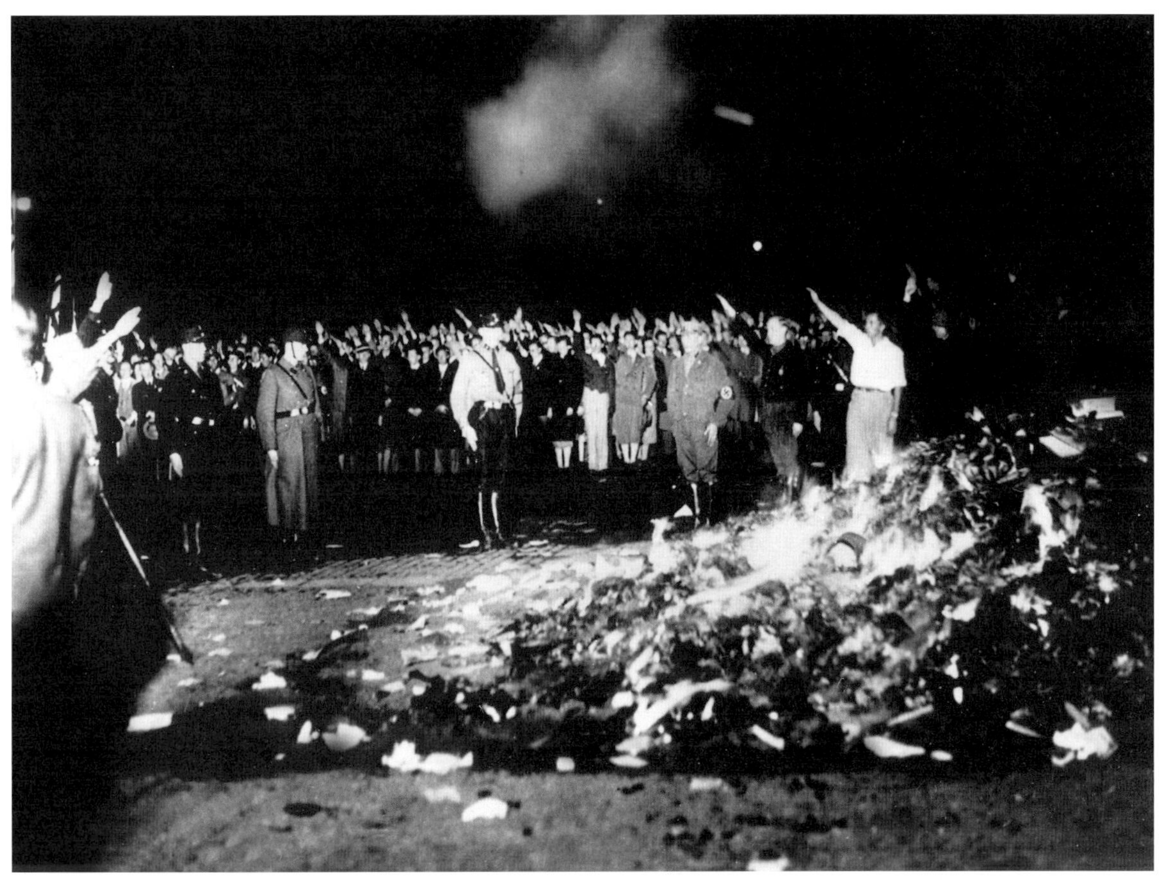

Verbrennung in Berlin. The 10 May 1933 book burning organized by the Nazis at the city's Opernplatz, now Bebelplatz.

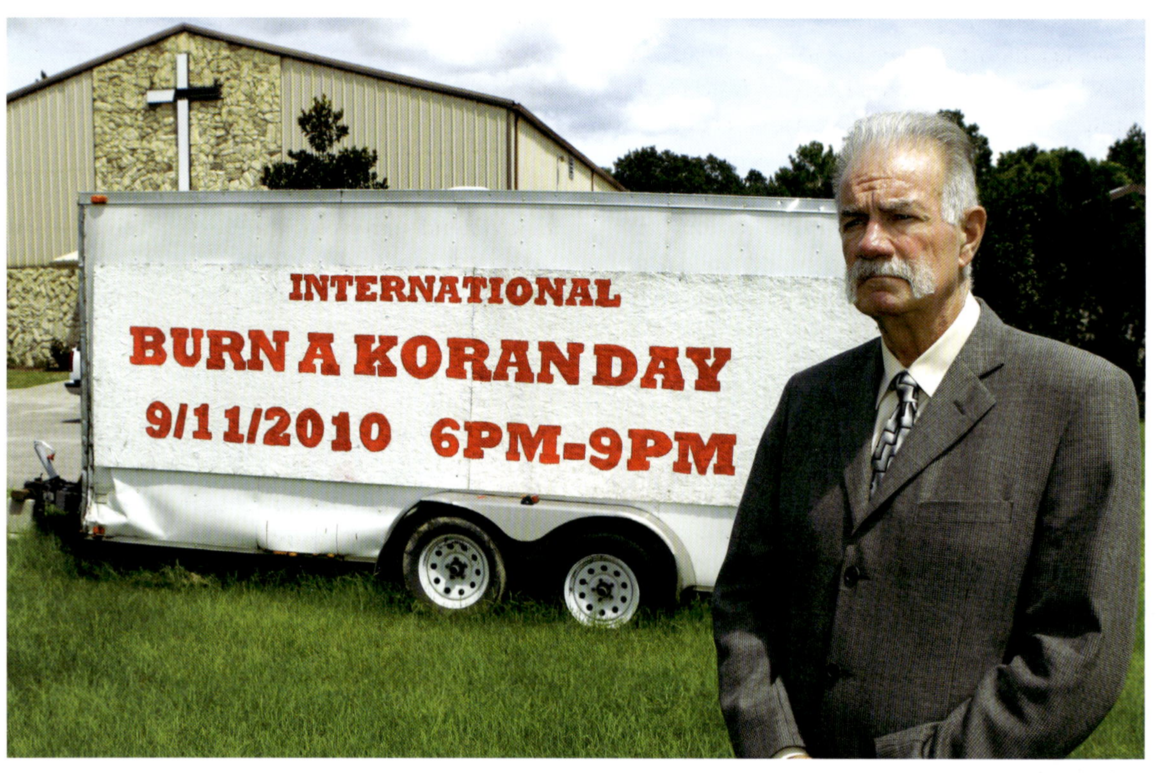
INTERNATIONAL
BURN A KORAN DAY
9/11/2010 6PM-9PM

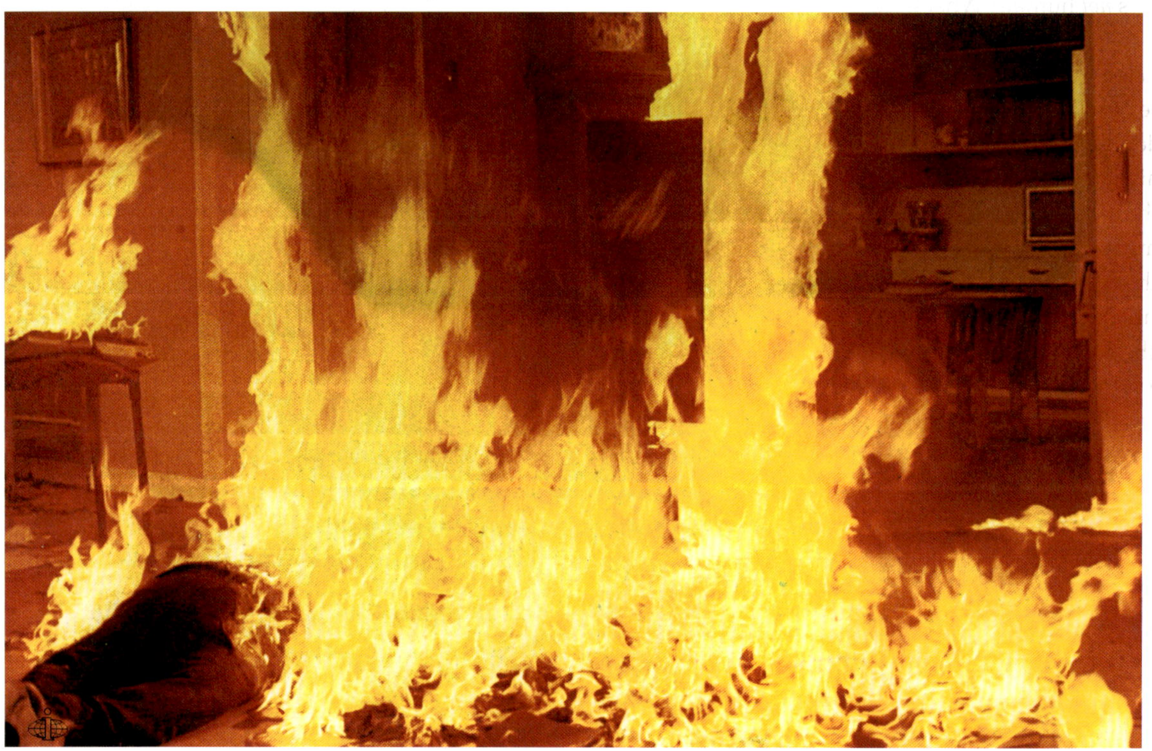

Heidegger assumed the "truth" of nationalist dictatorship. In this way, Heidegger renounced the power of the book—not just those that were burned but also his own.

Book burnings are therefore not simply acts that substitute for the destruction of particular people, no matter what form of fanaticism provokes them. Anti-Semitism, certainly an aspect of the bonfires in 1933, is, in Theodor Adorno's analysis in *The Authoritarian Personality*, an ideology tethered to what Freud called drive, a component between psyche and body beyond all control. He quotes Gotthold Ephraim Lessing's *Nathan the Weise*: "Tut nichts! Der Jude wird verbrannt." The Jew must burn no matter what he does. But a sexual component is often concomitant with persecution. Symptomatically, in Lessing's play, fire is a figure for strong sexual desire and for the fantasy of purification at the same time: the Christian Templar who saves Nathan's daughter from perishing in flames feels himself stained and compromised, as if he should have left her to burn. Fire is the Lacanian Imaginary glued to the Real; a figure for the drives shifting between pleasure and death, sexuality and aggression, affect and extermination.

But what in the book do bonfires seek to destroy that is *not* human? What in book burnings is irreducible to ideology, psychology, or political and religious statements? As an act, they appear to touch the very core of what Jacques Lacan calls the Symbolic, the order that sustains the desire of thought and language against the drive. The primary signifier for this order is the phallus. In Lacanian thought, castration is the symbolic installation of the prohibiting law of the Father through which the signifier substitutes for the phallus. At the same time, paternal law is the guarantor of the symbolic power of the phallus, the phallus being the primary signifier of desire. Given that books are bestowed with an extraordinary power by those who burn them, it is clear that it is the Symbolic itself, and the law of the Father, which is being both claimed and challenged. What one attempts to burn then is not the object, but the signifier itself. Bonfires of books do not only demonstrate hatred; they illuminate a central anxiety at the heart of this gesture of destruction. Unlike the material book, the hand of Satan cannot burn. What emerges with the bonfires of books, then, is a double gesture: on the one hand, a majestic incorporation of the law sustaining a fundamental prohibition against unlimited enjoyment of certain acts or objects, and on the other, an anxious denegation of the existence of such a law. What is at stake is a formidable enjoyment that can neither be had for oneself nor allowed for the other.

LITERATURES ON FIRE

The concept of sovereignty has been the subject of much attention in recent years, and not simply in its original sense as a symbolic dimension of the law. There is an intrinsic relation between literature and the concept of sovereignty, one explored by Georges Bataille in his 1957 book *Literature and Evil*.

In 1946, the journal *Action* had published an issue in which they asked: Should Kafka be burned? Certainly, Kafka had by then already been burned, but the question pertained not to the acts of 1933, but to the fact that Kafka wanted to have his manuscripts destroyed after his death by his friend Max Brod. (They ended up in the National Library in Tel Aviv in 2015.) Bataille answered the question posed by *Action*: Kafka's authorship was itself a kind of slow burning out of life, as well as an interminable practice of enjoyment.

Bataille writes that although Kafka, who lived in the shadow of his father, led a life that seemed to be founded on everyday normalcy, his "real" existence took place alongside it—in the dream, in writing, in fantasy. Kafka's writings became a world of absolute irresponsibility, of "the unrestrained caprice of his heroes, their childishness and carelessness, their scandalous behavior and obvious lies."[8] Through this act, Kafka's writings develop in a state of sovereignty that is not unlike that to be found in the writings of the Marquis de Sade: a sovereignty that entails both the setting of the law and the absence of laws, "suffused with useless liberty."[9] In his writings, Kafka enjoys the clandestine pleasure of opposing the father through the erection of his own fantasmatic laws.

For Bataille, sovereignty comes in the form of expanse, an excess that will continuously emerge as

---

Opposite above: Terry Jones of the Dove World Outreach Center in Gainesville, Florida. In July 2010, Jones announced that he would stage an International Burn-a-Koran Day that September on the ninth anniversary of the 9/11 attacks. Though he later canceled the event, the following March he staged a mock trial of the Koran, after which an associate burned a copy of the book. Opposite below: Film still from *Fahrenheit 451*, 1966, directed by François Truffaut.

new forms and paths. This may seem to go against the psychoanalytic doctrine that posits lack as the origin of desire. However, as Lacan has shown, desire and drive both originate at the impossible object, the *objet petit a*. And although the psychoanalytic notion of drive cannot be equated with the organic powers that stream from the Bataillean notion of excess, the Lacanian drive must also be seen as excessive energies, akin to the staggering and explosive movements of the literature of sovereignty in Bataille. To psychoanalysis, the subject of literature—the subject engaged with it—evades the Symbolic order of economic, legal, and social structures and escapes into the world of dreams and fantasy. Here, we touch upon what Bataille calls sovereignty; its very condition means that it cannot be represented, but it is attached to the structural components of the law, and is expressed as enjoyment.

Simone de Beauvoir also used the trope of book burning, in a text that in many ways can be seen as a pendant to Bataille's text on Kafka: "Must We Burn Sade?" She examines a logic of writing similar to that which for Bataille was an expression of sovereignty: the sexuality of the writing subject, she argues, is to be found at the level of pure fantasy, in the system of literature that for Sade was "demonic." It is a life beyond "space, time, prison, the police, the void of absence, opaque presences, the conflicts of existence, death, life and all its contradictions."[10] Sade, like Kafka, exercises a "useless liberty" of exuberant submission to a specific kind of enjoyment.

So what is the sovereignty of literature? The subject of literature reflects, but not from a position of rupture or lack but rather from behind a mask—a pretense or a theatrical role of some sort, a position of marginality. The subject of enjoyment can never present itself directly; it can only do so through the means of an aesthetic elaboration—for instance, a theatrical mask, a narrative, or a portrait. The book-as-signifier and the subject of enjoyment are tied to each other. Here we confront an ineffable aspect of enjoyment: as the subject of literature becomes signs to others, it becomes ineffable to itself. The enjoyment of writing demands its own *mimesis*; this is to be found, although transformed, in the fantasy world of the work operating though its own laws of signification. In a Lacanian register, a subject comes into being through a signifier that represents the subject for another signifier, meaning that subjectivity and language support each other.[11] The subject of literature is not the author of his enjoyment; the enjoyment of writing must always pass through the desire of the enjoyment of the Other. At the same time, literature is a signifier that does not represent the Symbolic order, but rather extends an invitation into another order, of fantasy, desire and enjoyment. In literature, enjoyment is produced not by succumbing to the desire of the Other, but by the erection of a self-imposed Other. It is at this point, also, that the sovereignty of literature emerges, as a point of freedom. Literature makes a claim not to representation, but rather to the possibility of undermining any claim to representation; the sovereignty of literature is the undoing and redoing of the Symbolic.

SOVEREIGNTY AND THE DRIVE

What we find in Bataille's question, as well as in Beauvoir's—must we burn Kafka? must we burn Sade?—is an exploration of the enjoyment that follows literature as a signifier of sovereignty. With what right does literature pose as sovereign? Certainly neither Bataille nor Beauvoir would be found burning books. Their titles are, rather, rhetorical hints at what books might be seen to perform: claiming a scandalous right to enjoyment while undoing the law of the father as the unquestionable focus of sovereignty. Approaching literature as a discourse beyond content, genre, or expression of subjectivity, both Bataille and Beauvoir touch upon the enjoyment of writing as the scandalous core of the signifier of the book.

Lacan has described this kind of enjoyment in his analysis of James Joyce's *Ulysses*, a book burned, as we saw, for unleashing the unclean and the obscene in the United States of the 1920s. To Lacan, it is Joyce's approach to naming that allows him a form of writing close to the limit of psychosis. It is at this limit that a continuous exploration of enjoyment is possible, an enjoyment that is not phallic but linguistic. *Ulysses*, Lacan writes, bears witness to the way in which Joyce remains rooted in his father even as he denies him: a figure echoing Kafka, as depicted by Bataille.[12] The names of the father are displaced, moved around and hidden in all of Joyce's books: Jacob, Abraham, Daedalus, and so on. It is in this continuous circuit of displacement that Joyce's symptom is to be found: an enjoyment of the act of writing itself.[13]

To Lacan, there is no enjoyment to be had without the payment of anxiety. In his *Seminar X*:

Fra Angelico, "The Dispute of Saint Dominic and the Miracle of the Book," detail from the predella of his altarpiece *The Coronation of the Virgin*, ca. 1430–1432. This image depicts an episode from the life of the saint in which he threw his own book and a book containing a number of heretical Albighensian doctrines into a fire; his own leapt from the flames, while the other was consumed.

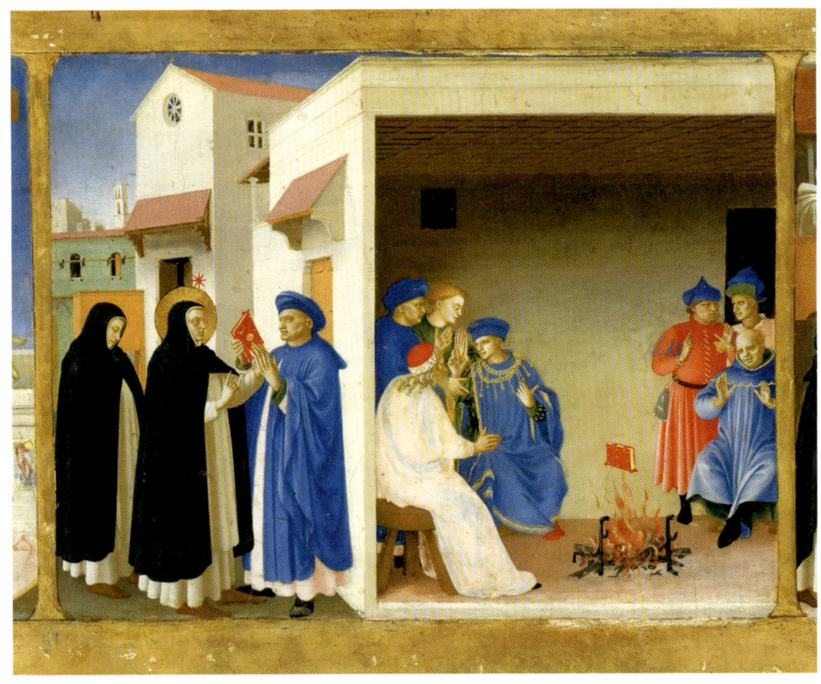

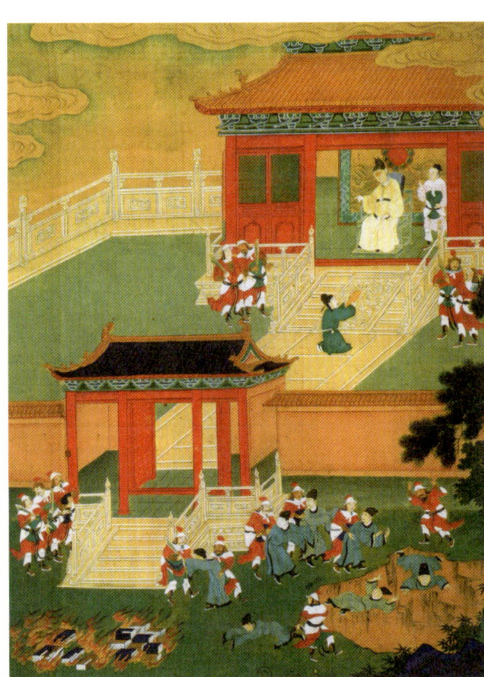

An eighteenth-century painting of an episode in the third century BC when Shi Huangdi, the first emperor of the Qin dynasty in China, purportedly ordered the burning of Confucian books and the live burial of Confucian scholars.

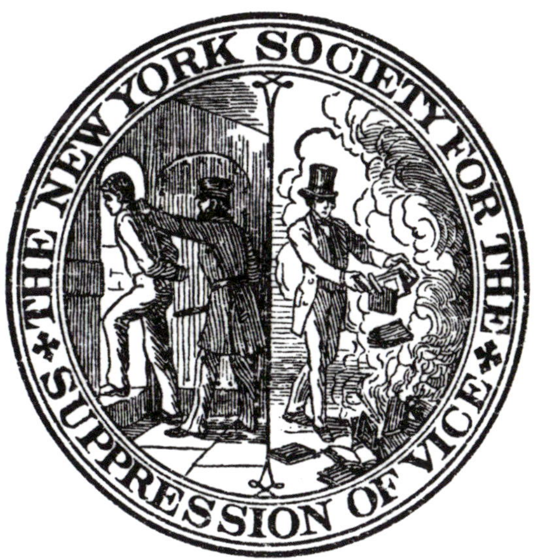

Official seal of the New York Society for the Suppression of Vice, founded by Anthony Comstock in 1873.

Anxiety, he demonstrates that the Other is there as an "un-consciousness that is constituted as such."[14] This means that the Other cannot provide me with the answer to the question, "What do I desire?" The Other "involves my desire in the measure of what he is lacking and that he does not know."[15] Still, it is this same Other that commands me to search. In *Anxiety*, and in the short seminar *On the Names of the Father*, Lacan makes clear that the Other is a signifier that, above all, commands: it may appear as "the sovereign good God, a delusional conception of Plato" or as "the God of the Jews," a God who demands the *jouissance* of the subject. This is the source of anxiety: "To this order '*Jouis!*', I can only answer one thing, which is: '*J'ouis* (I hear).' Of course, but naturally I do not enjoy so easily for all that."[16] The Other imposes a command to which the subject can never fully respond. If it attempts to, it will itself fade. That is why for psychoanalysis, sovereignty can never be the God of command; it must always be the law of the father, of prohibition, of castration.[17]

BOOKS FOR THE FUTURE

Bonfires of books are performed not by literature lovers but by religious and political fanatics. They are acts that serve a command: the punishment of literary sovereignty. The fanatic seeks an answer to the question of anxiety: What does the Other desire? The literary work appears as an irresponsible and flippant answer. The bonfires of books complete the fantasy of a punishing Other. The fire appears to produce an enjoyment in the fanatic who obeys the Other of command. It does not work particularly well. The result is dry and barren, loaded with tension in the face of an Other whose desire remains unknown.

The book is treated like a Prometheus who has stolen fire from the gods and must be punished in flames. Certainly, books stand in for the hatred against the other, the wish to excommunicate or extinguish beliefs and people. But the Promethean quality of the book permeates the whole scene. Book burnings are not simply replacements for the destruction of a people; they are attempts at destroying the book, the enjoyment of literature. In book burnings, it is not a given book but the Book itself that produces a doctrine of destruction. As Giorgio Agamben has noted in his book on literature, *The Fire and the Tale*, both reading and writing are metaphysical acts that serve to de-biologize any notion of the human. Both reading and writing are acts of creation that carry traces of a metaphysical dimension. This metaphysical dimension leaves material traces through the blankness of the page: traces that we can find, for instance, in the elliptic contractions of Kafka's parables, or in the short notes of Simone Weil's diaries. In writing and reading books, in thinking and fantasizing with them, we are dealing less with a human capacity than with the power of literary language, something that lies both within and beyond the material aspects of the book. The "book" is what takes place neither in the book nor in the world, says Agamben, and therefore, it carries the virtual capacity of ruining both itself and the world concomitantly.[18] When books burn, something more than human lives of the present are being destroyed. Insofar as the book also conditions past and future lives, it is ultimately the possibility of new and emergent forms of life that is being targeted.

1 Haig Bosmajian, *Burning Books* (London: MacFarland & Company, 2006), p. 7.
2 Ibid., p. 193.
3 Ibid., p. 195.
4 Rebecca Knuth, *Burning Books and Leveling Libraries: Extremist Violence and Cultural Destruction* (Westport, CT: Praeger Publishers, 2006), p. x.
5 Eva Gesine Baur, *Eien Spurensuche* (Vienna: C. H. Beck, 2008), p. 178.
6 See <library.arizona.edu/exhibits/burnedbooks/documents.htm#herrmann2>.
7 Page duBois, *Sappho Is Burning* (Chicago: The University of Chicago Press, 1995), p. 193.
8 Georges Bataille, *Literature and Evil*, trans. Alastair Hamilton (London: Marion Boyars, 1985), p. 158.
9 Ibid., p. 165.
10 Simone de Beauvoir, "Must We Burn Sade?" in *Simone de Beauvoir, Political Writings*, ed. Margaret Simons and Marybeth Timmermann, trans. Kim Allen Gleed, Marilyn Gaddis Rose, and Virginia Preston (Urbana: University of Illinois Press, 2012), p. 69.
11 Jacques Lacan, *The Four Fundamental Concepts of Psychoanalysis*, trans. Alan Sheridan (New York: W. W. Norton, 1978), p. 207.
12 See Jacques Lacan, "Le Sinthome," trans. Luke Thurston, p. 21. This unofficial translation of Lacan's Seminar 23 of 1975–1976 is available at <lacanonline.com/index/wp-content/uploads/2014/11/Seminar-XXIII-The-Sinthome-Jacques-Lacan-Thurston-translation.pdf>.
13 Ibid., pp. 30–31.
14 Jacques Lacan, *Seminar X: Anxiety*, trans. A. R. Price (Cambridge: Polity Press, 2016), p. 23.
15 Ibid.
16 Jacques Lacan, *On the Names of the Father* (Cambridge: Polity Press, 2013), p. 272.
17 As Lacan has shown in his analysis of Joyce, this occurs in a way that uncovers the eternal truth: there is no Other of the Other. See Jaques Lacan, "Le Sinthome," p. 18.
18 Giorgio Agamben, *Le Feu et le récit*, trans. Martin Rueff (Paris: Payot & Rivages, 2015), p. 115.

SCHLOSS MURNAU, HOLLYWOODLAND, CA 90068

Volker M. Welter

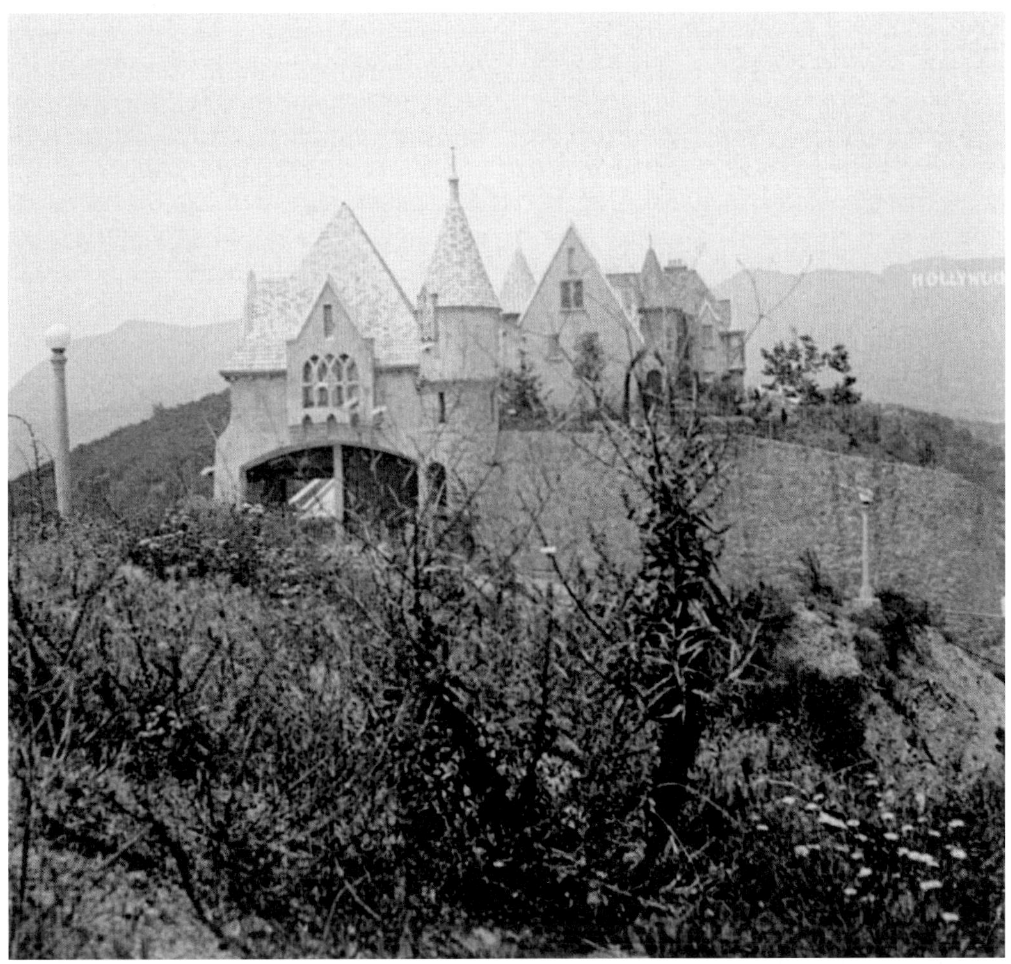

Above: Friedrich Wilhelm Murnau, photograph of Wolf's Lair, Hollywood Hills, ca. 1928–1929. Courtesy Deutsche Kinemathek–Sammlung Murnau.

Castles, palaces, and stately manor homes provide the setting for many movies by Friedrich Wilhelm Murnau (1888–1931), the German silent film director who is today probably best known for *Nosferatu: A Symphony of Horror* (1922).[1] One of Murnau's earliest films, *The Blue Boy* (1919) is set in Vischering Castle in Westphalia, which dates back to the thirteenth century. *The Haunted Castle* (1921) takes place in a neoclassical manor house, and much of the plot of *The Burning Earth* (1922) happens in and around a castle in Silesia. For Nosferatu, Murnau picked Orava Castle in Slovakia, a building with roots stretching back to the thirteenth century, as the site of Count Orlok's home. And while the location of *The Expulsion* (1923) is only a crofter's home on a faraway mountaintop, its isolation recalls the privacy of the moated Vischering Castle.[2]

Murnau arrived in California in early July 1926 and stayed there, except for a few months back in Berlin in 1927, until mid-May 1929. It was then that he sailed for Tahiti to shoot his last movie, *Tabu: A Story of the South Seas* (1931), returning to California by October 1930. A few months later, on 11 March 1931, Murnau died from the injuries that he had suffered in a car accident just north of Santa Barbara the previous day. For parts of his sojourn in California, Murnau made his home in Los Angeles in a building that contemporaries called a *Schloss* or castle. The edifice and its whereabouts have thus far remained unidentified and its importance and meaning for Murnau, accordingly, obscure. Considering Murnau's profession, to move into a castle-like home seems to be another case of movie settings determining private architectural taste. However, Murnau's fascination with castles harks back much further than his rise to one of Weimar Germany's foremost movie directors. Castles held for Murnau private, positive associations rather than just being sites of inexplicable events or even horror, as some of his movies might suggest.

In 1917, during the Great War, the military unit to which Murnau belonged occupied near Verdun "a beautiful, but rather melancholy château, abandoned by its owners. … [Murnau] had the largest room in the château, arranged in perfect taste. Everything in it was clean and well-appointed; when you went to see him you forgot about the war, and made a polite and civilized visit."[3]

In Berlin, Murnau lived in a suburban version of a home that looked as if it had been lifted from a castle precinct in a walled medieval city. It was the family home of the poet Hans Ehrenbaum-Degele (1889–1915), Murnau's friend, and perhaps lover, who had been killed on the battlefield. After the war, the poet's mother had invited Murnau to stay in the home in Berlin's Grunewald neighborhood and some time later transferred the property to her son's friend. The building at Douglasstrasse 22–22a consists of two grand, attached townhouses, erected in 1901–1902 by the builder Wilhelm Körner, with Murnau occupying number 22. The tall, timbered roof, darkly paneled entrance hall, and the heavy masonry around the lower exterior walls may recall the past, but Murnau transformed his abode into a place evoking a future life elsewhere. Murnau lived there with the painter Walter Spies—a close friend, perhaps even another lover—and together the two men filled the home with artworks such as Asian marionettes and a mural depicting Persian-style hunting scenes that Spies painted in Murnau's study; in short, objects and motifs telling of dreams about living elsewhere.

Giving in to his long-felt *Fernweh*, Spies (1895–1942), left Murnau and their mutual home in 1923, seeking a new life in Bali. *Fernweh* is the opposite of *Heimweh* (homesickness) or a nostalgia for the past. It afflicts upon its sufferers a heartbreaking longing for distant shores where they hope to find solace, if not a new self. Unsurprisingly, numerous Germans experienced that condition during the postwar years, though *Fernweh*'s history reaches back further to the Romantic period and beyond, as evidenced by many German fairy tales. Leaving for California was Murnau's answer to his *Fernweh*, a longing he had probably felt for some time, changing his surname, as he did, from Plumpe, which in German evokes notions of clumsiness, to Murnau, a Bavarian village that had been home to an artists' colony in the late nineteenth century. Ultimately, California could not satisfy Murnau's *Fernweh*, as his later journey to Tahiti was supposed to take him even further, on to Bali, and back to Spies.

When Murnau returned briefly to Berlin in 1927, he asked the architect Dieter Sattler (1906–1968) to redecorate the interior of the Grunewald home in advance of his arrival.[4] Together with a mutual friend of both men, the cellist Francesco von Mendelssohn, Sattler created a historicist interior that fused sixteenth-century and baroque antiques, contemporary furniture, wallpapers, and soft furnishings, and paintings by Picasso and Cézanne into the image of a stately home that generations of owners had filled with objects and art works. The interior, as published in the fashionable magazine *Die Dame*, did not depict Murnau as in any way being interested in modernism in architecture and interior design.[5]

Fictional and real castles, stately manor houses, and visually rich, eclectic, and historicist interiors were the settings of much of Murnau's private life. From early on they were associated for him with men and with lovers, and expressed his desire for privacy, as illustrated by his decision to set *The Blue Boy* in Vischering Castle. The title references Thomas Gainsborough's 1770 painting of the same name, which plays an important role in the Dorian Gray–like plot involving a young man and a precious stone. In Germany's gay circles at the turn of the century, however, prints or copies of Gainsborough's painting were also used to signal their owners' sexuality. Recollections of Murnau by friends and contemporaries often describe him as a quiet, polite, and mannered gentleman, an image more of a member of the landed gentry in a manor house than of exalted gay Berlin during the Weimar Republic. Finally, the stylistic distances these private homes and interior spaces kept from the modernist architectural-artistic concerns of the period express not a nostalgic longing for a past—either lost or out of reach—but emphasize

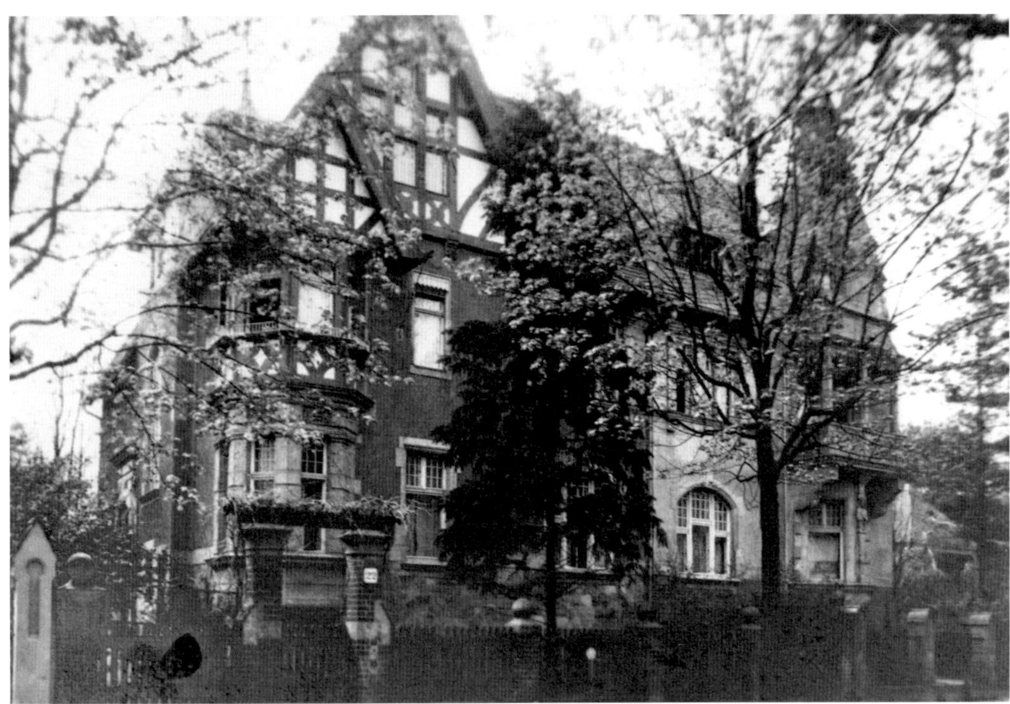

An undated photograph by Murnau of his semi-detached villa (left half), Douglasstrasse 22, Berlin. Courtesy Deutsche Kinemathek–Sammlung Murnau.

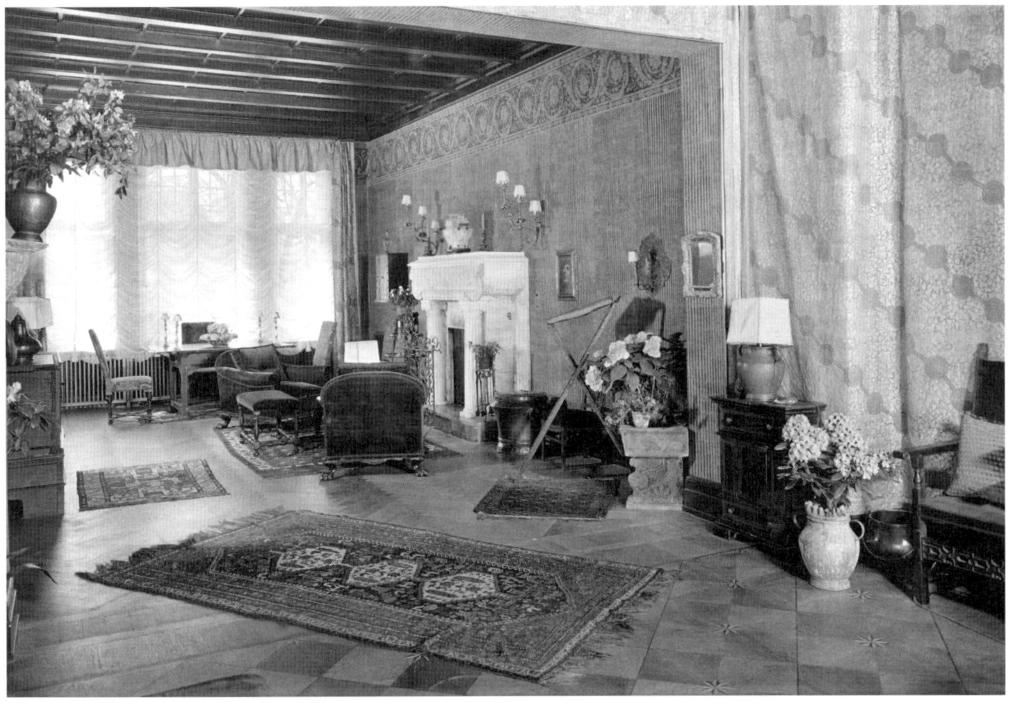

Interior of Murnau's living room at Douglasstrasse 22, ca. 1927, after redecoration by Dieter Sattler and Francesco von Mendelssohn. Photograph by the firm of Zander & Labisch. Courtesy Ullstein Bild.

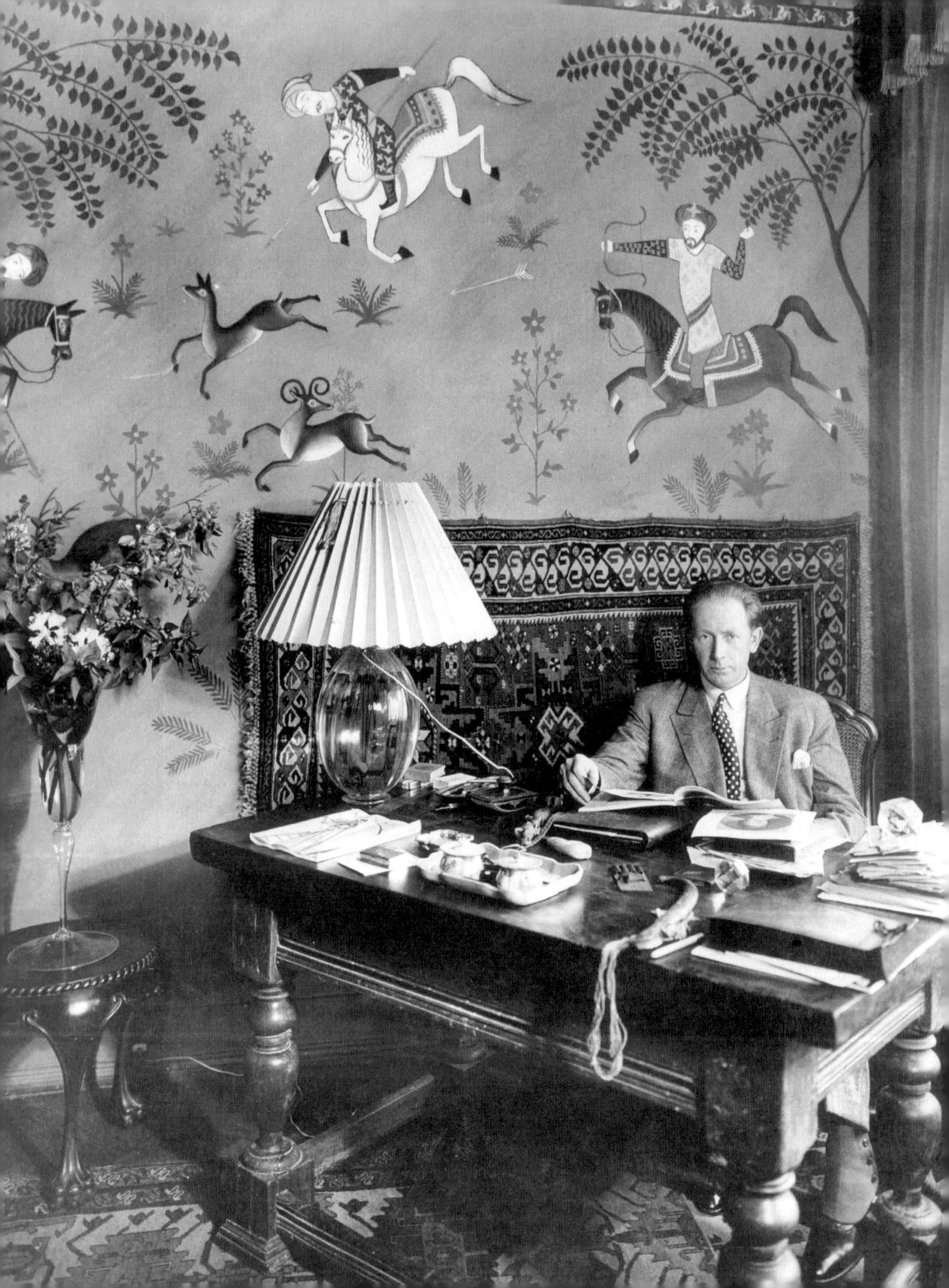

Murnau's *Fernweh*. Murnau's *Schloss* in Los Angeles, a building designed in a French Normandy revival style, perfectly matched that longing.

To trace Murnau's private life in California, one has to go to Berlin. The Deutsche Kinemathek preserves in its Murnau collection a series of photographs of a young nude posing for Murnau and his camera in and around a house that is located in the hills above Los Angeles.[6] Subsequent to the publication of a selection of Murnau's private photographs in 2013, the young man was identified as the actor David Rollins (1907–1997), whom Murnau considered, but ultimately did not pick, for a role in *Four Devils*, a movie he shot between January and May 1928.[7] In various interviews later in his life, Rollins told how Murnau, "a great friend of mine," kept inviting him to his private abode.[8]

In the photographs, Rollins smiles in and out of a pool; inside the house he looks dreamily toward the outside, and appears in general at ease with his nakedness. "I was never ashamed of my body," he states in one interview, even though, according to the interviewer, "Murnau's desire to see David [Rollins] in the nude [...] both puzzled and surprised him."[9] Some of Rollins's poses show the photographer's knowledge of art history, a subject Murnau had briefly studied at university. Sitting on a small bridge over a pool, the model mimics, for example, *Boy with Thorn*, an antique sculpture now in the Capitoline Museums in Rome that, for gay men in the nineteenth and early twentieth century, also made coded reference to homosexual desire. Yet where in Los Angeles was this house in the seclusion of which Murnau could shoot such private, intimate photographs of a friend?

There is a description of a home occupied by Murnau that matches the location in the hills captured in these photographs. It comes from David Flaherty, a brother of the movie director Robert Flaherty; both men were in early 1929 in discussion with Murnau about shooting an independent movie in the South Seas, which would become *Tabu*. Writing in 1960, David Flaherty recalled that right after his return from Tahiti—where he had been on an exploratory visit for a different movie—Murnau asked him over for dinner. "Murnau lived alone with his servants in a castle perched on the highest hill in Hollywood. I felt flattered to be the only guest at the long table, which gave an eagle's-eye view of the lights of Hollywood and Los Angeles far below."[10]

With Flaherty's topographical description of the house's site in hand, and by examining the edges and corners of the house visible in Murnau's private photographs, I searched for "castles in Hollywood" online, and was soon able to identify the edifice as standing in the Hollywood Hills at 2863 Durand Drive. Photographs by Murnau of the entire house, which I eventually saw in his archive in Berlin, confirm this identification. Locals know the building as "Wolf's Lair," perhaps a fitting name for a home temporarily occupied by a German.

Further up the hills rises the "Hollywood" sign. In 1923, when it was first erected, it read "Hollywoodland,"[11] flashed annoyingly with thousands of light bulbs, and advertised the hillside development below where engineers were cutting roads and leveling building sites. Among the developers was Leslie Milton Wolf (1894–1972), who acquired lots 1 to 4 in Block 2 of Tract 6450, numerical co-ordinates that translate to a triangular piece of land wedged between Durand Drive and Wetona Drive. There, Wolf erected as early as 1924 a two-story building of nine rooms in a French Normandy style, which meant plenty of corner turrets, steep roofs, and an irregular roofline. Access to the isolated spot was via Durand Drive, where a round tower marked the entrance to the lot. Already by December 1926, a second tower had appeared at the rear of the house.[12] And by March 1927, Wolf was expanding the original short entrance tower into a full-blown gatehouse to accommodate servants and automobiles. Beside the now-tall tower, mock medieval tracery and a dovecote were cramped underneath an elongated, hipped roof in a French castle mode. The gatehouse is visible in some of Murnau's photographs, dating his tenancy in the castle to after the completion of the former.

Two more photographs in Murnau's archive show the swimmer (and later *Tarzan* movie star) Johnny Weissmuller with and without Murnau in the garden of Wolf's Lair.[13] According to the *Los Angeles Times*, Weissmuller visited the city from 17 to 24 May 1928, which would place Murnau in the house in early spring of that year, around the time when the filming of *Four*

Opposite: Murnau at a sixteenth-century Italian writing desk in his home office at Douglasstrasse 22, ca. 1927. The mural is by Walter Spies. Photograph by the firm of Zander & Labisch. Courtesy Ullstein Bild.

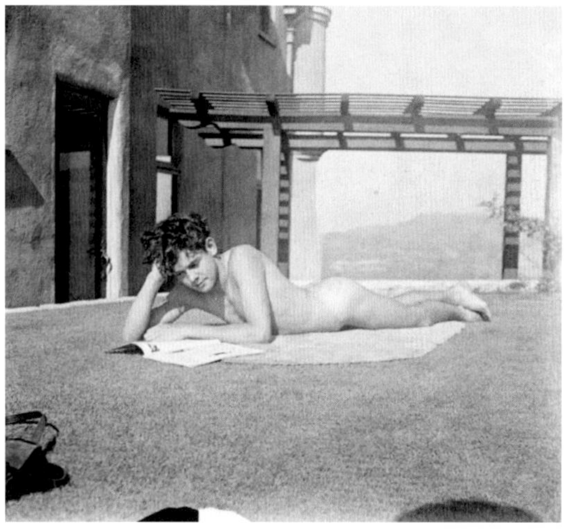

Murnau's photograph of the young actor David Rollins in the garden of Wolf's Lair, ca. 1928–1929. Courtesy Deutsche Kinemathek–Sammlung Murnau.

Devils ended.[14] Taking into account that Murnau had arrived back in the US in early October 1927, he may have moved into Wolf's Lair as early as late 1927. Assuming David Flaherty's recollections are chronologically correct, the dinner with Murnau happened at the earliest after 15 February 1929, the day when the *SS Tahiti*, on which Flaherty traveled, arrived back in San Francisco.[15] This would put the dinner most likely toward the end of Murnau's residency at Wolf's Lair, but absent further sources, the date of his leaving the *Schloss* currently has to remain undetermined. That the Los Angeles City Directory from 1929 lists his address as 9 Laughlin Park only adds to this uncertainty, especially as it is neither known when the information for the directory was compiled nor when the volume was published.

Erhard Bahr remarks in his book *Weimar on the Pacific: German Exile Culture in Los Angeles and the Crisis of Modernism* that as "a city without historical memory," Los Angeles has always attracted those who wanted "to escape history."[16] Many of the émigrés escaping (National Socialist) history in the 1930s and 1940s, however, could not find a life without history in Los Angeles, despite Southern California's reputation, because they in fact missed the very historic background against which they had habitually debated the merits of modernism. But for other immigrants, Murnau for example, this absence was neither cause for lament nor a shortcoming, but the attraction of California.

Already in 1827, Goethe had written "America, you've got it better" in a poem about the carefree living that came with freedom from history and remembrance. Still, the poem ends with a stern warning not to re-erect the past, as might happen when a young artist sets out to write poetry: "Protect him [...] From tales of bandits, ghosts and knights."[17] Others, such as the American landscape painter Thomas Cole, severed any reflexive linkage between old stories, historic buildings, and references to the past. In his 1836 "Essay on American Scenery," Cole points out that the associations that come to the mind of an observer of contemporary American landscapes generally have to do with the present and the future, but not the past. "Looking," Cole writes, "over the yet uncultivated scene, the mind's eye may see far into futurity." As an example of the associative images emerging from that distant future, Cole imagines that "on the gray crag shall rise temple and tower"; thus, historic building types like castles and palaces morph into symbolic images of the future.[18]

In Berlin during the 1920s, when architectural modernism took off, Murnau never succumbed to the lure of naked cubes, horizontal windows, flat roofs, and other signs of architectural modernity, and the life that accompanied it—a life Walter Benjamin once described as one without traces insofar as it was conducted between hard, shiny surfaces. But Murnau was not ignorant about the changes modernity wrought on the perception of (architectural) space and the human life conducted within it. Just the opposite: as early as 1924, he had discussed how the moving, rather than static, movie camera would make visible "the symphony of the melody of [human] bodies and the rhythm of space."[19] As an art historian, however, Murnau also knew that new techniques of camera usage were mere means for creating images. His trust in the power of images was so strong that he predicted in 1928—wrongly—that "the ordinary picture, without movietone accompaniment, without color, without prismatic effects and without three dimensions, but with as few subtitles as possible, will continue as a permanent form of the art."[20]

In the same article, Murnau reflected on contemporary America's love affair with war movies, which made the country appeal to him, "the most extreme pacifist," because of his longing for romance. The latter, in turn, also sheds light on the fascination castles and manor houses held for the movie director. Murnau

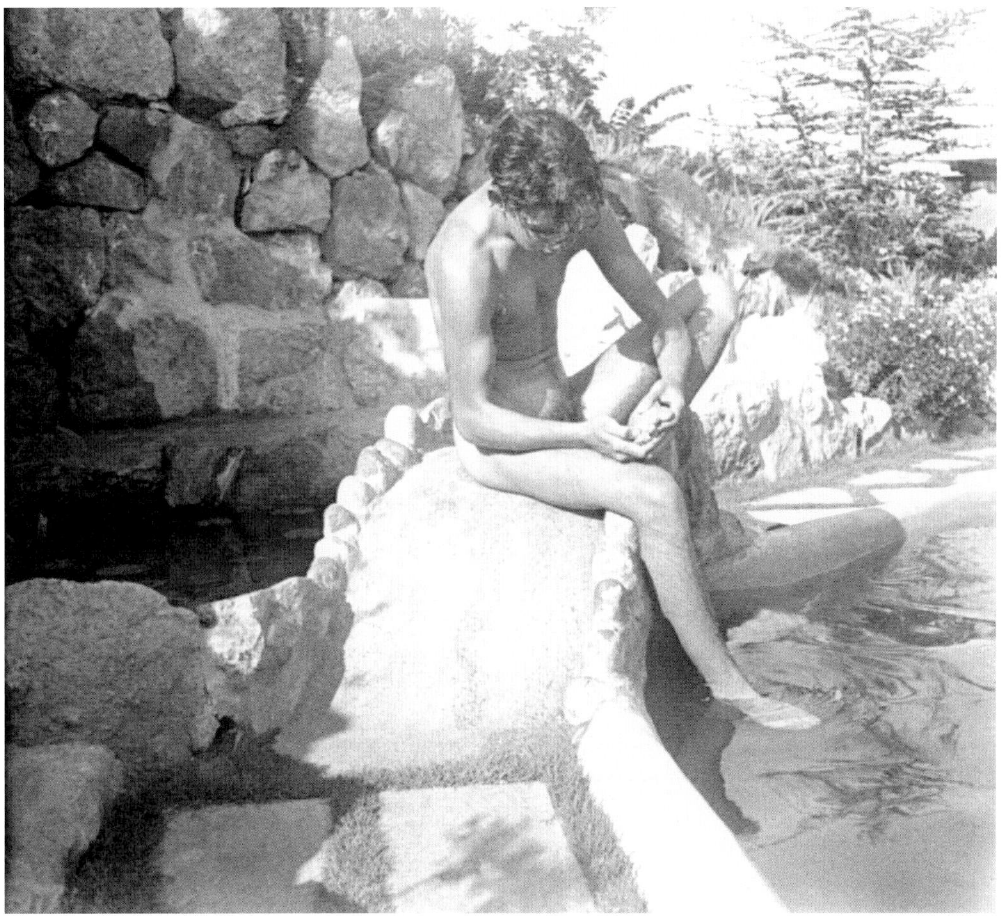

recognized in America's voluntary entry into the Great War a "demonstration of bravery, loyalty and martyrdom, each of these attributes a thread in the cloth called romance." Postwar Europe was no longer capable of seeing that romance, which, however, had not ceased to exist, even during the darkest time of warfare.[21] Murnau captured that romance when he arranged his room in the occupied French manor house into an image of a time when war was over. He experienced it again, when he lived in his *Schloss* in Hollywoodland, and he lived the romance whenever he created a private home for himself.

Finding the site of Murnau's tragic accident on California's Pacific Coast Highway north of Santa Barbara—on a section of the freeway now known as US Route 101—entailed a visit to a regional archive of the Department of Transportation of California, CalTrans, located in a nondescript office building on the outskirts of the city of San Luis Obispo. According to the coroner's report, Murnau's rented car was traveling north, toward Monterey, late in the afternoon of 10 March 1931.[22] The driver was Eliazar Garcia Stevenson, Murnau's approximately thirty-one-year-old valet, with John R. Freeland, a twenty-six-year-old chauffeur employed by the car rental company, in the passenger seat. Murnau was sitting on his own in the back. Driving on a stretch of road that was leading uphill in a slight right curve, the car tried to avoid an oncoming truck that was traveling downhill on the wrong side of the narrow, two-lane road. The maneuver failed. The limousine careened to the left, ejected all three passengers, flipped over along the far edge of the road, and came to rest upside down in a filled-in depression between the road and the adjacent train tracks. The valet and chauffeur were injured, but survived; Murnau

Above: Murnau's photo of David Rollins at Wolf's Lair posing in the manner of the subject of the antique sculpture *Boy with Thorn*, ca. 1928–1929. Courtesy Deutsche Kinemathek–Sammlung Murnau.

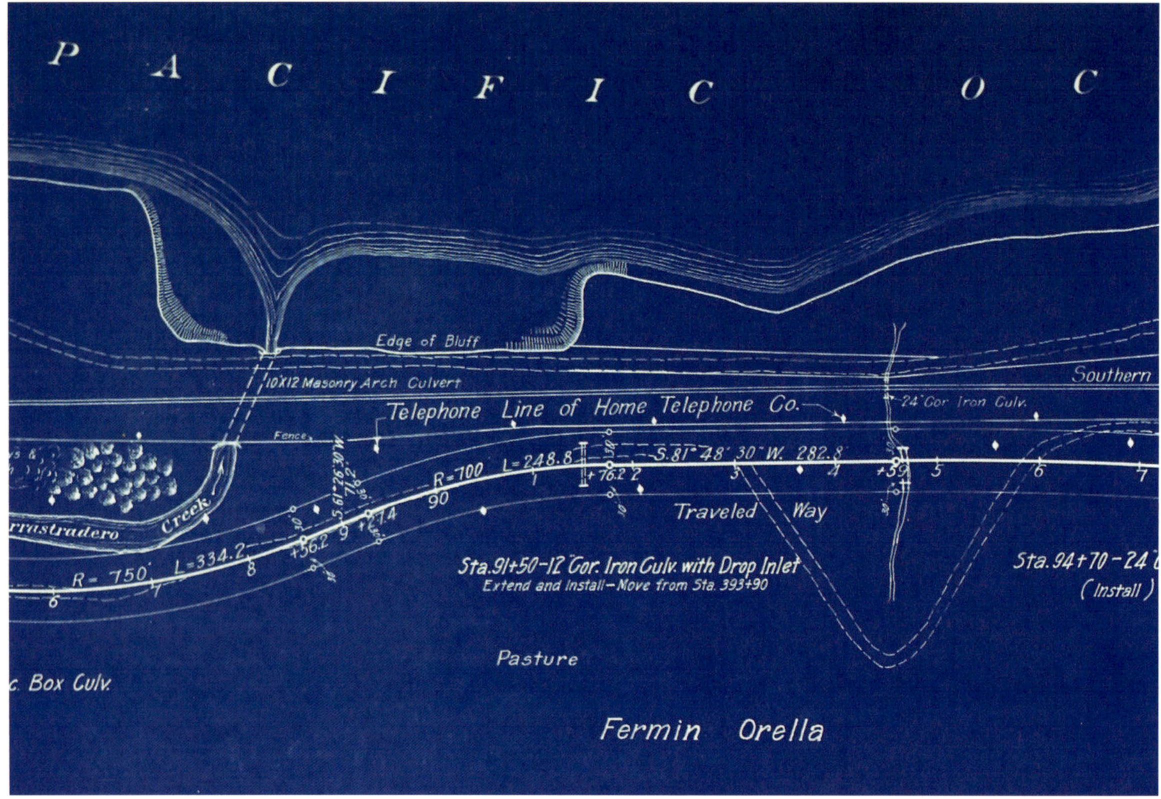

died the next day in Cottage Hospital in Santa Barbara.

The police officers tending to the victims estimated the site of the accident to be approximately a mile away from El Capitan Canyon. Historic blueprints from the early twentieth century in the CalTrans archive record how engineers gradually transformed a meandering coastal pathway into a modern road mostly following the contours of the coast and the profile of the land. Poring over one such map from 1914, an area about one-and-a-half miles out from El Capitan Canyon toward San Francisco stands out. There, the lower end of Cañada del Venadito, or "Canada El Arrastradero Creek" as the 1914 map calls it, crosses under today's route 101, the southbound lanes of which broadly follow the two-lane road Murnau traveled on. As laid out in 1914 and built in the subsequent decades, the road began there to take its first, gentle curve to the right past El Capitan Canyon while also moving upward. Standing at the side of the road in roughly that spot today, one can still match the coroner's description of the accident site to the broad lay of the land, including that filled-in canyon between the road and rail track in which the car landed.

Murnau's final resting place is in Südwestkirchhof Stahnsdorf in the southwest of Berlin. The artist Karl Ludwig Manzel (1858–1936) designed a tripartite, bold travertine wall that bears Murnau's name; a grave monument far more modern than any of Murnau's private homes had ever been. Indeed, it is far too modern, even too masculine for the lover of castles, romance, and men who lies buried there. In the center of the wall, Manzel placed a bronze portrait bust of Murnau. From there, the moviemaker's last gaze goes into the distance, the *Ferne* where California, Tahiti, and Bali lie.

Above: Detail of a 1914 blueprint depicting the course and layout of a new highway, US route 101, in the Rancho Canada del Corral area, Santa Barbara County, California. It was along this stretch of road that Murnau's fatal accident occurred. Courtesy Christopher Mancini, California Department of Transportation District 5 Archives.

Opposite: Karl Ludwig Manzel's 1931 grave monument for Murnau in the Südwestkirchhof Stahnsdorf, near Berlin, 1931. Photo Volker M. Welter.

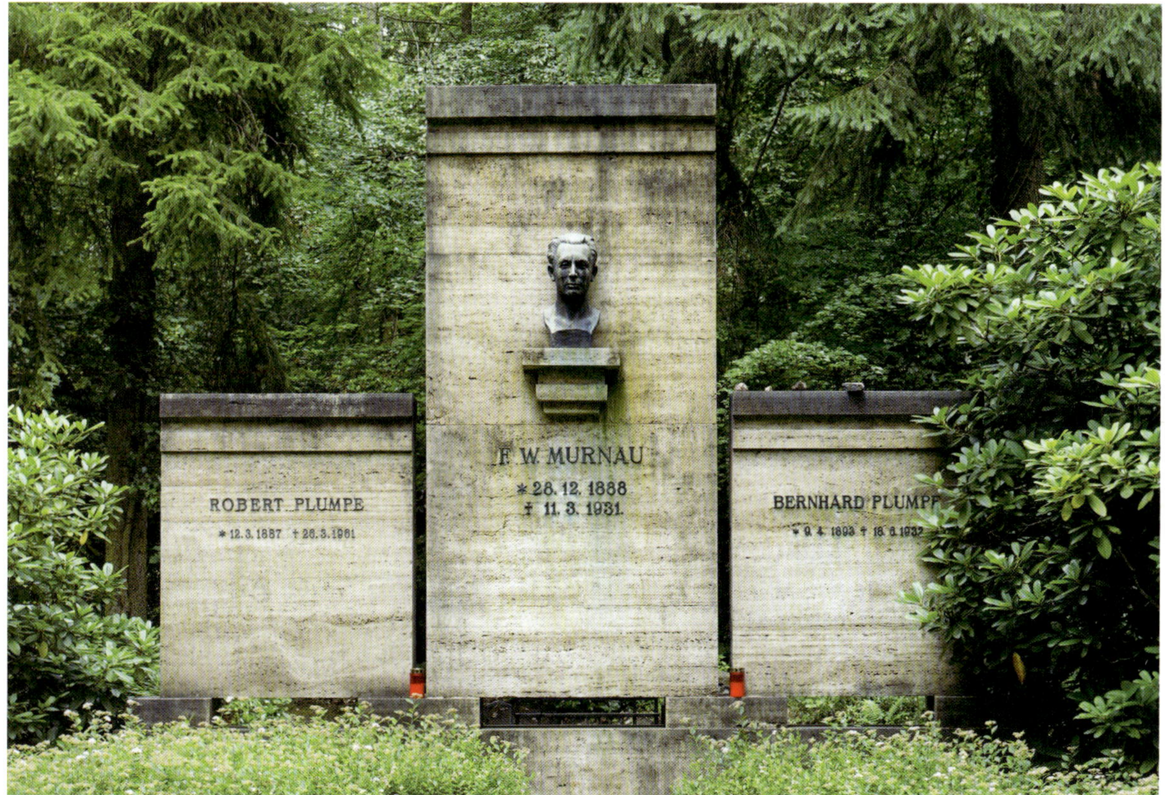

1 I would like to thank Professor Janet Bergstrom at UCLA; Les Hammer; Professor Bruce Robertson, UC Santa Barbara; Steve Vaught; Sian Winship, Society of Architectural Historians/Southern California Chapter; Deutsche Kinemathek, Berlin; and Chris Mancini and the Regional CalTrans Archive, CalTrans District 5, San Luis Obispo, for their help with and comments on the text.

2 I have followed the English translations of the original German titles given in Lotte H. Eisner, *Murnau* (Berkeley: University of California Press, 1973), pp. 273–277. In the case of *The Haunted Castle*, Eisner does not provide a translation, simply using the original German title–*Schloß Vogelöd*. In this instance, I have followed the translation offered by Kino International, which released an English-language DVD of the film in 2009.

3 This account of Murnau during the war by Wolfgang Schramm is published in Lotte H. Eisner, *Murnau*, p. 18.

4 Ulrike Stoll, *Kulturpolitik als Beruf: Dieter Sattler (1906–1968) in München, Rom und Bonn* (Paderborn: Ferdinand Schöningh, 2005), p. 49, n. 53.

5 "Eine Künstlerwohnung in Berlin-Grunewald. Das Heim des Regisseurs F. W. Murnau", *Die Dame*, no. 20 (July 1927), pp. 8–11.

6 *Friedrich Wilhelm Murnau: Die privaten Fotografien 1926–1931 Berlin, Amerika, Südsee*, ed. Guido Altendorf et. al. (Munich: Schirmer/Mosel, 2013), pp. 60–73.

7 Professor Janet Bergstrom kindly alerted me to this identification.

8 Tony Villecco, *Silent Stars Speak: Interviews with Twelve Cinema Pioneers* (Jefferson, NC: McFarland, 2001), p. 166.

9 Tony Villecco, *Silent Stars*, p. 166.

10 David Flaherty, "A Few Reminiscences," *Film Culture*, no. 20, 1960, pp. 14–15.

11 The word "land" was removed in 1949.

12 Steve Vaught kindly shared copies of the building permits for 2863 Durand Drive.

13 Guido Altendorf et al., *Die privaten Fotografien*, pp. 54–55.

14 Olive Hatch, "Johnny Weissmuller Heads Aquatic Program at Hollywood Athletic Club," *The Los Angeles Times*, 17 May 1928; "Weissmuller Hulvey to Vie with Barfoot," *The Los Angeles Times*, 24 May 1928. An earlier visit to Pasadena is recorded for August 1927, but Murnau was still in Berlin at that time.

15 Passenger list of the SS *Tahiti*, departing from Papeete, Tahiti, 24 January 1929, and arriving in San Francisco, 15 February 1929; obtained from California, Passenger and Crew Lists, 1882-1959, an online database available at <ancestry.com>.

16 Erhard Bahr, *Weimar on the Pacific: German Exile Culture in Los Angeles and the Crisis of Modernism* (Berkeley: University of California Press, 2007), p. 289.

17 Available at <schillerinstitute.org/transl/trans_goethe.html#America>. Translation by David Platt.

18 Thomas Cole, "Essay on American Scenery," *The American Monthly Magazine*, vol. 1, no. 1, (January 1836), p. 12.

19 Friedrich Wilhelm Murnau, "…der frei im Raum zu bewegende Aufnahmeapparat," *Die Filmwoche*, no. 1 (3 January 1924). Quoted in Fred Gehler and Ullrich Kasten, *Friedrich Wilhelm Murnau* (Berlin: Henschelverlag Kunst und Gesellschaft, 1990), p. 141. My translation.

20 Friedrich Wilhelm Murnau, "The Ideal Picture Needs No Titles: By Its Very Nature the Art of the Screen Should Tell a Complete Story Pictorially," *Theatre Magazine*, vol. 47, no. 322 (January 1928), p. 41.

21 Ibid.

22 Les Hammer kindly shared a copy of the coroner's report of 17 March 1931, which is filed at the Superior Court of Santa Barbara County. Hammer's *F. W. Murnau for the Record* (Morgan Hill, CA: Bookstand Publishing, 2010) offers the most detailed account of the accident and corrects the sordid rumors surrounding Murnau's death.

THE DESERT

THE DESERT IS A STATE OF MIND CAST OVER THE EARTH

Michael Marder

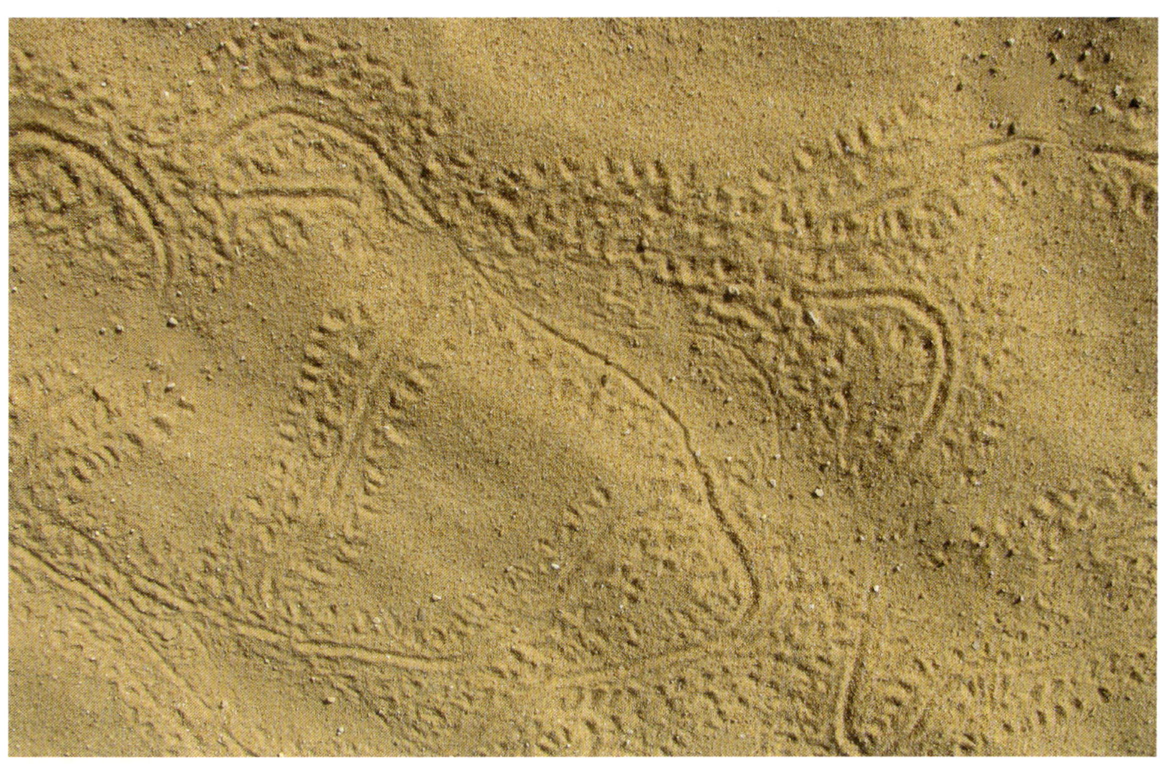

The desert is an invention, a creation of emptiness in the plentitude of existence, an introduction of barrenness into the fecundity of being. However dry this biome, it is never entirely vacant. Besides containing rocks or sand, the actual desert from Atacama to the Sahara and from the Gobi to Mojave is propitious to certain animals (coyotes and scorpions, chipmunks and rattlesnakes) and plants (barrel cacti and Joshua trees, tumbleweeds and ironwood) that find themselves at home there. It would be the height of arrogance to deem these and countless others of its inhabitants so insignificant that they are sidelined or forgotten, leaving only the vast vacuum, the expanding nothingness, that the ecosystem in question has come to denote. An automatic association of the desert with lifelessness betrays precisely such forgetting and neglect, which are, in my view, the side effects of a devastating project—refashioning the earth in the image of abstract thought. "The" desert is abstraction realized, cast over the world at the expense of biological, ecological, and ontological diversity.

When I write that the desert is an invention, I am alluding not only to how emptiness is interpolated by our manners of thinking into the *plenum* of what we, in a convenient shorthand, encode as "nature," but also to how, in the literal sense of the Latin *invenire*, the desert is called forth and comes into the world thanks to the accumulated impact of human industries on the environment. Our unique geographic imprint, our intergenerational signature, it constitutes our legacy and lasting contribution to natural history. The desert, to be sure, preexists and will endure long after the planetary dominance of *Homo sapiens*. But, at the same time, it grows as a result of human-induced climate change, threatening the earth with desertification, which is accompanied by ever more acute and widespread water and food shortages, conflicts over increasingly scarce resources, and skyrocketing extinction rates. Properly understood, an invention is not a mere figment of imagination, and, even if it were something of the kind, it would not preclude the real work of shaping actuality, whether destructively or constructively.

There is no desert. The desert is everywhere. We must find a way to hold onto both of these statements at the same time without experiencing the cognitive dissonance their paradoxical coincidence induces. Ultimately, in purely geographical terms, the desert is undefinable and, hence, indefinite, indeterminate, un-delimited. Although aridity may be its key feature, oxygen-starved "ocean deserts" are far from dry; despite pointing toward the absence of life, the desert is, as we have seen, populated by distinct plant and animal species. What, then, gives the desert its identity? Whence does it draw its meaning?

If the desert has no clear-cut identity as a noun, then it may well be that what lends it some degree of coherence is the verb form "to desert" and the attendant passive voice "deserted." Needless to say, the assumption that deserts are deserted by all forms of life is erroneous. Instead, the areas we relegate to the status of deserts are abandoned by our instrumental rationality, to which they appear useless. They are deserted to the extent that we no longer care for and about them, let alone about their autochthonous plants and animals. Unfit for the habitation of the very humans who've had a hand in their spread, deserts seem to be the areas of the world so vacant that they register as little more than black holes on the radars of our concerns. That is why the beings living there, too, are voided, rendered invisible, disregarded, forced to merge with nothing. Theirs is the fate of everyone and everything sacrificed to the arid abstraction of thought, indifferent to the singularity of existence.

The desert, then, is a state of mind that levels difference and treats everything as the formally equal and interchangeable parts of the void. Actual deserts are, of course, awash with differences in terrain and mineral composition, in altitude and degrees of denudation whereby the terrestrial surface wears away, and in the flora and fauna whose habitats they are. But the desert represented, presented, and indeed produced as the earthly incarnation of abstraction is homogeneous; in effect, it is homogeneity as such. Only on its ideally lifeless, empty, windswept plains is the life of abstract thought possible. Only there does a mind closed on itself open unto the world, recognize itself in the harshest biome—which it sees merely as a concretization of its own drive toward abstraction—and then withdraw, desert-ing that enucleated place in the night it has made, one in which all cows (cacti, coyotes...) are black.

Traditionally construed as an exilic milieu rife with danger as well as opportunities for regeneration, the growing desert has been transformed into an indicator of our exile from being, above all from its diversity and existential vibrancy. That we neither care for nor deign to notice the beings populating its expanses is symptomatic, as Heidegger would doubtless confirm, of our lack of care for being itself. Abandoned, forsaken, left in the lurch there, in the total and blinding exposure to the elements (be they the sun or the wind), is the human duty—the sole duty still defining what remains of the human—to expose oneself to, be fascinated by, mirror, or channel all that is just as it is. In the etymological knot tying together the desert and (military) desertion, we may thus discern the devastating outcomes of abrogating humanity as a task still to be discharged. Opting for the indifference of abstraction instead of the involvement of care, we desert the world and ourselves, which is to say, desertify ourselves and the world.

The global exile currently underway will not last for forty years, as did biblical wanderings in the Sinai intended to cleanse two generations of slave mentality. The way things stand, our exile from being into the desert of abstraction, concretely reflected in the spread of deserts worldwide, will, like an object's approach to the outer edge of a black hole, take an infinity to be completed. And, at the end of this interminable itinerary, the actual will finally become rational, the deserts that consume the earth turning indistinguishable from the desert of abstract thought.

TITANIC IN THE DESERT

Emilio Distretti

Beginning in the seventeenth century, colonialism materialized as a power capable of transforming "other" worlds, territories, and landscapes that it saw as empty lands. Since the nineteenth century, these have been categorized as *terrae nullius*, a legal designation that voided these areas of any intrinsic value and deprived the indigenous people of land titles as a step toward justifying the seizure of land. The perceived emptiness of the desert was a model for those conceptualizing *terra nullius*, presenting it as abandoned, uncultivated, and outside any economy. The desert was thus never only a physical reality but also occupied a central place in the formation of the colonial imagination.

The desert played an important imaginary role for two settler-colonial movements that emerged in the first part of the twentieth century—Italian Fascism, which sought to colonize the northern Libyan Sahara, and Zionism, in its quest to colonize the Naqab.

Across a few decades—between the 1930s and 1950s—Fascism and Zionism incubated colonial discourses and practices based on the desire to domesticate the desert and "make it bloom." In both discourses, wild deserts were not simply a metaphor for wilderness but were understood to be the outcome of abandonment caused by the idleness and negligence of their current inhabitants. Each revolving around narratives and myths of return—the return of, and the return to, ancient glory and patrimony—both Fascism and Zionism justified their projects by taking the desert as their starting point. From a spatial point of view, the desert was understood as the *tabula rasa* where the imagination proliferates; from a historical-political point of view, it was seen as the degree zero of a new order. The nationalist myths respectively claim that the Italians were returning to the Libyan coasts, where the Roman Empire had previously flourished, while the Zionists claimed their return to Eretz Israel after centuries of exile. In these discourses, positioned as reactions to the carelessness of the deserts'

Below: An Italian agricultural village being constructed in the Libyan Desert, date unknown. Courtesy Department of Art History and Archaeology, Columbia University.

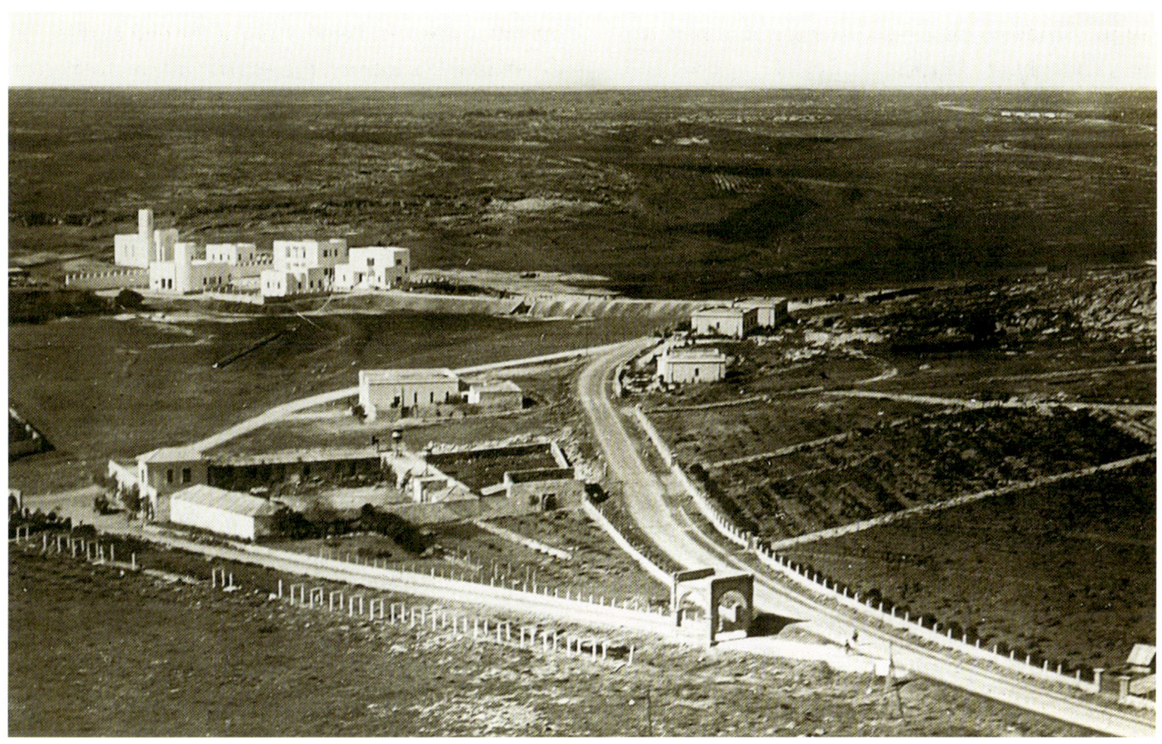

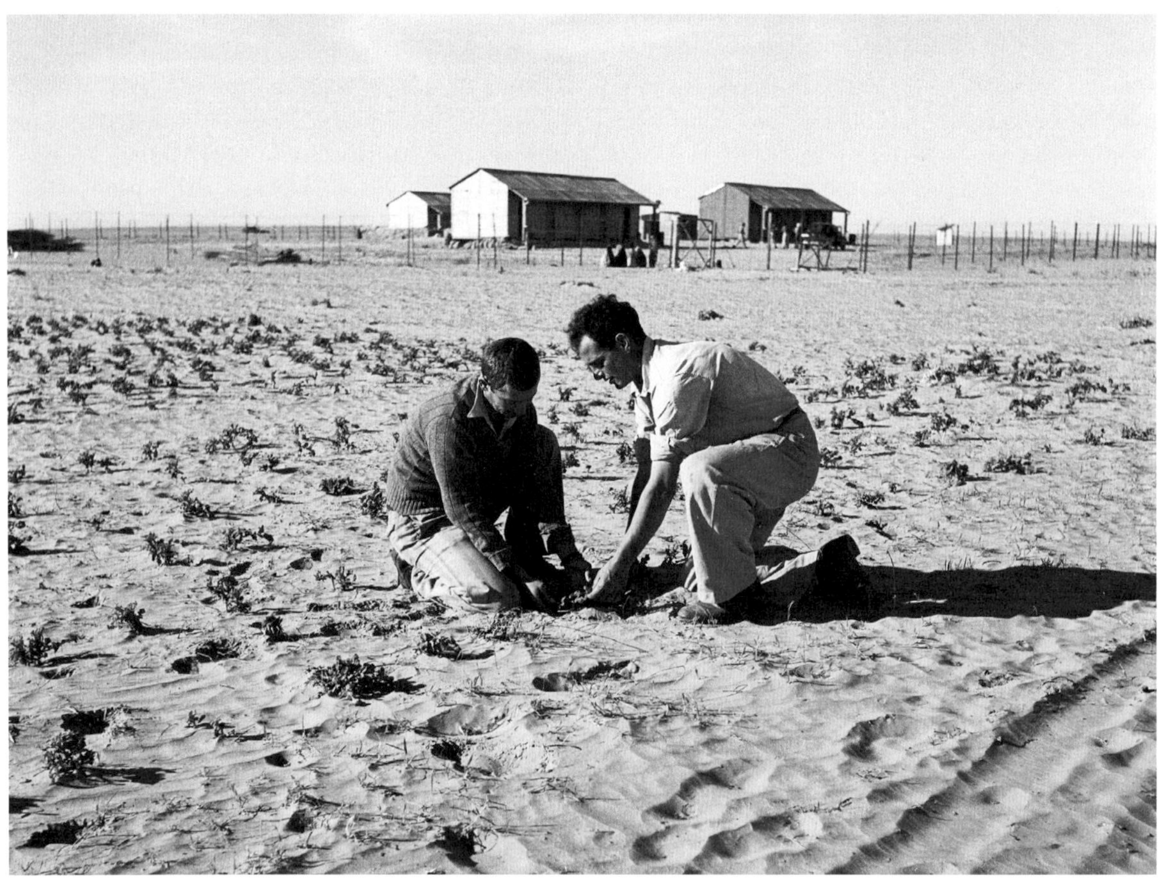

Jewish settlers at work in a potato field at the farming community of Kibbutz Urim in the Naqab (Negev) Desert, Mandatory Palestine, September 1946.

custodians, settling the terrain became synonymous with resurrection. Needless to say, the colonial imaginary disregarded and dismissed the presence of significant native populations in both deserts. The fulfillment of these latter-day colonialist dreams came, of course, at their expense.

Along the desert boundary that connected the archaeological sites of Leptis Magna, Sabratha, and the Arch of Marcus Aurelius in the center of Tripoli, the Italian nationalist discourse of the 1930s aspired to tie the Roman ruins, proof of the great ancient civilization, to the grand expectations of a future hegemonic Fascist empire. Archaeological investigations conducted by the Italians before and after their conquest had not only uncovered monuments, but also fossilized seeds and land-use infrastructure from Roman times such as canals and aqueducts, all of which were celebrated as a manifestation of ancient Roman agricultural expertise.

Before David Ben-Gurion invoked it in the 1950s, Benito Mussolini used the biblical metaphor of "making the desert bloom" to imagine the Fascist revitalization of Libya, which until then had been mocked as a "great bowl of dust." Fascism envisioned a new ecology for the Libyan desert based on an agrarian revolution, where the hunter's spear, seeking the odd rat or lizard, would give way to the plough of the settler. After the 1938 state-driven mass migration of twenty thousand Italian settlers, the so-called *Ventimila*, governor-general Italo Balbo's *fanterie rurali*, or "rural infantry," built new villages, houses, roads, and aqueducts. These squads of workers, who were depicted with a spade in one hand and a gun in the other, became the emblem of the Fascist settler. The Libyan desert had to be transformed into the new "granary of Rome," producing high living standards through the use of ecology and architecture. In 1940, a special issue of the popular magazine *L'Illustrazione Italiana* was published as a way to celebrate Libya as a new destination for a bourgeoisie eager to escape their urban cage. One of the magazine's reporters praised the way in which the tourist industry had begun to counter "romantic" expectations of wilderness and savage nature by promoting how the colony in fact offered a comfortable experience in keeping with metropolitan Italy:

The butter is always here in little rolls, the milk is fresh, the salad is crisp and slowly we learn that cows have just arrived from Tripoli on a lorry, and that the salad represents the victory of modernism over barbarity, the victory of the water taken from the artesian well over millenary sands.[1]

A few years later, the Zionists similarly sought to establish agricultural settlements and awaken the desert from an imagined millenary "emptiness": Israel's nation-building project combined the myth of "back to the land" after centuries of exile with the slogan of "turning the desert green," an agenda that has been pursued by the Jewish National Fund since 1901 through planting trees, ferrying water, and developing settlements all over historic Palestine.

The settling of the Naqab and the Arabah started long before the establishment of the state of Israel in 1948. Prior to the partition of Palestine, eleven "points" of Jewish settlement were established overnight in October 1946 in order to assure the inclusion of this area in the future Jewish state; later, the Israeli Defense Forces (IDF) completed the occupation of southern Palestine.[2] The conquest of the desert between 1948 and 1949 was undertaken by the Nahal, an IDF program instituted by Ben-Gurion, which similarly to Balbo's *fanterie rurali* combined military service and the establishment of agricultural settlements, fighting and farming. Under the supervision of Nahal officers, enlisted men worked on farms and paved roads, and planted eucalyptus trees, acacia, and jujube while the road to the Red Sea was being laid down.

While ideology and agricultural expansion have been historically considered the common ground shared by both colonial models, I recently uncovered a story that revolves around a different intersection of these two colonial worlds, and a character who in fact moved between them. Creating the basis for a literal juxtaposition of colonial geographies between Libya and Palestine, this story unveils a material relation between the Libyan Sahara and the Naqab.

I learned about this history when I was conducting interviews, both in Italy and in Palestine/Israel, during research on the Jewish Italian architect Umberto Di Segni, who, together with the better known Florestano Di Fausto, is considered to be the most prominent representative of modernist, and in fact Fascist, architecture in Libya. After the war, Di Segni emigrated to the newly established state of Israel. While trying to track—with little success—the traces of Di Segni's architecture in Tel Aviv and Netanya, I met Jack Arbib, a Jewish Italian-Libyan writer who documented Di Segni's life across Libya and Israel.

In our conversation, Arbib incidentally mentioned his uncle Pio Nahum, another Italian-Libyan Jew who emigrated to Israel after 1948. His is a story of migration and colonization—narrated by the material history of ruined war materiel strewn across the desert. It is also a story that connects the two distant deserts, and could be read as a mythical, biblical fable and a conjunction of two colonial histories.

Complementing Arbib's memories, Guido Nahum, the youngest son of Pio, shared more anecdotes from his family history. This story could not have been written without both their testimonies.

• • •

Pio Nahum's family story is a typical tale of an elite Jewish family in Fascist-ruled Libya before and after the Racial Laws of 1938. While Ze'ev Jabotinsky's revisionist Zionism embraced Fascism in its early phase, the everyday life of Italian and Libyan Jews in the colony went through different stages. Clearly seen by the Italian authorities as the interface, and thus mediators, with the Arab "primitives," Jews played a crucial role in colonial affairs until 1938. In fact, Guido's story began by recalling the career of his grandfather, Aidan, who was a colonel in the Italian army between 1930 and 1934. More importantly, he was the personal interpreter of the governor of Cyrenaica, the notorious Marshal Rodolfo Graziani—later infamously known as "the butcher of Ethiopia" for his use of poison gas and other means to massacre the Ethiopian population under Italian occupation.

Despite the Fascist regime's recognition of Jews as the economic engine in Tripoli and Benghazi and as loyal to the ideology, the racial manifesto of 1938, drawn up largely under German influence but enthusiastically embraced by Mussolini, broke the illusion of integration and forced Jews to leave all public positions. But as his private correspondence with Mussolini reveals, Italo Balbo, recognizing the strategic economic position of Jews in Libya, played a key role in trying to defend their communities in the colony. While they lost all political influence, they managed to safeguard many of their financial interests. This may explain how the Nahum family survived the war, and even retained some of its economic status in postwar Libya. Interestingly, in our conversation, despite reflecting on the harshness of being a Jew in occupied Libya under the racial laws, Guido looked back nostalgically on those days in Benghazi before and after 1945, when his father made his fortune.

He told me about one Mr. Ziegler, whose name betrayed a different provenance—"a distinguished man in his late 50s, with aristocratic manners and fluency in French, a somewhat strange figure in postwar Libya." The unusual presence of this man in Benghazi in the aftermath of World War II had been a mystery for Guido for years. Ziegler lodged in their house for weeks as a guest of his father. Guido remembers that the man "played every evening with the children and paid generous compliments to Mrs. Nahum for her cooking skills." But he never exchanged a word with his father in public or in front of the family, as if they did not have anything to speak about. A few years after the formation of Israel, when the Nahum family emigrated there, the identity of Ziegler was revealed: he was a member of the Jewish Agency who had come to Libya to convince Pio to move his assets from Libya to the newly created state and invest his capital there.

The story of Nahum's fortune is in fact a story of waste, and in two senses: the waste of war, here to be found in the "wastelands" of the desert. Our notion of waste is defined both spatiotemporally—waste is matter considered to be "out of time" and "out of place," doomed to dispersion or perdition—and territorially, best exemplified by the desert, which functions as a topos reflecting the threshold of rationality and the dead end of human projects. Both conditions are marked by abandonment, uselessness, and unproductiveness.

Yet it was precisely junk in the desert that was the source of Nahum's fortune. After Rommel's army was defeated at El Alamein by Montgomery's troops in 1942, the Libyan desert was left scattered with the residue of war: among the many abandoned bodies of dead soldiers, there were hundreds of truck and tank carcasses, an excellent source of iron. The British authorities asked for bids to clean the desert of all its waste, and Pio Nahum won the contract. This junk soon became a truly profitable business: iron and steel were in dire need to feed the blast furnaces of European factories, the new industry of global peace. He was turning waste into gold.

But Nahum's workers and diggers, screening the Libyan Sahara for war residue, also found a surprising

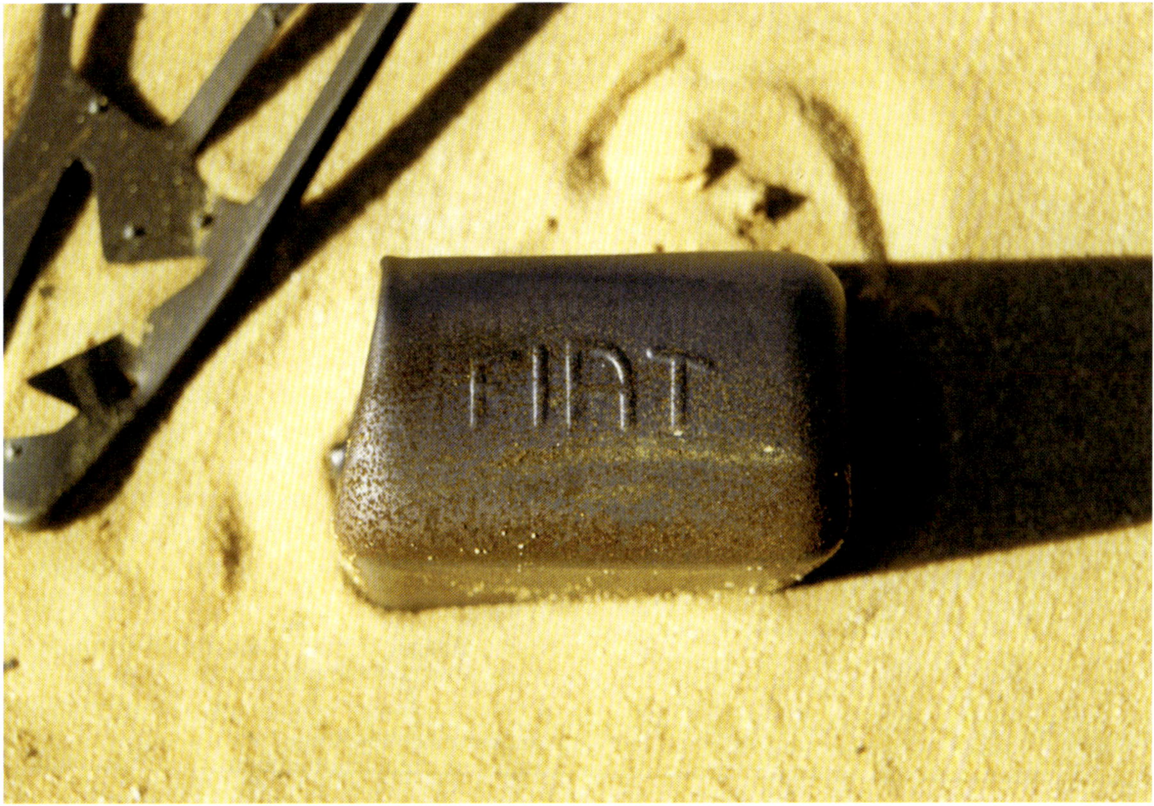

form of waste: dozens of abandoned trucks that they could easily repair and return to use. Many were abandoned by German and Italian soldiers in an attempt to escape the lethal strikes of the British Spitfires. In 1942, these planes were targeting convoys along the Litoranea, the east-west coastal highway—built by Mussolini in 1937 at the time of Italian occupation—that followed the edge of the desert. Many of the trucks still had gas in their tanks. After being recovered and repaired, the trucks were put back into service in the regions of Cyrenaica and Tripolitania. Nahum quickly became the most successful entrepreneur in postwar Libya. On this basis, a secret cooperation between Nahum, Ziegler, and the Jewish Agency began to develop. But the rumors of a Libyan Jew supporting the Zionist cause in Palestine prompted Libyan nationalists to put a bounty on his head. In 1946, Nahum and Ziegler agreed that there was no more time to lose, and things unfolded rapidly thereafter. Nahum stayed in Libya to organize a secret transfer of his operations, while his family temporarily found refuge in Italy. He wanted, of course, to take his wealth with him. He split his fleet in two: half the trucks were sent on boats through the Mediterranean port of Benghazi, and from there to the port of Haifa, at the time still under the British Mandate. The other half was sent through the desert. There, a group of Libyan Jews who were experienced desert drivers were given the mission of smuggling the trucks through Egypt and into Palestine through the Sinai and the Naqab. Between 1946 and 1947, seventy trucks entered Palestine illegally.

According to Guido Nahum's memories, his father's migration clearly echoes a sense of biblical wandering, where the desert acts as the theater in which Zionist ideology could find its completion. But as this story

---

Above: Remnants of war materiel can still be found in the Libyan desert to this day. Part from a World War II–era Fiat truck abandoned in a valley in the Jebel Sherif mountains, Libya. This Fiat truck was a casualty of an engagement between Italian ground and air forces and the British Army's Long Range Desert Group on 31 January 1941. Photo Harald Woeste.

Overleaf: Remains of one of the Chevrolet trucks used by the British Army's Long Range Desert Group during their encounter with Italian forces in January 1941. Photo Harald Woeste.

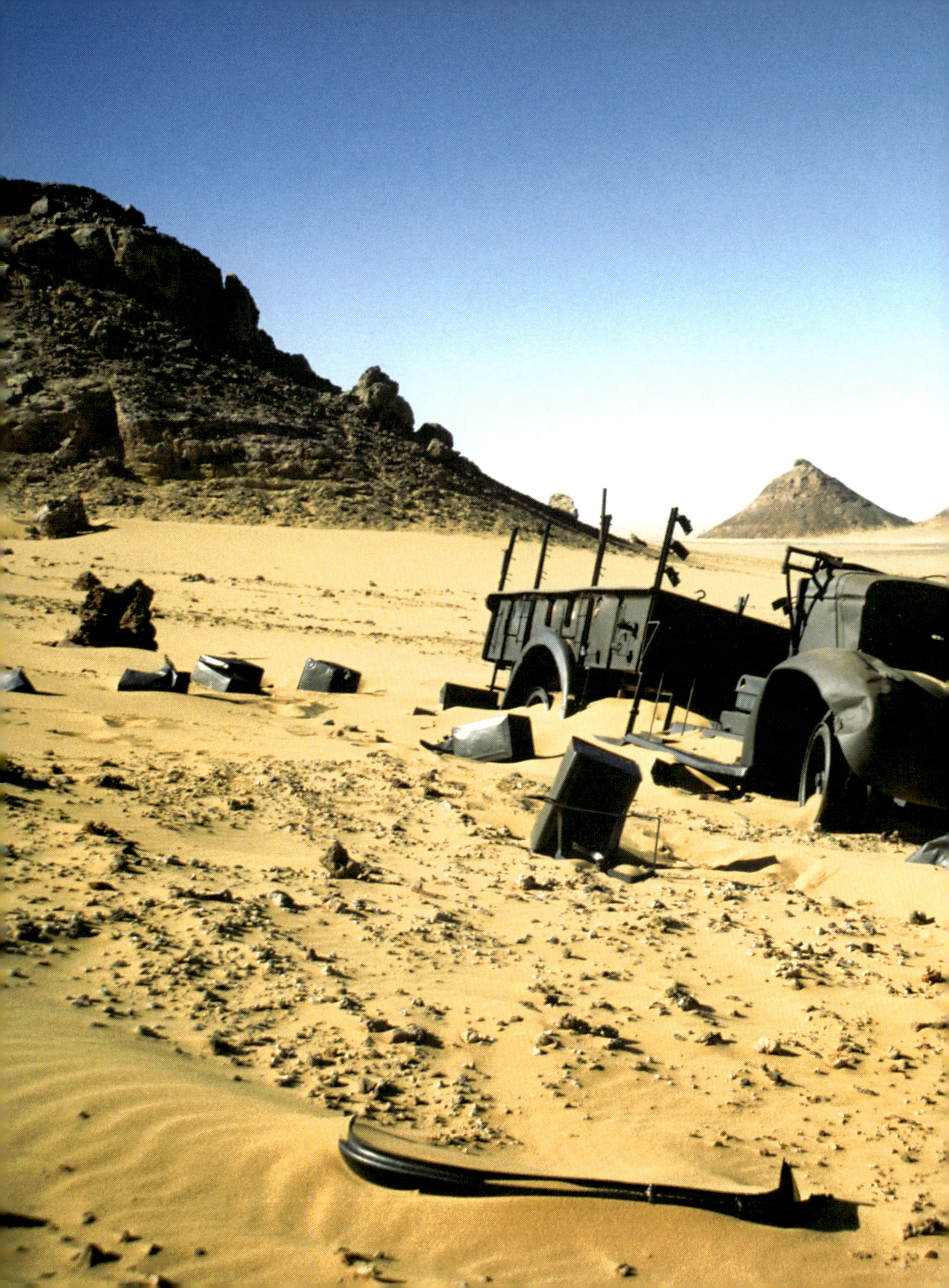

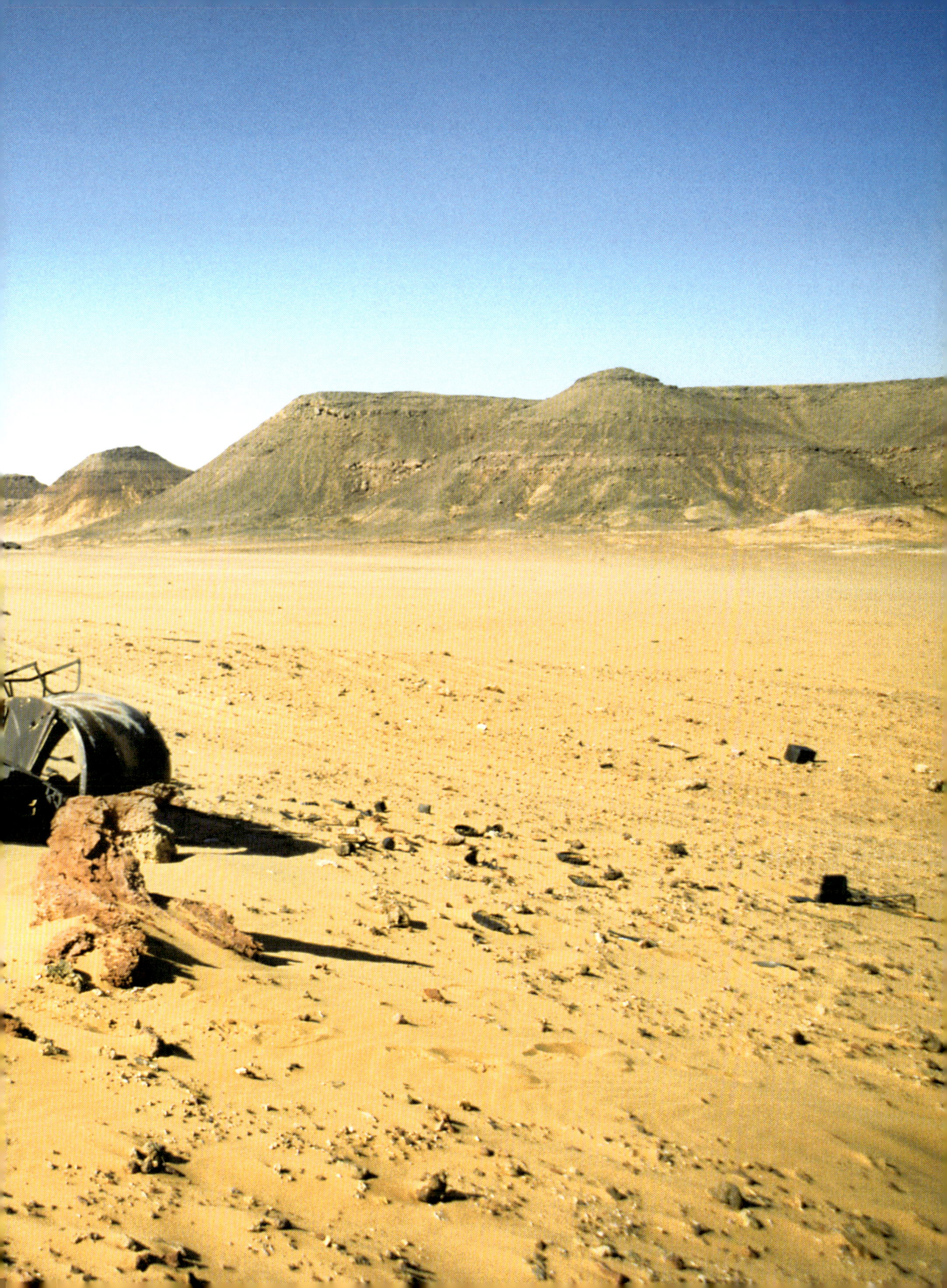

shows, the wandering is not representative of a human drama only; it also relates to a furious circulation of iron, steel, and war refuse from Libya to Palestine at a time of shifting ideologies and massive political transformations. Interestingly, in Guido Nahum's recollection, this movement and trade of metals, engines, and wheels actually started in Italy, before World War II reached North Africa. In order to understand deeply the interconnections between Fascist Italy and its peripheral colonial world, let us trace the metal back through history to see how it got to the desert in the first place, before it made Nahum a fortune.

• • •

"Oro alla patria!" or "Gold to the fatherland!"—the slogan that accompanied the 1935 colonization of Ethiopia (after Eritrea, Somalia, and Libya) and Italy's imperial ambitions—supported Mussolini's vision of an autarkic economic regime. Even as it was on its way to Addis Ababa, the Fascist state organized a mass parade in the streets of Rome to gather funds for Italy's war efforts and colonial plans: crowds of Italian women swarmed Piazza Venezia in Rome to donate their golden wedding rings to the fatherland. In return, they received steel rings to symbolize the union with the nation. But the national collection of gold was not enough. The regime also called upon its citizens to donate iron and other metals to support the war industry: copper pots from family kitchens, metal fences from farms, and bronze bells from churches were all used to produce cannons, vehicles, and armament. In the Fascist imaginary, the colonial lands became the theater in which the union between metals and men could be staged as a way to celebrate the military, economic, and spiritual power of the nation. Through autarky, propaganda, colonialism, and war, metal eventually became synonymous with politics.

It was Fiat who first began to employ these donated metals, using them to manufacture cylinder heads for cars and trucks to support the war and the colonial enterprise. The Fiat 626 truck, which was ideal for desert routes, became the most popular vehicle in Libya and Ethiopia for both civilian and military purposes. There they ran and there they died after being abandoned by soldiers retreating in 1942. At this point, it might have seemed that the "Fascist metal" had completed its life cycle, starting in the furnaces of Fiat's factory in Turin and ending in the Libyan desert.

But in the hands of Pio Nahum, heterodox desert archaeologist and entrepreneur, this war waste was to find a second life: the metal, the components, and the trucks were all revived, inspiring a new nexus between North Africa and the Middle East. Indeed, through a visionary union of colonial landscapes, Nahum's transit from one desert to another broke the temporal and spatial distance between two alien colonial worlds: one that had just passed and another that was about to come into being.

After the creation of the state of Israel in 1948, Nahum founded Titanic—the first Israeli transportation company to run on the Tel Aviv–Eilat line, which connected the metropolis at the center of the country to the Red Sea in the south. By the early 1950s, Titanic had become the preeminent civilian transportation company for crossing the Naqab and the Arabah deserts. Thanks to the experience of their Libyan drivers, who had expertise in navigating desert routes, mule tracks, and border roads, the trucks traversed Scorpion's Ascent, an old Roman desert road connecting the Naqab to the Arabah. Nahum's convoys comprised a line of six trucks with armed guards and two military jeeps, one at the front and the other at the back, so as to safeguard them against possible attacks from Palestinian fighters along the border with Jordan.[3]

While serving various purposes (transport of mail, goods, cement, and timbers for the new settlements in the desert), Titanic worked closely with the Israeli Ministry of Defense, backing the Engineering Corps in their renovation of the old, crumbling Roman, Ottoman, and British desert roads. It was the first company to bring Jewish settlers to the shores of the Red Sea, where the city of Eilat was founded in 1951.

Driven by entrepreneurship, ideology, and the capitalist spirit, Nahum's journey contributes to a redefinition of the image of the wanderer in desert spaces. Representations of deserts typically refer to theology and the prophets of the monotheistic religions to explain the sense of bewilderment caused by the act of wandering—"the wilderness was where Moses had wandered with his people for forty years, and where they had nearly abandoned their God to worship a golden idol," says environmental historian William Cronon.[4] Against this image, the wanderer of Nahum's story, who has lost his place in the world, meets the settler and embraces an ideology of expansion. Here, deserts evolve from being a "primitive" and "worthless" place into a laboratory for building a nation-state. From transport to cultivation, deserts must be "redeemed" by the settler's labor and technology. In both Fascist and Zionist discourses, such "redemption" was justified as the reaction against the Arab presence, which has been marked as the cause of disorder and neglect. "Making the desert bloom" was a slogan of civilization, one that refused the passive contemplation of wild nature and instead imposed order on a "chaotic" landscape, on "wasteland."

• • •

Titanic did not survive long as a company. By 1961, it had gone out of business. Presumably, this was partly connected to the prolonged drought that hit vast areas of the Naqab between 1956 and 1962, forcing settlers, agricultural enterprises, and other ventures to retreat from the region. But in Guido Nahum's memory, the closure of the business was mainly the result of growing competition in the transportation sector and the high maintenance costs involved in sustaining the old Titanic fleet, which was severely damaged over the course of many difficult trips across the desert. With time, and the refusal of the Israeli government to support Titanic financially to replace the vehicles' broken parts, the fleet fell into disrepair. Unlike other local companies that could rely on brand new vehicles, Titanic's old trucks were of course of Italian origin and spare parts for them could only be imported.

Following the trajectory of the Fiat trucks from Italy to Palestine, the line drawn in the various deserts by Nahum indicates how this story cannot be simply reduced to a biography, as it adds an important epistemological aspect to the writing of history in the context of global colonialism. In this scenario, Nahum's story shifts the focus to the intersection of two settler-colonial worlds, where wandering sets the stage for settler-colonialism. The settler—embodying the passage from nomadism to civilization—eventually comes to inhabit a modern grid of infrastructure and agriculture that facilitate future migration, trade, and nation building. But in both Libya and Palestine, "making the desert bloom" required lands emptied to make room for new civilizations. This came with a heavy human cost to the indigenous populations. In this sense, the Bedouin Nakba—when the Israeli military expelled almost 90 percent of the hundred thousand Bedouins of the Naqab to the West Bank, Gaza, Jordan, and Egypt between 1948 and 1953—seems to echo the so-called military "pacification" of Libya. Conducted by the Italian army between 1923 and 1932 in Cyrenaica against the indigenous rebellion led by Omar al-Mukhtar, this campaign led to the ethnic cleansing of half of the population of Cyrenaica in order to clear space for Italian settlers. Importantly, ethnic cleansing is an ongoing reality in the Naqab. Thousands of Bedouins are still facing house demolitions, displacement, and resettlement in permanent towns to facilitate the Israeli state plan to domesticate the desert and reclaim it for their own settlements.

From occupied Libya to Palestine, Guido Nahum's memories and tales about the vicissitudes of his family clearly echo those of a biblical story, where the desert can represent both the beginning of and the end of exile. But these stories also situate us in the present, showing how in the colonialist epic, the desert—once traces of what existed before have been erased—can be made to perform as *tabula rasa*, as *terra nullius*, a place that offers, to quote David Ben-Gurion, "the greatest opportunity to accomplish everything from the very beginning."

1 Maria del Corso, "Gli alberghi della Libia," *L'illustrazione Italiana* (2 June 1940), p. 886. My translation.

2 This strategy echoes the *homa u'migdal*, or "wall-and-tower," settlement method that had been used by Zionist settlers during the Arab revolts of 1936 and 1939: using this rapid construction technique, which employed prefabricated materials, they could assemble an outpost overnight so as to circumvent Mandatory British restrictions on the construction of new settlements. According to Ottoman law, adopted by the British, constructions could be deemed legal if the roof had been completed.

3 Soon after the armistice agreements were signed in 1949, the phenomenon of Palestinian refugees attempting to return to their houses, villages, and fields, and to family members who were left behind, was commonplace. Israel always treated them as "infiltrators" and responded to these attempts with a shoot-to-kill policy. With time, Palestinians started forming armed escorts for refugees wishing to return, as well as organizing missions of attack and sabotage.

4 William Cronon, "The Trouble with Wilderness; or, Getting Back to the Wrong Nature," in *Uncommon Ground: Rethinking the Human Place in Nature*, ed. William Cronon (New York: W. W. Norton, 1995), p. 70.

ORPHAN UTOPIA
Reed McConnell

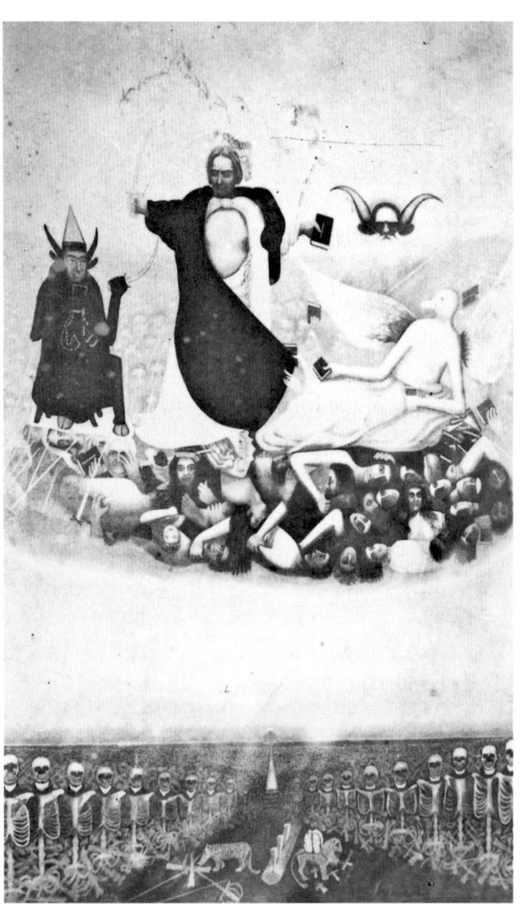

Reproduction of an undated painting by John Ballou Newbrough lost in a flood while in storage in El Paso, Texas. The complex iconography of the painting—said to be seventeen feet tall and ten feet wide—depicted a central tenet of *Oahspe*'s theology: that Christianity was founded when a powerful spirit usurped and distorted the teachings of the Jewish prophet Joshu/Jesus. Sometimes referred to as *The Three Worlds*, the painting depicts the three realms outlined in *Oahspe*—the work's lower third, where the skeletons can be seen, depicts Corpor; the false God-Christ figure occupies the middle region, called Atmospherea; and the now-faded upper portion represents Etherea, the higher heavens. Thanks to Leslee Alexander for her assistance with the captions for this article.

When the angels appeared to John Ballou Newbrough early one morning in 1881, he was nothing if not well prepared. A dentist and Spiritualist, he had spent the last ten years purifying himself for supernatural contact by abstaining from meat, bathing twice a day, and rising before dawn. The visit was expected.

The angels wanted him to buy a typewriter, a newfangled device—Newbrough described typing as writing "by keys, like a piano" in a letter to the Boston Spiritualist journal *The Banner of Light*—that would allow him to transcribe their account of the world's true spiritual history.[1] He obeyed, and for the next fifty weeks the angels visited him in his New York City apartment every morning before sunrise, taking control of his hands in sessions that lasted exactly fifteen minutes. By the end, Newbrough had produced a nine-hundred page manuscript called *Oahspe*: a history of world religions that exposed their lies and elucidated their fundamental interconnections.[2]

The dictating angels were nothing if not thorough. To supplement the text, they provided Newbrough with images of religious leaders, which he painted in the dark. Among those reproduced in the 1891 edition of *Oahspe* are the austere, mustachioed Zarathustra, with a cherub grinning behind his left shoulder, and a serenely smiling Confucius, hair stroked by a ghostly figure while an enormous eye floats in the clouds above him. These luminaries appear alongside diagrams and illustrations, everything from language trees to astronomical models to illustrations of ancient temples. (Newbrough claimed to have copied them, according to the angels' instructions, from technical books.)

Although Spiritualism was known and largely accepted in the New York of the time—séances were popular among the rich, and Newbrough had been hosting them in his apartment on West 34th Street for decades—some quarters received *Oahspe* with hostility. A "new bible" was a bit harder to reconcile with Christianity than simple communication with spirits, especially when that bible claimed that Jesus was actually a crafty angel named Looeamong who had tricked the other angels and minor deities into electing him chief divinity of the universe. A *New York Times* article from 1883 describes an interaction

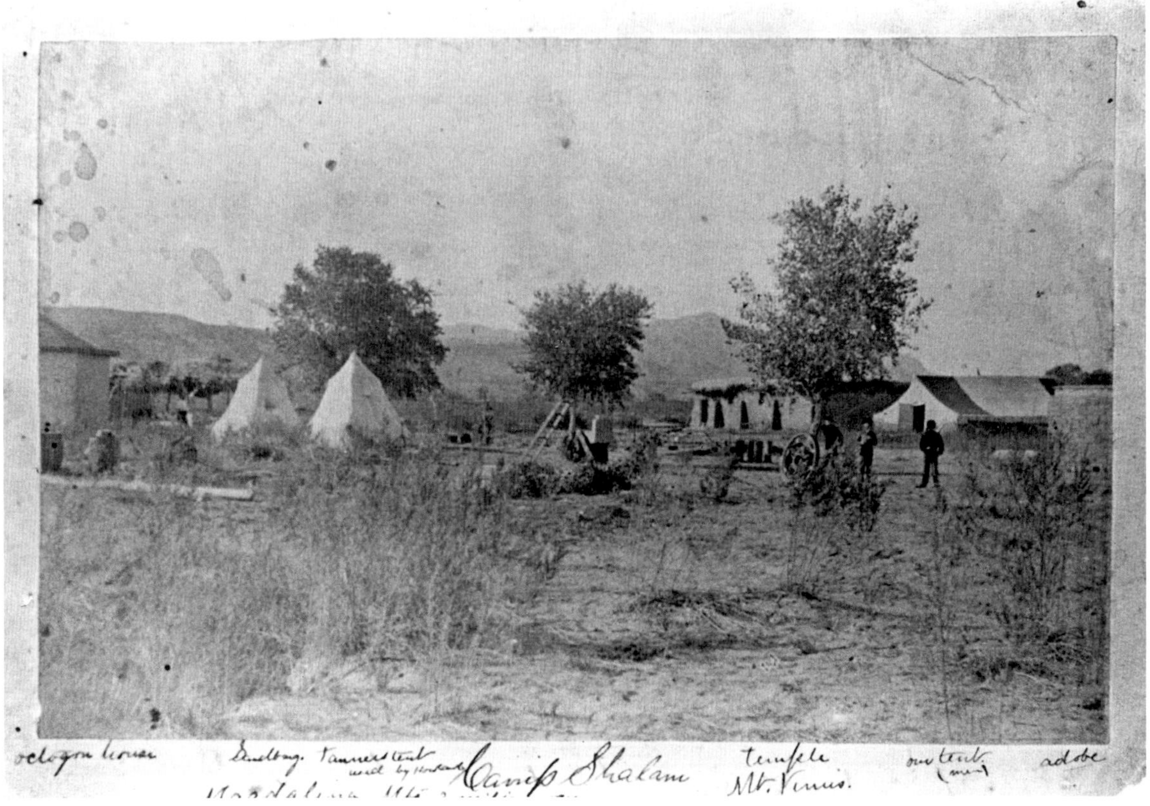

between Newbrough and a heckler at an early meeting introducing *Oahspe*:

Dr. Newbrough: You are out of order. We do not open discussion.
Mr. Lightburn: Do you wish the Old Bible to be thrown aside? If Christianity is not true I want to know what is.
Dr. Newbrough: You are out of order, Sir.
Mr. Lightburn: Of course I am. Everybody is. You had no right to make such announcements if you cannot substantiate them. Give me my hat.[3]

What most fascinated the newspapers, though, was Newbrough's intention to found a colony. *Oahspe* enjoins its followers—called Faithists—to gather orphans and raise them to be independent, vegetarian, and spiritually pure, as preparation for leadership of a New World Order. The *New York Times* reported that "all that was asked of the members was that they should buy tracts of land in order that head-quarters might be established and people removed to them from the profanity of the world," and at the time of the article's publication, the search was already underway for a site in the southwestern desert.[4] Shalam, as Newbrough ultimately named the colony, would be a religious community and a refuge for thousands of indigent babies, far from the corruption of cities. As they prepared to leave a year later, the *New York Times* reassessed the colonists' aims: "[the Faithists] have given no intelligible idea of what they want or seek to accomplish."[5]

• • •

Newbrough actually had a very clear sense of what he sought to accomplish. The bedrock of his venture was his concern for the destitute, a fixation with roots in his early life. Born in rural Ohio in 1828, he witnessed the health consequences of poverty while working as an

Above: The earliest known photo of Shalam Colony, ca. 1885. The handwritten captions along the bottom margin identify both structures in the camp—such as "octogon house" and the "temple," which was likely the first building erected at the site—as well as natural landmarks including Robledo Peak, known at the time as Mount Venus. All images courtesy New Mexico State University Library.

assistant to a dentist in Cleveland during his high school years. After graduating, he attended medical school and finally became a dentist himself, moving to New York with the goal of tending to the oft-neglected dental problems of the urban poor. He then traveled the world, making a fortune in the California gold rush before traversing Europe and Asia. His journeys gave him a pronounced sense of poverty's misery, and compounded his determination to do something about it.[6]

Newbrough's obsession with babies (or *babes*, as he called them) has less obvious sources. But its ramifications are evident in every aspect of his new faith. The section of *Oahspe* that warns against theft focuses not on food or livestock but babies: "Now, behold, a certain rich man coveted his neighbors' children, and he went about and captured many of them. And withal he was mighty above his neighbors, and none of them could regain their offspring."[7] *Oahspe* also prohibits abortion, referring to aborted fetuses as babies "slain by their mothers and fathers."[8] Newbrough's passion for babies was not limited to those in almshouses—it seems that he wanted as many as possible to come into being.

"I wish I were where ten thousand babies fenced me in on every side," wrote Newbrough to a friend in 1883, the year before he arrived in New Mexico and established Shalam.[9] In a subsequent letter, he describes the living conditions in orphanages that made his efforts to acquire babies for the colony so urgent:

We lost one little babe, which we brought away from the almshouse—though it was nearly dead when we received it . . . To me it is perfectly appalling how these little things are slaughtered in this city. We hope to save many, and to raise them up in the right way, so as to have a new race by and by.[10]

Surprisingly, Newbrough's conception of a "new race" was free from the scientific racism then prevalent. At a time when eugenicist notions of racial purity were ascendant in American society, Newbrough took in all the babies he could get ahold of—baby boys and baby girls of any race and class. However, the number of babies he was able to bring to Shalam was not high. Few of the settlers entering the colony already had children, and bureaucratic hurdles made it hard for Newbrough to adopt.[11] In a letter of 1883, Newbrough writes that "there is so much round about red tapism to be gone through in order to get a child out, that it dies by the time the permit is granted."[12] A *Southwestern Farm and Orchard* profile of Shalam written ten years after its establishment counts only twelve babies living there, "among them ... a negro and at least one mulatto."[13] Before the colony's demise, the Faithists also adopted a baby of Chinese descent.[14] The children had one thing in common: all had been orphaned, and most were among the poorest of the poor. Such were the children that John Ballou Newbrough hoped would inherit the earth.

• • •

The search for a place to start the colony took some time. Newbrough looked in California, but his attempts to acquire land there fell through. Returning from an exploratory trip, he stopped in Las Cruces, New Mexico, and there found many acres of arid land available very cheaply. The colonists pitched their first tents in late October 1884.[15]

Shalam's colonists knew almost nothing about farming, and their first months in Mesilla Valley were hard. Growing vegetables in the unirrigated desert was a monumental task, and the Faithists, who adhered to a vegetarian diet, suffered. There were no buildings on the land—the construction of dormitories, kitchens, and a school began a year later—and the villagers had to spend the first few months living in tents. But with the indispensable aid of villagers from Doña Ana, just south of the colony, Shalam ultimately built an irrigation system: sixteen miles of piping and a seventeen-thousand gallon reservoir.[16] People from Doña Ana also taught the colonists how to cook beans and chilies, and worked on the commune when the Faithists were overwhelmed. Within a few years, Newbrough and his partner in the venture, Andrew Howland, were supervising a (mostly) self-sustaining commune.

Opposite above: Undated photograph depicting the ruins of Shalam's Fraternum, a dormitory building for the colony's adults. The mostly adobe structure contained more than forty rooms, including a kitchen and dining room, a library, and a laundry room, all built around a large central courtyard. As was the case with most buildings at Shalam, the front entrance to the Fraternum faced east.

Opposite below: Photos of Shalam's infants published in the second edition of *Oahspe*, 1891. A number of the infants came from New Orleans, where Newbrough had opened a temporary "receiving station" to accept foundlings.

While there is near universal consensus in the scientific community that global climate change is accelerating the pace of desertification around the world, there is less agreement about what precise climatological conditions constitute "desert" aridity. Most contemporary models draw on the work of the Russian-German scientist Wladimir Köppen (1846–1940), who in 1884 published the first version of his climate classification system. Köppen's scheme—which he revised in 1900 and then a number of additional times until his death—divides the world into five different climatic zones based on temperature, and the amount and seasonal particularities of precipitation in a given place. Dry biomes, which fall into Köppen's category B, are further divided into arid and semi-arid zones, which are additionally differentiated by whether they are hot, mild, or cold. Later work by climatologists added a variety of nuances to Köppen's original classification, including the crucial component of evapotranspiration, the amount of water that evaporates from the land plus that which is transpired by plants into the atmosphere. For the purposes of more general geographical and political distinctions, however, the definition of aridity is often shorthanded into a simple accounting of annual precipitation. While 200mm per year is sometimes given as the threshold, the 2007 Intergovenmental Panel on Climate Change—a joint project of the World Meteorological Organization and the UN's Environment Programme—adopted as its standard for a desert biome a mean annual precipitation amount of less than 250mm, coincidentally the exact vertical dimension of *Cabinet*.

ORPHAN UTOPIA

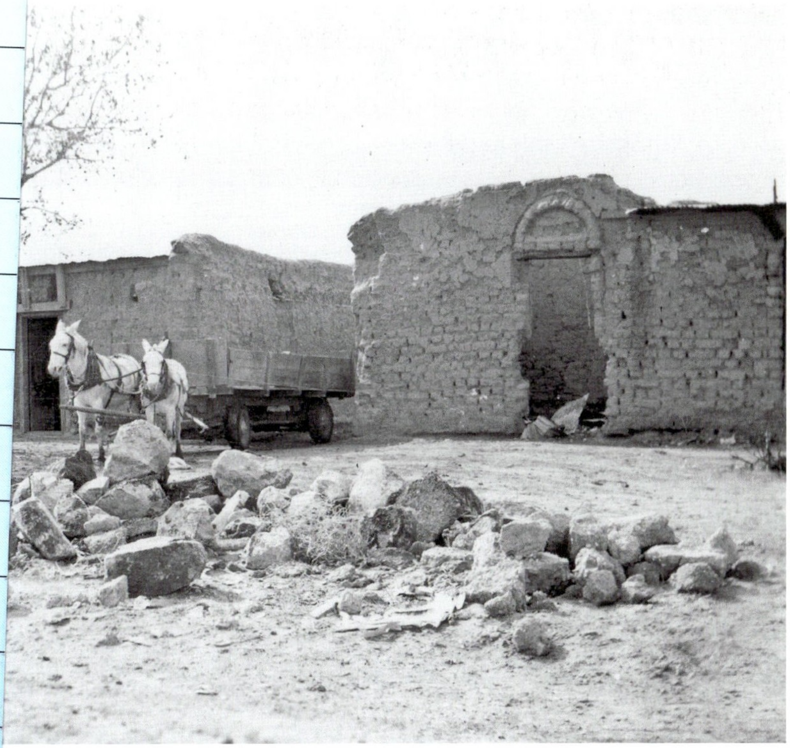

'YA. THALE. FIATISI. VOHU.

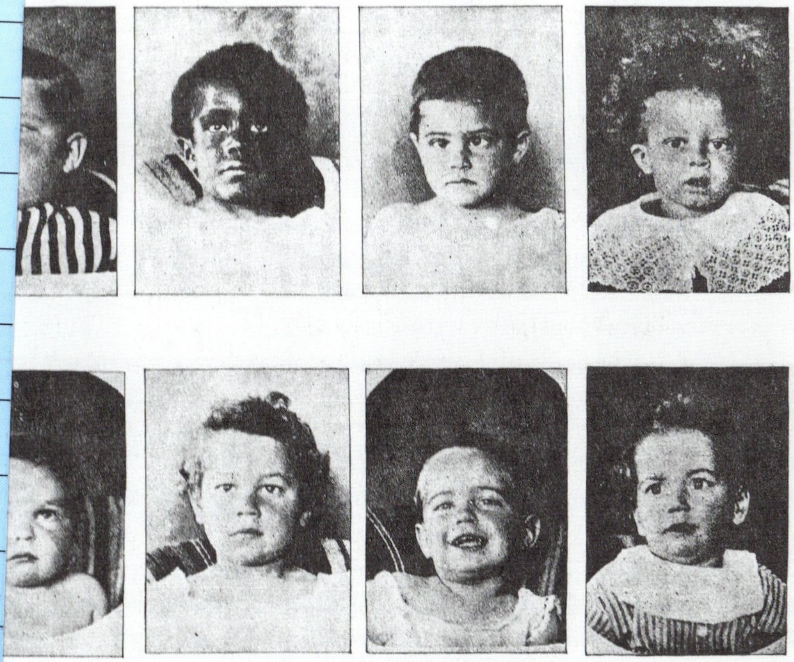

HAGA. HA'JAH. PATHODICES. DIS.

But Shalam remained small, and so, despite a lack of emphasis on proselytizing, Newbrough and his wife began to travel the country on baby-collecting missions. In New Orleans, where they spent several months, the Newbroughs established a "receiving home" with the slogan "Children Wanted and No Questions Asked." Other Faithists established similar homes in Kansas City, Chicago, and Philadelphia.[17]

The 1894 *Farm and Orchard* profile of the colony described the twelve children on the farm as "mostly about 8 years of age . . . fed entirely on vegetable food, with a liberal allowance of fruit and nuts. Their clothing consists of a little linen tunic, and they wear no hats or shoes. They receive a bath twice a day."[18] The adults, too, wore little: in "Shalam: Utopian Desert Paradise," Ann Hufstedler writes that "Shalam was considered by some to be practically a nudist colony, as the men worked in the fields in white trousers, barefooted, bareheaded, and shirtless. Their long hair would naturally add to their unusual appearance. Howland was once arrested in El Paso, Texas, for indecent appearance."[19]

Although the commune's children were raised in a highly ascetic environment, *Farm and Orchard* observed that they appeared healthy ("although not robust"), also remarking "one note-worthy fact about them. We have made several visits to the colony and never saw one of the children crying or looking unhappy. They are always running about at play and they are the most cheerfully obedient lot of children we ever came across."[20]

• • •

Tensions abounded, however, among Shalam's adults. Communal labor was difficult; irrigation ditches had to be dug, vegetables had to be harvested, and while members of the colony did not pay for room or board, they also received no wages—which made transitioning back into life outside an exceedingly difficult prospect.

In 1891, a man named Jesse M. Ellis claimed to have been deceived by the colony, and sued. His case made it to the New Mexico Supreme Court, which ruled in favor of Shalam. Justice A. A. Freeman's decision is written in such florid prose that it has raised speculation that he was inebriated when he wrote it. He makes fun of both the plaintiff and *Oahspe*:

The most that can be gathered from the declaration is that the defendants . . . had christened [their] newfound Vale of Tempe the "Land of Shalam:" had sent forth their siren notes, which, sweeter and more seductive than the music that led the intrepid Odysseus to the Isle of Calypso, reached the ears of the plaintiff at his far-off home in Georgia, and induced him to "consecrate his life and labors, and all his worldly effects," etc., to the new gospel of Oahspe.[22]

Freeman proceeds to scrutinize one of the central stories in *Oahspe* (the book was entered as evidence) in which the world's deities gather to elect a god to be worshipped above all others—essentially, their president. It's quite an assembly: Buddha attends, as do Mars, Jove, and Shiva. Thirty-seven candidates vie for the position of supreme god, of whom only fifteen are listed. The names of the remaining twenty-two, the judge remarks, "are not given, and, therefore, there is nothing in the record to support the contention of the counsel that the list includes the names of Bob Ingersoll and Phoebe Coussins [*sic*]."[23] Supernatural deliberations continue for one year and five months, after which the exhausted deities let the lower angels make the decision—handy for Christ, or "Looeamong," head of the lower angels. He is elected unanimously, which seems to have bothered Justice Freeman:

We think this part of the exhibit ought to have been excluded from the jury, because it is an attack in a collateral way on the title of this man Looeamong, who is not a party to this proceeding, showing that he had not only packed the convention (council) with his friends, but had surrounded the place of meeting with his hosts, 'a thousand angels deep on every side,' thus violating that principle of our laws which forbids the use of troops at the polls.[24]

• • •

Jesse Ellis may have been the first former member of Shalam to publicly express discontent with the colony, but the years after the verdict in his case were tumultuous. In 1891, Newbrough died in an influenza epidemic; Andrew Howland married his widow and assumed leadership.[25] Howland created a sister colony called Levitica on the same tract as Shalam, consisting of twenty houses, each with their own acre of land, set aside for full families who wished to join the commune. But after many of the families in Levitica refused to do the work necessary for its upkeep, Howland dissolved it, chartering a train for the emigrants.[26]

Mooching was a problem that Shalam, like many other utopian communities, was unable to avoid. Though some were drawn to New Mexico by the opportunity to work in harmony with like-minded, determined individuals, others exploited the colony's resources. And while Faithist boosters predicted that Shalam would eventually adopt two to three thousand babies, the number of children adopted never rose above twenty-eight.[27] In a July 1970 article in the *New Mexico Historical Review*, Daniel Simundson suggests that the colony's failure was mostly a consequence of insufficient human and financial capital: "Its labor force was inadequate. Newbrough's band was largely comprised of romanticists and amateur metaphysicians who had little aptitude for physical labor. Finally, although the Oasphe [*sic*] bible had indicated that converts would be inevitable, they never appeared."[28] The lack of adequate labor force was then compounded by the loss of financial backing: over the course of his involvement with Shalam, Andrew Howland had sunk his entire fortune into colony upkeep and unprofitable agricultural ventures, and by 1900, he was reduced to selling cookies called "U-Like-Ums" door-to-door in the neighboring village of Doña Ana as a last-ditch attempt to support Shalam's two dozen children.

The colony dissolved in 1901. Howland, who had put the deed to the colony in the name of the children, successfully sued to have it transferred back to his own name,[29] and sent them off to foster homes and orphanages—a heartbreaking development for a group of children who had, by all accounts, had a loving upbringing.[30] Shalam might have "failed," but for seventeen years it provided twenty-eight orphans with a safe and happy home.

• • •

Shalam has left only traces in the Las Cruces of today. The colony's former campus is now owned by farmers, and where there were once fields and houses and babes there are now acres of trees planted in straight rows. The dry and unforgiving land that once gave the Faithists so much trouble is now used entirely for pecan farming.

The colony's most enduring legacy is religious, or ideological, rather than physical, and in fact the movement never died out. But its numbers have remained static. Unlike Mormons, for instance, Faithists do not aggressively proselytize, instead quietly waiting for people to join them of their own accord, or else sending out friendly pamphlets. After the dissolution of Shalam Colony, believers continued to pass the faith on to their children and the very occasional convert, and new communities were steadily established in locations ranging from Arizona to as far east as Massachusetts.

In the 1950s, a directory of religious organization listed a Faithist group called the Essenes of Kosmon operating a colony in Montrose, Colorado: "In May, 1954, the group included eight people, four men, two women, and two children. New members are desired. The requirement for membership is to know *Oahspe* and follow its teachings. A year of probationary residence is required before acceptance as a resident member."[31] Archived newsletters from the group indicate that its numbers never grew beyond ten.[32] For a while, a Faithist named Virginia Howard operated a very small commune in Tiger, Georgia, but she passed away in 2010, and the colony with her. There have been no active colonies for several years.

• • •

The age of the frontier is over. In *Wasted Lives*, the philosopher Zygmunt Bauman writes that "the planet is full," and that this "signals the disappearance of 'no man's lands,' territories fit to be defined and/or treated as void of human habitation as well as devoid of sovereign administration—and thus open to (clamouring for!) colonization and settlement."[33] We are as a world now awake to the inhabited nature of most livable space. The world is devoid of perceptible voids, places where one might imagine starting with a blank slate because the place itself is understood as a blank slate.

But place was always incidental to Shalam Colony. Newbrough chose the New Mexican desert not because it had sacred significance (as was the case for Mormon settlers in Utah), but because it allowed the Faithists to establish a community removed from the dictates of the outside world. A provision in *Oahspe* instructs Faithists that when they erect buildings in their communities, they should never be built to last, because each generation should have the chance to build something new, with their own hands: "Man buildeth a house, and it perisheth. Succeeding generations must also build, otherwise the art of building would perish. Better the building perish, than the art of building."[34] The community, in any given iteration, is not supposed to last forever. What matters is that the ideas and the passions of the Faithists live on.

There are about twelve practicing Faithists remaining in the world, scattered from Japan to New Mexico to Massachusetts.[35] They keep in touch electronically, holding weekly prayer meetings via Skype. The Internet is perhaps the closest thing to a frontier that exists today—a placeless space where our dreams of a better world can imprint themselves upon the endless, neutral network. Failing that, the next frontier is space. And on that score, *Oahspe* was ahead of its time. Although it was written in the late 1800s, the book dreams of spacecraft, of visitors from other worlds floating down to earth in "etherean ships."[36] Heaven's reaches are boundless, and who knows what humanity might discover as it continues to traverse them: new planets, new stars, or benevolent new gods entirely concerned with children, with their health and well-being, and the opportunity for every one of them to flourish.

1 Cited in "John Ballou Newbrough," in *The Encyclopedia of Occultism and Parapsychology*, vol. 2, 2nd ed., ed. Leslie A. Shepard (Detroit: Gale Research Company, 1984), pp. 950–951.

2 Ibid.

3 "Faithists in Convention: Delegates from Eleven States at the First Session," *The New York Times*, 25 November 1883.

4 Ibid.

5 "The Sect of Faithists: The Followers of Oahspe and Some of the Plans and Practices," *The New York Times*, 21 November 1884.

6 Lee Priestley, *Shalam: Utopia on the Rio Grande* (El Paso: Texas Western Press, 1988), pp. 5–7.

7 John Ballou Newbrough, *Oahspe: A New Bible in the Words of Jehovih and His Angel Embassadors* (New York: Oahspe Publishing Association, 1882), p. 804.

8 Ibid., p. 207.

9 John Ballou Newbrough to Mr. and Mrs. Arthur Bates, 6 April 1883. Opal Lee Priestley Papers, Archives and Special Collections, New Mexico State University Library.

10 John Ballou Newbrough to Mr. and Mrs. Arthur Bates, 26 April 1883. Opal Lee Priestley Papers, Archives and Special Collections, New Mexico State University Library.

11 The Faithists sometimes mailed proselytizing literature directly to children. In 1885, one Atlanta paper reported sightings of a Faithist book that had "the appearance of an almanac, and thereby slips through the hands of watchful parents. Within the past few days, however, several of them have fallen into fathers' hands and as many complaints have been made to Postmaster Wilson." See "Fathers Get Mad: Because Their Children Receive a Book. A Pamphlet Mailed to Atlanta Children Creates Sensation–The Inducements Offered to Live in Shalam–The Religious Belief of the People Who Live There, Etc., Etc.," *The Atlanta Constitution*, 1 October 1885.

12 John Ballou Newbrough to Mr. and Mrs. Arthur Bates, 6 April 1883.

13 "The Shalamites," *Southwestern Farm and Orchard*, vol. 1, no. 7 (September 1894), p. 1.

14 Lee Priestley mentions that "a Chinese child found a private home" after the dissolution of the colony. See Priestley, "Shalam: Land of the Children," *New Mexico Magazine*, vol. 39, no. 6 (November–December 1961), p. 46.

15 Ibid, p. 22.

16 Ibid, p. 23.

17 Ibid, p. 22.

18 "The Shalamites," *Southwestern Farm and Orchard*, p. 1.

19 Ann Hufstedler, "Shalam: Utopian Desert Paradise," *Las Cruces Citizen*, 28 April 1960. Hufstedler was a senior at Las Cruces High School. Her essay won first place in the Katherine D. Stoes section of a student writing contest hosted by the Las Cruces Writers' Club and was subsequently published in the *Citizen*. Stoes was one of the first journalists to research and publish significant work on Shalam Colony, and her papers reside at New Mexico State University. The footnotes and bibliography of Hufstedler's article were not printed in the newspaper.

20 "The Shalamites," *Southwestern Farm and Orchard*, p. 1.

21 "The higher court's decision was couched in terms which still are rated as the most scintillating example of juristic humor extant in any language–so unusual in legal proceedings that snickering lawyers now suggest that Justice Alfred A. Freeman, who wrote it, must have been inspired by spirits of the liquid variety." Wallace Perry, "The Glorious Land of Shalam," *Southwest Review*, vol. 38, no. 1 (Winter 1953), p. 40.

22 Ellis v. Newbrough, 1891-NMSC-028, 6 N.M. 181, 27 P. 490 (S. Ct. 1891), p. 2. Page number refers to the digital version of the decision available at <nmcompcomm.us/nmcases/NMSC/1891/1891-NMSC-028.pdf>.

23 Ibid. Bob Ingersoll and Phoebe Couzins were both prominent lawyers in the late 1800s, he an orator famous for his defense of agnosticism and she one of the first female lawyers in the country. It is likely that someone involved in the suit made a joke about the list of candidates being so long that it probably included the names of famous legal figures like Ingersoll and Couzins, and the judge is taking this at face value, whether tongue-in-cheek or not.

24 Ibid.

25 Lee Priestley, "Shalam: Land of the Children," p. 23.

26 Ibid.

27 See "Fathers Get Mad" for the Faithists' optimistic estimates, and Wallace Perry, "The Glorious Land of Shalam," p. 43, for details on the number of orphans adopted by the colony.

28 Daniel Simundson, "Strangers in the Valley: *The Rio Grande Republican and Shalam*, 1884–1891," *New Mexico Historical Review*, vol. 45, no. 3 (July 1970), pp. 205–206.

29 "End of the Shalam Colony," *New-York Tribune*, 27 April 1901.

30 See Ann Hufstedler, "Shalam: Utopian Desert Paradise," and also Lee Priestley's "Shalam: Land of the Children," p. 46. Priestley claims that a black child from the colony was sent to live with Booker T. Washington after its dissolution. However, it is impossible to locate the source for this dubious claim.

31 Directory of communes, n. d., folder 10 ("A Survey of Mutualistic Communities in America"), Opal Lee Priestley Papers, Archives and Special Collections, New Mexico State University Library.

32 "A Friendly Talk," *The Kosmon Pioneer Bulletin*, vol. 9, no. 8 (August 1951), pp. 3–4.

33 Zygmunt Bauman, *Wasted Lives* (Cambridge, UK: Polity Press, 2004), p. 5.

34 John Ballou Newbrough, *Oahspe*, p. 290.

35 Interview with a Faithist, 11 November 2015.

36 John Ballou Newbrough, *Oahspe*, p. 55.

ARTIST PROJECT / DETAILS ON THE RARE EARTH FRONTIER

Elizabeth Knafo

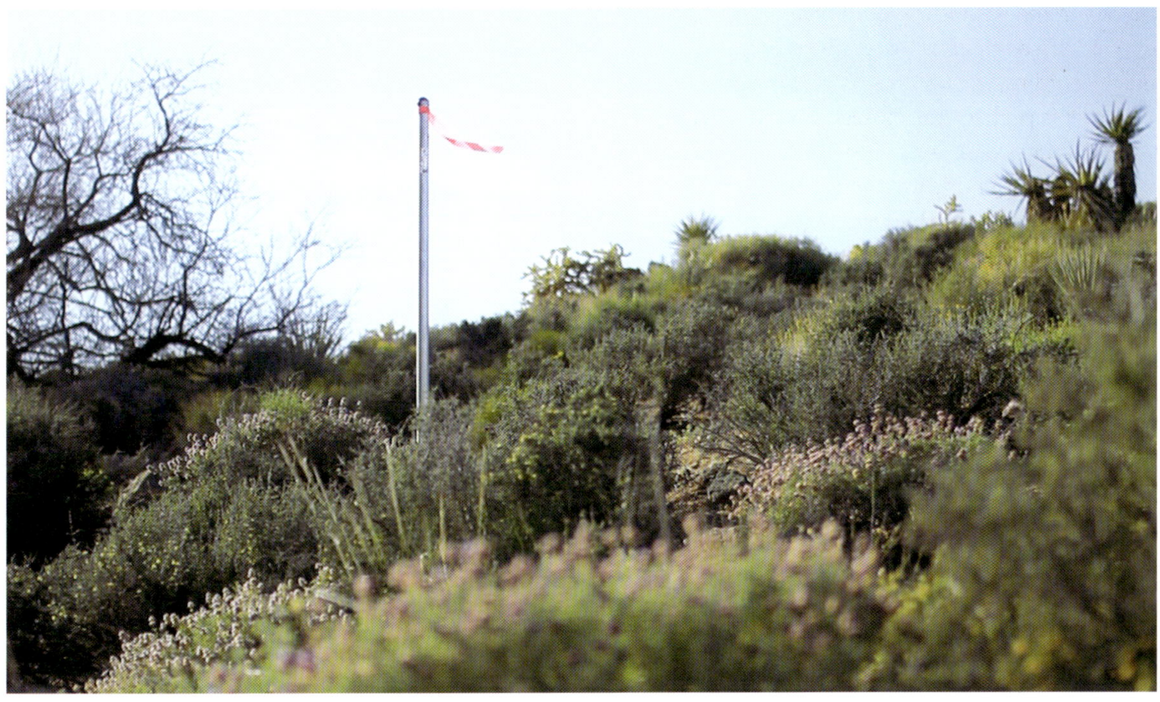

At a place called Mountain Pass in the Mojave Desert, just outside California's Mojave National Preserve, is a recently bankrupt rare earth mine and processing plant. There are seventeen rare earth elements, which are divided into "heavies" and "lights" based on their relative atomic weights. The heavies are crucial components in consumer electronics and military technology, in the physical infrastructure and digital capabilities of the internet, and in surveillance tools. They are used in the computing, display, and maintenance of systems of global trade, digital warfare, and militarized policing, as well as in the storage servers where social media sites and digital surveillance data are warehoused. Heavy rare earths, which Molycorp, Inc., the company that owned the mine in California, was hoping to extract, are, at this time, irreplaceable ingredients in all things digital. Light rare earths, on the other hand, are used in more mundane industrial applications, such as UV window coatings and petroleum production.

The rare earth mine had been in operation for fifty years, but was closed in 2002 by environmental regulatory agencies. The operation was reopened and expanded in 2010; the project was dubbed "Project Phoenix," presumably in reference to the resurrection of the mine. (At the time of its 2002 closure, the operation had in fact been owned by another company of the same name; the newly formed company behind the 2010 reopening purchased the name and the site in 2008.)

At the groundbreaking ceremony, Molycorp emphasized "green" energy and national security as their rationales for beginning to mine again. Those speaking on behalf of the company touted the uses of rare earths in wind turbines and electric cars, and asserted that the mine would help make the United States independent of China's rare earth supply. (Over 90 percent of the rare earths on the world market comes from Chinese mines). Neither Molycorp nor the politicians at the event made any mention of the

Above: A Molycorp mining claim near their mine in Mountain Pass, California. All images from Elizabeth Knafo, *Rare Earth*, 2014.

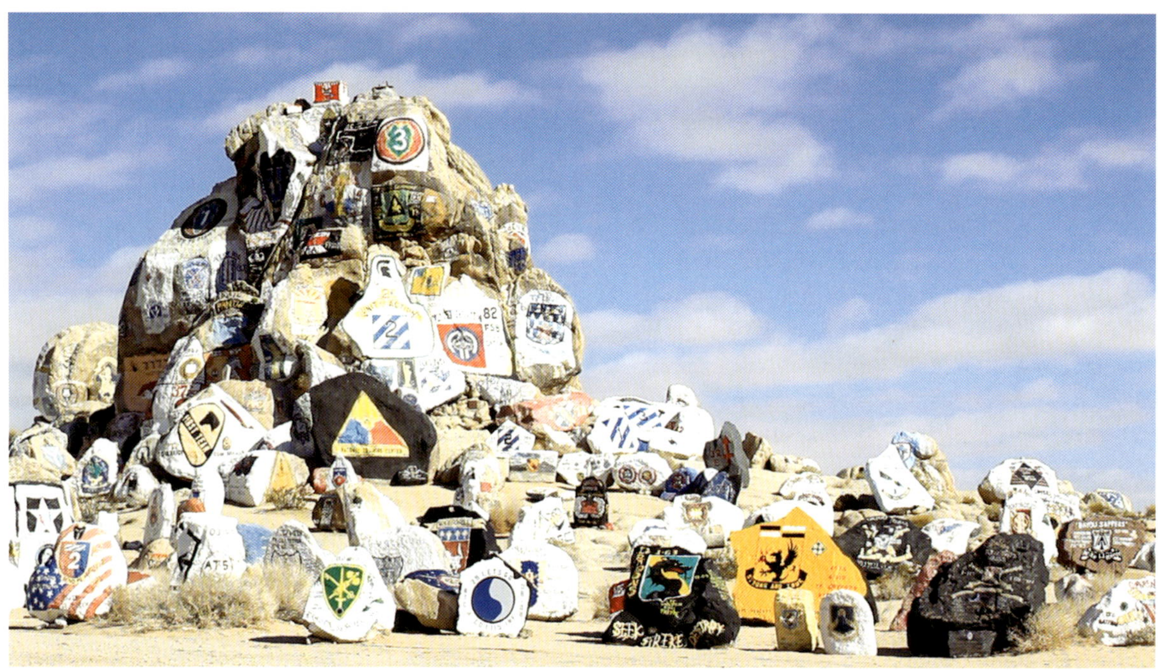

radioactive waste generated in rare earth processing. Nor did they mention the fact that in 1986, the company town at Mountain Pass closed down after workers and their families started to get sick. There is a dearth of public information on what effect the radioactive dust plaguing the mine's surroundings had on the town's closure, and what effect it has on the area to this day. For their part, the mine's management claimed that the cost of running the town became prohibitive once the mine's profits began to fall, in part due to a federal government decision to make unleaded gasoline—the production of which did not require a particular rare earth mined at the site—the official standard in the United States.

Soon after the reopening, metal poles started to dot the hills surrounding the pit as the company began staking new mineral claims in search of additional deposits, especially those containing higher concentrations of lucrative heavy rare earths. Such claims are part of a legal framework—originating in the late nineteenth century and fundamental to white advancement into the western parts of the continent—that introduces public land into the marketplace by allowing industrial mining concerns to lease or even purchase that land if they can prove it has mineral value. The land and mineral claims surrounding Molycorp's pit mine are examples of how US frontier narratives and economics are accompanied by a supporting bureaucracy designed to push the US project westward. These extractive enterprises, premised on racial hierarchies and land dispossession, operate to produce, and then exploit, rarity—an outlook that helps make the very possibility of human life on earth increasingly rare. The project presented here revisits material from a documentary I made between 2011 and 2014 that examined the way in which the Mountain Pass mine has permanently altered the desert by depositing its radioactive waste there. This work considers the "rare earth frontier"—a term I have borrowed from Boston University professor Julie Klinger—the parameters of which are industrial in pace, ubiquitous in terms of technological application, and global, even extraterrestrial, in scale.

To grasp the scope of the United States' fundamental relationship to geology, it is important to remember that pressure on rock is always also pressure on the softer, more permeable, forms of life—humans, plants, animals. These enterprises, European-colonial at first, and later a collaboration between the state and corporate interests, formed the basis for the settlement of the country and rely on

Above: Military insignia painted on boulders in the Mojave Desert outside Fort Irwin, California.

the commandeering of natural resources and the use of exploited labor, both on the land and hundreds of feet below it.

A geologist described the global media and investment frenzy of 2010 surrounding rare earth prospecting and mining as "rare earth fever." This allusion to gold fever, and the California gold rush of 1848, connects geology to the notion of the frontier and the ways in which it has functioned as a premise for transforming spaces, conceptual or physical, into sites of extractive, capitalist production. The frontier sits adjacent to the current territory, territory being distinct from terrain in that it serves as the marker of colonial, racial, economic, and cultural rule. Scarcity of resources must be enforced in order to push settlers and investors to the frontier, where its resources are then transformed and subsumed into the economic system. Settlers, prospectors, and investors take the land; time and time again, they are the foot soldiers of the dispossession of the indigenous. Rather than being a previously undiscovered space, the frontier is a ground created through an orchestrated and projected emptiness, an assigned uselessness: a generative narrative that allows a privileged race and class to accumulate and circulate resources and capital at the expense of the people and other forms of life already resident in these places.

This ideological narrative, formed during the colonial period, remains operative today in an economic context that propels us toward catastrophic global climate change under the inequities of racial capitalism. The rare earth frontier is the frontierism of our enduring neoliberal era, a time of increased police militarization, global surveillance, and increasingly extreme privatization and extraction. Though similar to the frontier mentality of the nineteenth century, the narrative now includes not only digital technology and weaponry but also an "end-of-the-world" ideology that determines and sustains its form and method. It is distinctly post-9/11 in its particular paranoias and aspirations, yet it is also rooted in the visions of total surveillance from earlier epochs of American paranoia. This projection of endless surveillance and war is a crucial component of what allows the supposed wasteland of the desert to be "recuperated" through continued investment.

The Molycorp mine's management had promised investors and local politicians that the minerals processed at Mountain Pass would facilitate the creation of equipment not only necessary for green technologies but also for the American military. But even though none of the rare earth elements for the manufacture of military equipment was actually in the ground at Mountain Pass, the "critical minerals" narrative worked long enough to raise millions of dollars in investments.

In the Mojave Desert, the mining pits and shafts of the past centuries' prospecting are scattered around the parklands and desert roads. Through the many eras of US history, mineral matter has been fundamental to the generation of power: social, ideological, militaristic, and energetic. With the incorporation of rare earth

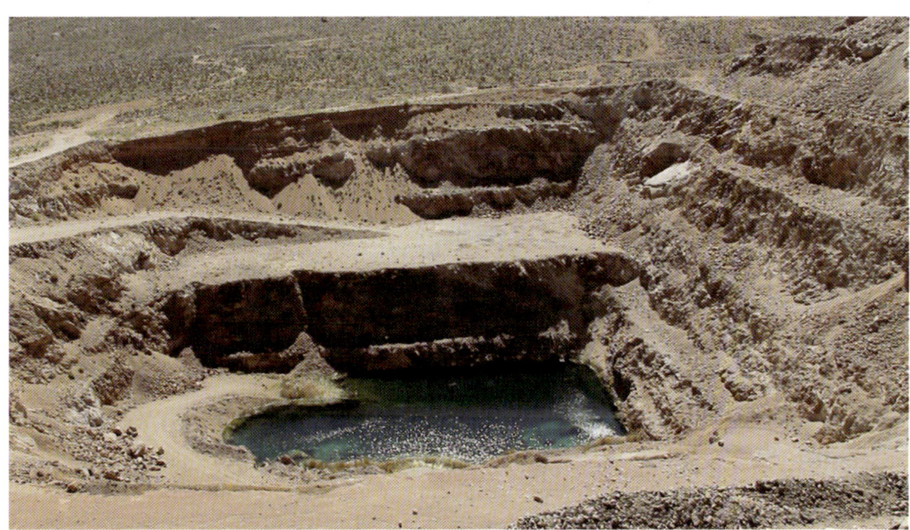

The Morning Star pit mine, at the bottom of which the desert water table is visible. The mine, closed in 1993 by Vanderbilt Gold Corporation after a series of environmental violations, is on land that is now within the boundaries of the Mojave National Preserve, California.

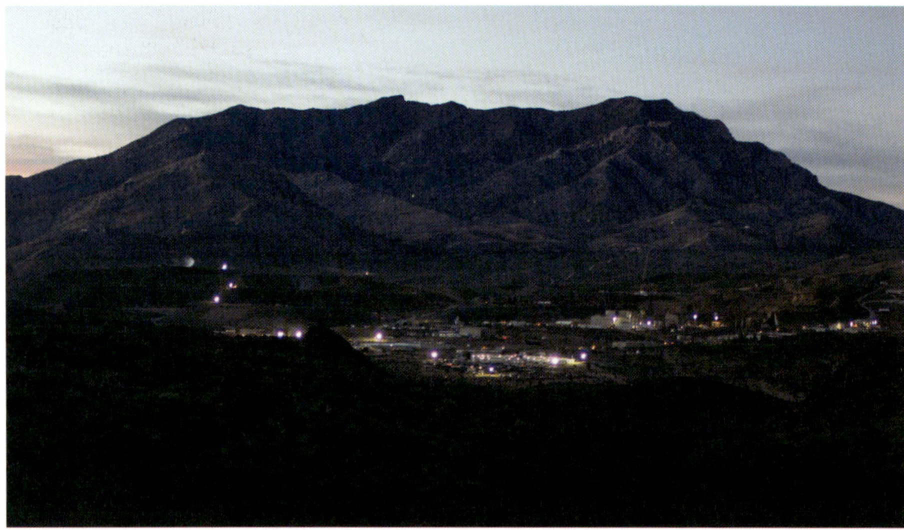

Opposite: An open-pit excavation truck.

Left: The Molycorp rare earth pit mine and processing facilities at the base of Clark Mountain.

technologies, these powers course through the flicker of location services, data mines, and surveillance servers, through our screens as we watch ourselves and the state and its corporate affiliates find new ways to ensure their power by watching us back.

CLARK MOUNTAIN

The Mountain Pass mine sits at the foot of Clark Mountain, which consists in part of rock more than a billion years old heaved up from deep beneath the earth's surface as a result of the collision of the North American continent with the oceanic crust beneath the Pacific Ocean. The mountains and playas of this desert lay bare the planet's elemental story—Earth's four-billion-year-old creation visible in its seams, transitions, and uplifts of stone. And the landscape is abundant with minerals; limestone, basalt, granite, turquoise, zinc, tungsten, borax, lead, copper, silver, and gold are all present.

The indigenous peoples knew an overland route from the area around present-day Santa Fe to the Pacific Ocean that crossed through this part of the desert, but it eluded the Spanish until they learned of it from their Mojave guides. The survival of the Spanish missionaries and gold-seeking soldiers relied heavily on the knowledge that the Mojave, Serrano, Paiute, Chemehuevi, Hualapai, and Vanyume peoples shared with them.

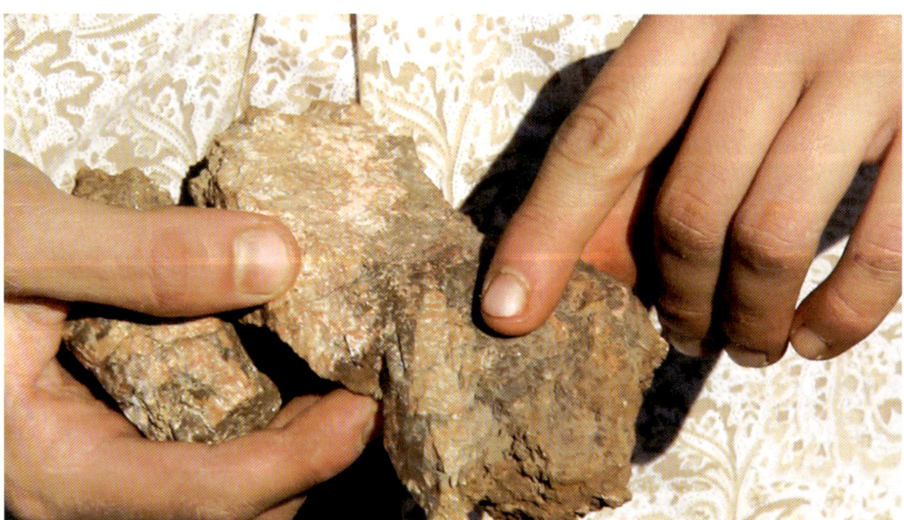

Bastnasite, a rock containing rare earth minerals, as well as radioactive orium.

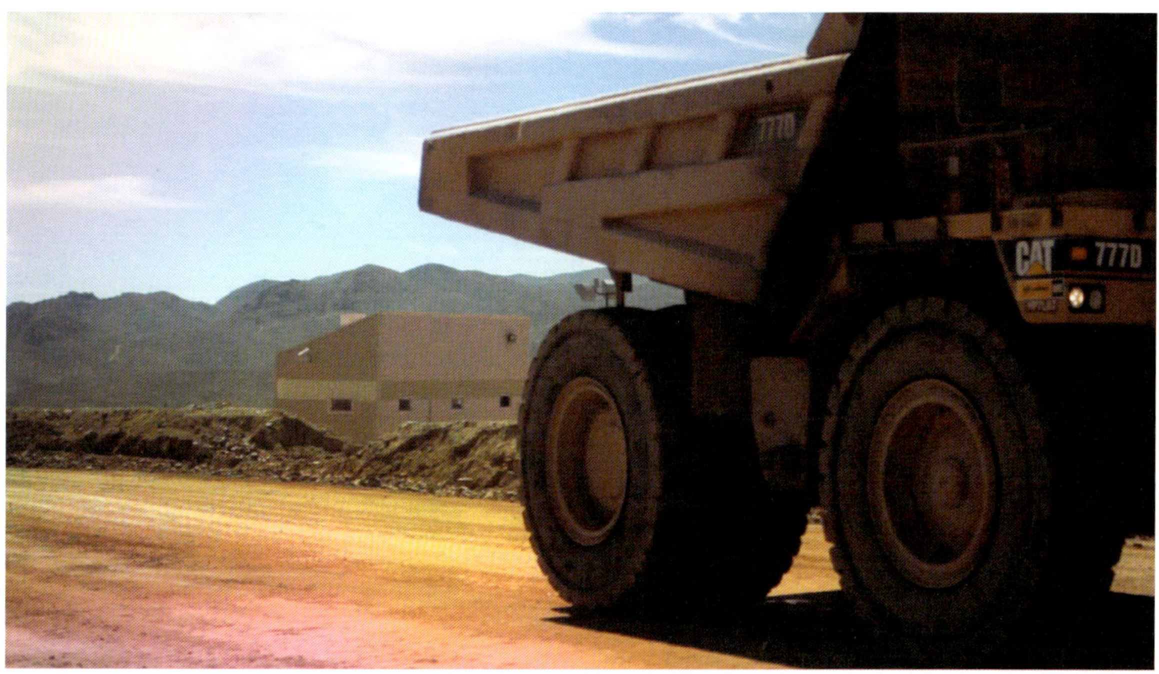

Gold was once mined beneath this mountain, as were copper, zinc, and lead when prices for those metals rose steeply during World War I. The US government classified this land as public land when it took control of it, but its later, industrial use was facilitated by provisions such as those in the 1872 General Mining Law, which were designed to encourage the expansionist programs of "manifest destiny" and the mining booms of the Gold Rush. These laws sanctioned the forcible and violent conversion of Native American lands into American territories, which was often achieved for the US government by proxy via the miners, homesteaders, and ranchers who raced west and tied their livelihoods to these contested lands. Often, though, before the miner or settler made it west, speculators had already laid claim to huge tracts of land, seizing it at cheap prices, often under different names, thereby skewing supply and demand and creating some of America's first real-estate bubbles.

In the 1940s, a Nevada prospector, inspired by a government newsreel entreating citizens to seek uranium, took his Geiger counter out to an area around the abandoned gold mine at Clark Mountain, where he located a radioactive vein. What the prospector found wasn't uranium, but a deposit of radioactive host rock containing one or more of the seventeen rare earth elements. Shortly after the Molybdenum Corporation of America (later renamed Molycorp) opened a mine there in 1952, two rare earth elements were found: europium and yttrium, both of which are necessary to create a bright red phosphor used in color television cathode tubes. The mine's management claimed that every color TV in the United States manufactured after 1966 got its red from this mountain.

In 1994, when Mojave National Preserve was established, Clark Mountain was included within its boundaries. But the adjacent, operational mine, as well as the claim areas surrounding it, was placed within a zone of exception, which meant that the Mojave National Preserve would be divided into two, noncontiguous areas. And in the drone era, the mining claim at Mountain Pass became a primary military concern because of the critical role played by rare earths in the manufacture of components used in digitally enhanced arsenals.

RARE EARTHS

Rare earths are found compacted together with bearing rock, but once crushed and chemically separated through a complex and toxic process, they are capable of a wide array of functions. They are the only known substances that can create the phosphors and luminescent conductivity of fiber optic cables;

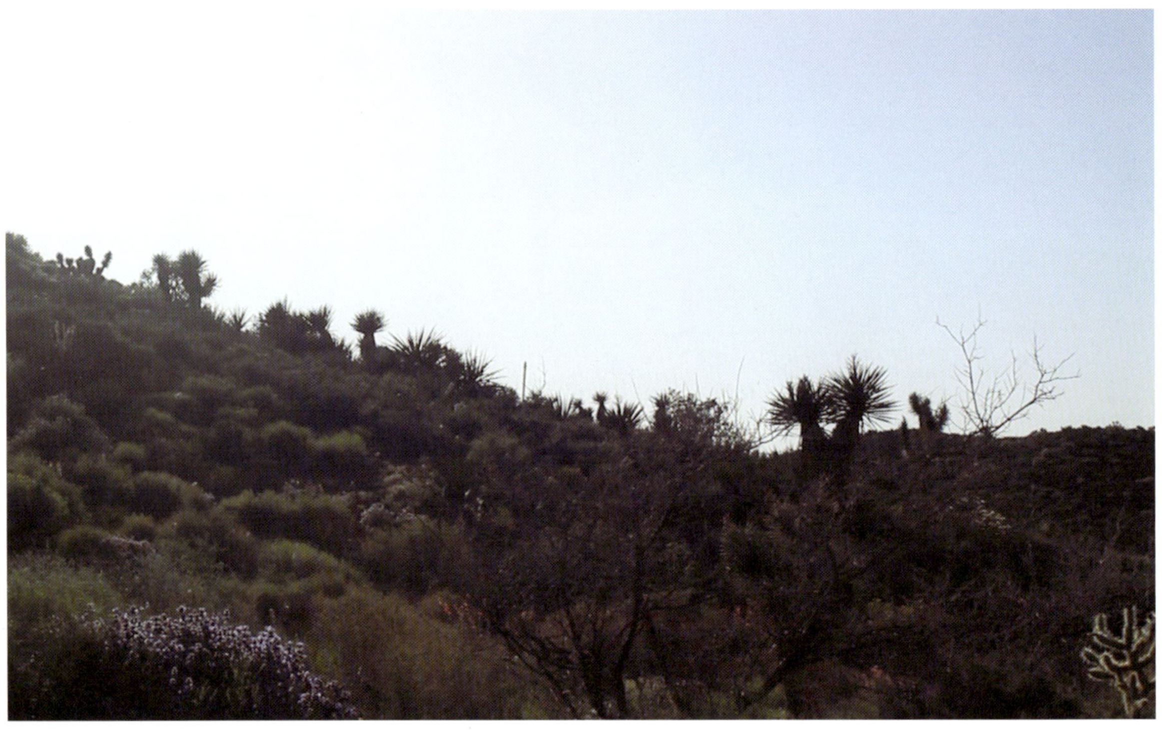

A Molycorp mining claim on land south of its mine.

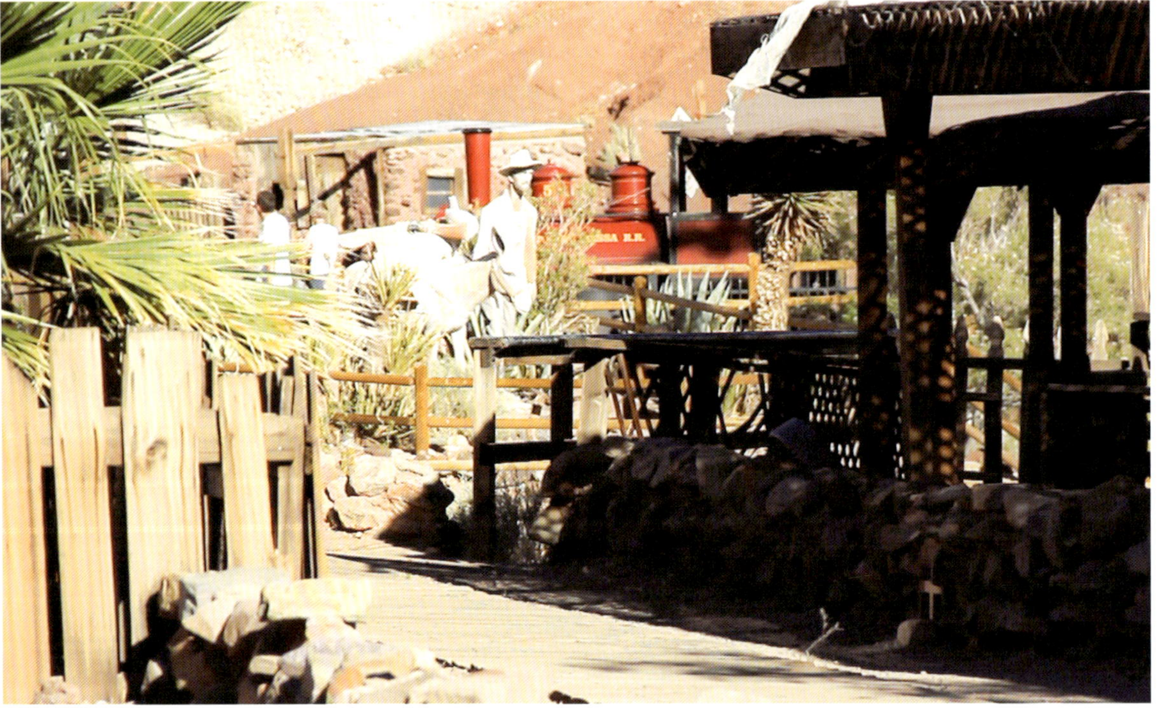

Statue of a prospector in Calico, a now-abandoned former silver mining town in the Mojave Desert.

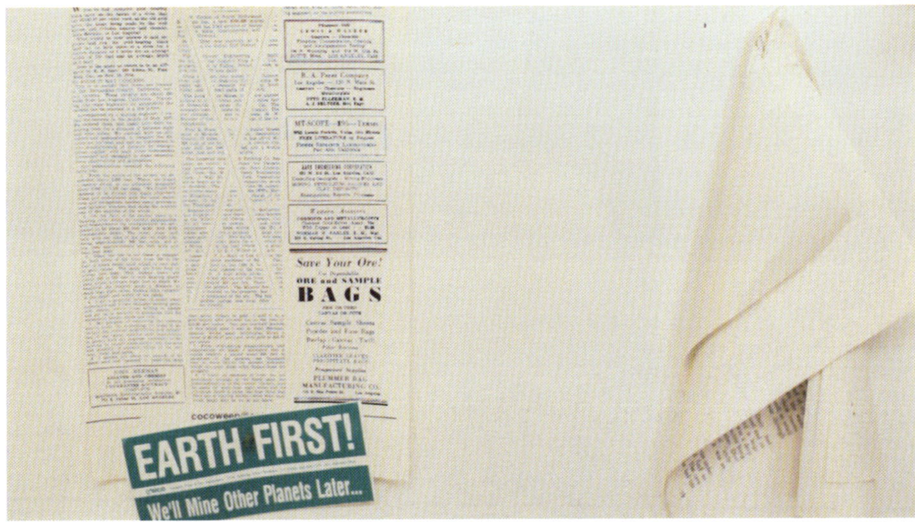

"Earth First! We'll Mine Other Planets Later..." Bumper sticker on wall of a gold-hunting camp near the Molycorp mine.

the supermagnetic forces enabling nanotechnology; and the remote control mechanism for surveillance satellites and unmanned aerial vehicles. They are instrumental in the manufacture of touch screens and global positioning satellites. Yttrium and europium are today used to create color phosphors for LED lights and screens; gadolinium facilitates the magnetic resonance waves of an MRI and is fundamental to creating various forms of digital memory for hard drives and microchips. And neodymium is used to make exceptionally small, strong magnets for the batteries and engines of electric cars and wind turbines, though each of these products' clean-energy claims are contradicted by the vast quantity of radioactive waste generated in the production of all rare earth elements.

Rare earths aren't actually rare. Yet while they are present throughout the earth's crust, they are expensive and laborious to process. At the same time that mining and energy companies, as well as politicians, insist on "rare earth scarcity," large volumes of rare earth–laden objects quickly become obsolete and move into landfills where their chemical and geologic journey will continue in aquifers, air, and soil. The chemicals and elements in objects that do land in e-waste recycling centers will enter the lungs, kidneys, and central nervous systems of workers in Ghana, India, China, and elsewhere during the toxic process of mining electronics for valuable parts.

The Mountain Pass rare earth mine first closed in 2002, after fifty years of operation, when state water regulatory agencies discovered that its owners had covered up a radioactive wastewater spill. And radioactive wastewater remains an issue at the site. Molycorp was forced to file for bankruptcy in the wake of a 2012 class action lawsuit from investors after the company failed to find heavy rare earths in large enough quantities to sustain the business; the mine was closed a second time in 2016. But the corporation was required to maintain the water pumps that help contain the radioactive wastewater—presumably necessary *forever.* A permanent program of maintenance is needed to prevent waste from a now defunct mine from once again seeping into the desert air and aquifers.

The portrayal of the desert itself as "wasteland," and as a place where waste can be discarded, is premised on a conflation of harshness of climate with a lack of life. The subtle colors of sand vegetation, the camouflaged reptiles, and the burrowing and mountain-dwelling mammals are dismissed if we accede to a framework that sees "nature" only in lush and verdant landscapes. The notion of the desert as an expendable space is a self-fulfilling prophecy in that once it is figured as a "wasteland," it can be transformed into one by extensive resource extraction, dumping, and military testing.

EXTREME EXTRACTION

Global prospecting for rare earth minerals drives territorial disputes, indigenous treaty violations, and unchecked industrialization in some of the most ecologically vulnerable spots on the planet. Deposits have been claimed by governments and mineral

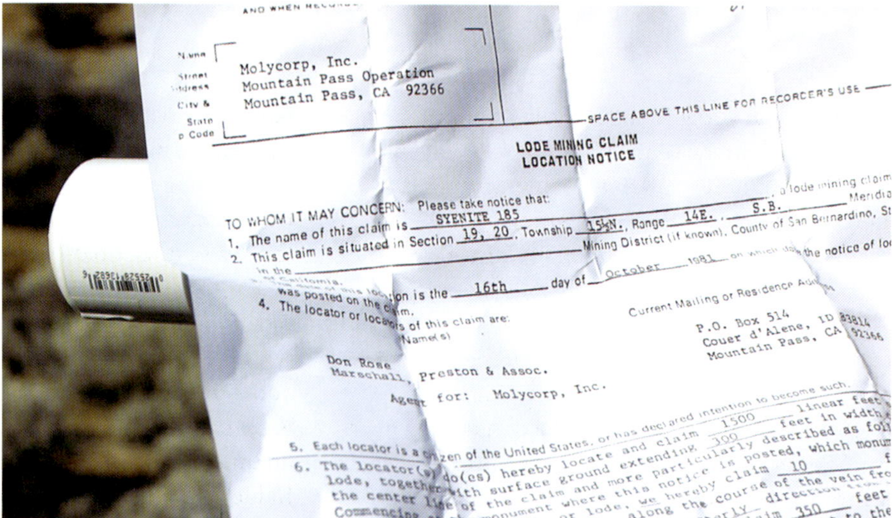

Molycorp, Inc.
Mountain Pass Operation
Mountain Pass, CA 92366

SPACE ABOVE THIS LINE FOR RECORDER'S USE

LODE MINING CLAIM
LOCATION NOTICE

TO WHOM IT MAY CONCERN: Please take notice that:
1. The name of this claim is SYENITE 185, a lode mining claim
2. This claim is situated in Section 19, 20, Township 15½N., Range 14E., S.B. Meridian
Mining District (if known), County of San Bernardino, State of California.
on is the 16th day of October 1981 on which day the notice of location was posted on the claim.
4. The locators of this claim are:

Name(s) | Current Mailing or Residence Address
Don Rose | P.O. Box 514 Couer d'Alene, ID 83814
Marschall, Preston & Assoc. | Mountain Pass, CA 92366
Agent for: Molycorp, Inc.

5. Each locator is a citizen of the United States, or has declared intention to become such.
6. The locator(s) do(es) hereby locate and claim 1500 linear feet
lode, together with surface ground extending 300 feet in width
the center line of the claim and more particularly described as fol
Commencing at the monument where this notice is posted, which monum
we hereby claim 10 f
along the course of the vein fro
direction
claim 350 feet
to the

Document recording a Molycorp mining claim known as Syenite 185.

investors on First Nations lands across the Northwest Territories of Canada, as well as in India, Australia, Malaysia, Jamaica, Brazil, South Africa, Namibia, Mongolia, Kyrgyzstan, and Vietnam. An estimated one trillion dollars' worth of deposits are now being assessed by the United States Geological Survey in Afghanistan, while in the United States itself, claims have been staked in the Black Hills National Forest in Wyoming, on Apache and Ysleta del Sur Pueblo sacred lands in the high desert plains of New Mexico, and in Idaho, Missouri, South Dakota, Alaska, Nebraska, Montana, Florida, Arizona, California, and Texas. China, Australia, and the European Union are currently vying for access to the rare earth deposits recently discovered underneath Greenland's melting glaciers, and rich quantities of rare earths have been found in what is called "deep mud," now being dredged off the Pacific seabed by the Japanese.

Predictably, politicians and mining lobbyists from resource-rich countries often deride environmental protection regulations; in Baotou, Mongolia, for example, residents of the town surrounding a rare earth mine now suffer from infertile soil laced with heavy metals and radioactive thorium, as well as from high rates of cancer and tooth loss.

These same advocates of rare earth extraction are not confining their search to our own planet. Like all elements, rare earths are thought to be the coalesced remains of ancient supernovae, and laws regarding property and mining rights in outer space are currently being worked out in US legislation, such as the Asteroids Act of 2014. A year later, Congress passed an act that, contrary to the Outer Space Treaty of 1967, to which the US is a signatory, converts the previously unclaimable resources found in space into goods subject to property rights due to what the US Federal Aviation Administration has described as "the private sector's need to protect its assets and personnel on the moon or on other celestial bodies." And recent "off-earth mining" forums held in Australia have brought together businesses, university researchers, and governmental organizations like NASA to participate in panels exploring "Project Concepts for Near-Term Commercial Asteroid Mining" and "Offworld Robotic Excavation for Large-Scale Resource Extraction and Habitat Construction."

These new prospectors hope that one day "off-earth mining" will mark the ancient rocks of extraterrestrial bodies in the same way that earlier speculative booms are visible in the scraped remnants of ancient rock at Clark Mountain, gutted clear down to the desert water table. Their continued project of extraction and toxic redistribution is achieved, as it has always been, through an economic system that relies on the belief that its demands, processes, and outcomes are as natural and inevitable as the formation of mineral and stone.

GRAVE MATTERS

Maria Golia

Egypt is almost entirely desert; unless you happen to be somewhere in the central Nile Delta or Fayoum Oasis, it is never more than five kilometers away. The desert encouraged the sociability that characterizes Cairo, a city whose population has historically been concentrated as far away from it (and as close to the Nile) as possible. Only recently and with great reluctance have people begun to inhabit the outlying wastelands in significant numbers. Describing how "nature and climate affect the psyche of human groups," Egyptian social commentator Milad Hanna remarked that "the desert, with its infinite space, stimulates imagination and awakens fear of the approaching stranger."[1] The residential apartment blocks sprouting in Cairo's environs in fact stand shoulder to shoulder, huddled together as if for company. Surrounded by desert, Cairenes have lived in tight quarters for so long they've become agoraphobic.

Egyptians have long associated the desert with the strange and threatening. Although it was predominately desert in antiquity, Egypt was not as arid as it is now. The Nile delta was a marshland, labyrinthine groves of papyrus with tall, slender stalks and fan-like feathery tips. The river roiled with fish; fowl were so plentiful they were hunted with nets strung up between the five-meter-high papyri stems. The land flanking the river was carpeted with fields and the annual floods more or less guaranteed at least one big crop of grains, in addition to pulses, roots, vegetables, and fodder enough for a variety of domesticated animals. The river was understood as a godsend, an affirmation of divine will, yet at just an hour's walk from its banks, this verdant, animated realm came to an abrupt halt. At the edge of the floodplain lay an endless expanse of scorched hills and valleys. The desert was everywhere at the corner of one's eye: vast, empty, and silent, the negation of life, nature at its most fiercely indifferent. Cemeteries were always located there, west of the Nile where the sun set, the place of death. Like other natural phenomena observed by the ancient Egyptians, the desert was associated with a deity, in this case Seth, god of strangers and strange lands.

Son of Geb (father earth) and Nut (mother sky), Seth and his siblings Isis, Osiris, and Nephthys belonged to the Great Ennead, a group of A-list gods, but he was the family rogue. Lord of the tempest, he could raise the sand-laden winds that blocked the sun (the eye of Ra, the original god) and the rainsqualls that sent destructive streams of muck and rubble roaring down from the desert hills. Cold-blooded lizards that thrive on heat were said to be ruled by Seth, as were deadly scorpions who love the dark. Crocodiles and hippopotami, which were plentiful in the Early Dynastic Period (ca. 3000–2686 BC), were Seth's havoc-wreaking helpers. Seth himself was depicted as a man with the head of an unidentifiable, perhaps mythical or extinct, animal. In hieroglyphic writing, the Seth-animal was used in words such as illness, crisis, nightmare, rage, tumult, to boast, to be harsh, to roar, and to deceive. The figure was likewise used in hieroglyphic writing to designate "confusion," the opposite of order.[2]

The ancients were enamored of order and their ideology was rooted in nature's reliable cycles. The year officially began with the Nile flood that quenched the parched fields in summer (*akhet*). Planting season (*peret*) started when the flood withdrew, having deposited alluvial silt so rich it gave the nation its name: *Khmt*, "the black land." The harvest (*shemmu*) corresponded with spring, bringing the promise of prosperity throughout another year, until the floods came again and the cycle repeated. The Nile, however, could be capricious; too much or too little water spelled disaster. This element of disruption needed to be acknowledged, anticipated, and, ideally, held in check through a variety of tailored rituals. Yet Seth did not stand in mere opposition to order and the life-giving forces it encompassed:

His function in an archaic society is to add disorder to order and so make a whole, to render possible, within the fixed bounds of what is permitted, an experience of what is not permitted.[3]

Seth lent balance to portrayals of both nature and the gods, neither of whom were always beneficent. He was a murderer. He killed his brother Osiris out of jealous pique and tried to seduce Isis, Osiris's sister/wife. Reverberating heat and menace, Seth was highly sexed; his phallus was said to emit fire.[4] In the course of an epic battle, he buggered his young nephew, the falcon god Horus (son of Isis and Osiris), and stole one of his eyes. He was a thief, and in sexual and other matters "the enemy of boundaries."[5] And he was a sore loser. When Ra named Horus the battle's victor and ruler of the cosmic order, Seth was banished to the desert where he did his best to raise hell. He was nonetheless given his due as a powerful god. His cult lasted well into the Twentieth Dynasty (ca. 1186–1069 BC), not least in towns marking the departure point for desert caravans.[6] Only when Egyptian civilization had passed its prime did Seth become a scapegoat, an "enemy of the gods":

Robber! Lord of Lies; king of deceit; gang-leader of criminals.... [He] who creates rebellion; lord of looting, who rejoices at greed, master thief, who suscitates theft, who gives offense....[7]

The ideal Egyptian in social terms was a *ger ma-a*, literally "the silent man," a law-abiding "follower of Horus."[8] His antithesis, the "follower of Seth," is described in a text believed to date to the Twelfth Dynasty (ca. 1985–1773 BC). What Egyptologist John Romer refers to as "the first dispassionate study of a specific human character that has come down to us" is essentially the portrait of an angry man.[9] According to the text, Seth's followers were loners, hot-blooded, and unpredictable, given to drunken rage and violence, and probably redheaded. A compelling character, the follower of Seth is "beloved of women through ... the greatness of his loving them."[10]

The papyrus bearing a copy of this text was part of a library assembled by the scribe Qenherkhopshef (active ca. 1246–1195 BC) when the text was already ancient wisdom.[11] Qenherkhopshef lived and worked in Deir el-Medina, the village of the royal tomb builders on the west bank of Thebes (today's Luxor) whose ruins have yielded rich and piquant data about its inhabitants' lives. Tucked behind the sun-baked hills at the edge of the Theban Necropolis, the village was home to literate and highly skilled masons, carpenters, and artisans employed by a royal enterprise known as the "Institution of the Tomb" ("the Tomb" for short). Their title was "servant in the Great Place" (the necropolis), sometimes referred to as "the Place of Truth." They were responsible for building the pharaohs' "horizon of eternity," a task that began as soon as a ruler took over and lasted as long as he did. The tomb builders and their families lived in small stone houses packed tightly against one another in facing rows; they intermarried and knew each other's foibles well. The scribe Qenherkhopshef, for instance, took bribes for bureaucratic favors and the construction foreman Paneb bore the marks of a follower of Seth.[12]

Thanks to the survival of papyrus documents recording the complaints and court cases against him, we know that Paneb was a man of exceptional vitality. An accomplished foreman under whose supervision five royal tombs were built, he was a notorious philanderer, extortionist, embezzler, and suspected murderer. He "fornicated" with a variety of "citizenesses," and in one case had a foursome with his son, whom he'd named Aapehty, "great of strength," Seth's most common epithet. But Paneb's most grievous offence in societal terms was the violation of his oath as a servant of the tomb: "I shall not overturn a stone in the area of the great place of Pharaoh." He pilfered the contents of at least one royal burial, and dismantled blocks of existing tombs to reuse in his own burial place. He was accused of breaking into the burial chamber of Sethos II (which he had helped build), where he opened wine amphorae, hoisted himself atop the sarcophagus, and got drunk, perhaps in the belief that anyone named after Seth wouldn't mind.[13]

The "men of the gang," as the tomb builders called themselves, spent most of their time bivouacked in the desert, returning home every ten days for a two-day weekend. Their work required precise craft and brute labor; the royal tombs, often multiple rooms and passageways in addition to a burial chamber, were carved deep into the desert's stony bowels. That working conditions were harsh is an understatement. The builders suffered occupational hazards like scorpion bites, conjunctivitis, and the occasional rock-crushed limb, but perhaps the most insidious was aiding and abetting the burial of outlandish quantities of gold and precious goods. Treasure-laden tombs invited corruption, especially among those responsible for their building, stocking, and protection. Paneb's is but one of many documented cases of tomb raiding.

Opposite: Farming between the Nile and the desert. Mural painting from the tomb of Unsu, a grain accountant in the early Eighteenth Dynasty. The mural, which dates to ca. 1450 BC, depicts the agricultural operations in Thebes that Unsu had supervised. Courtesy the Louvre.

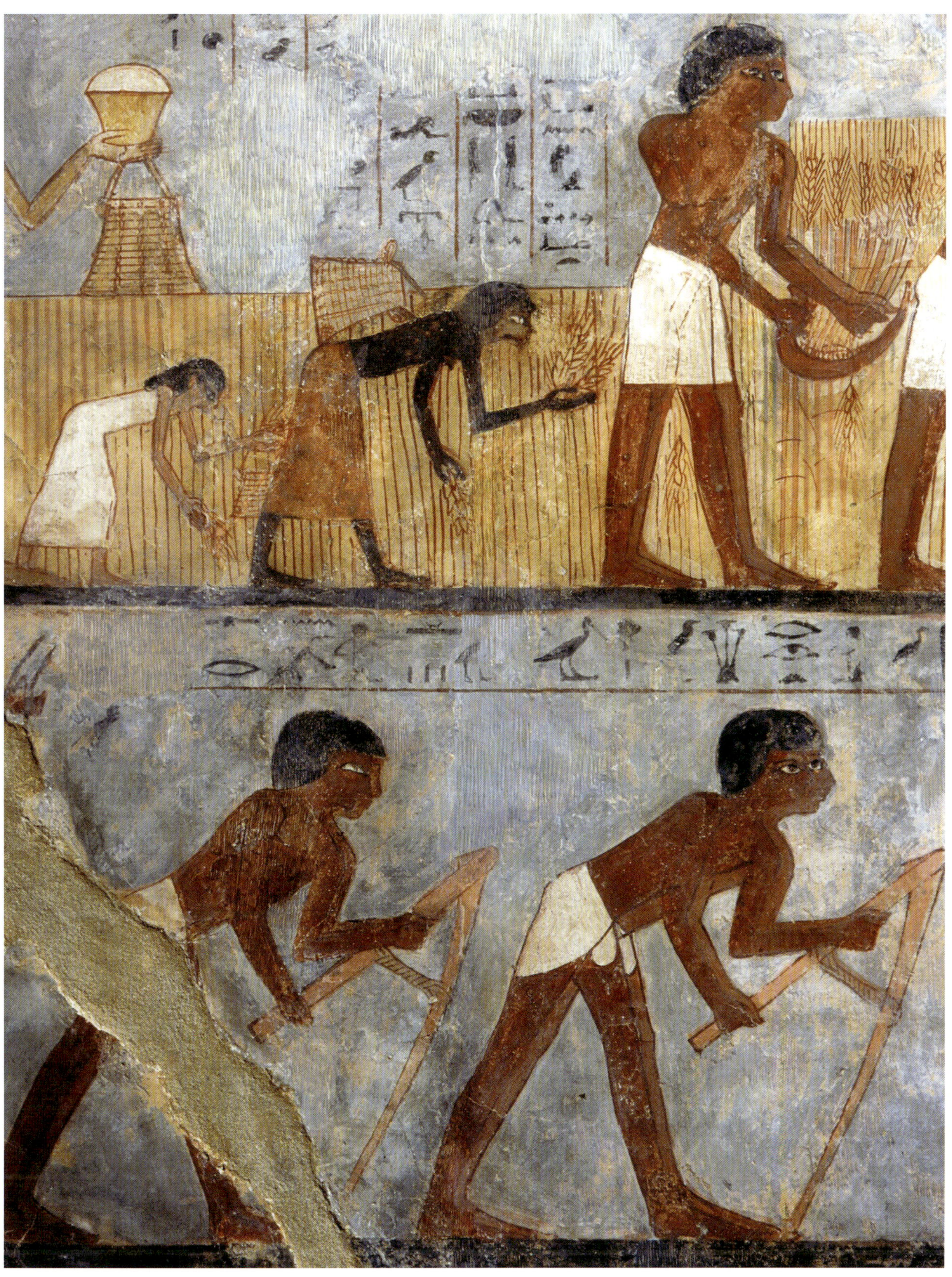

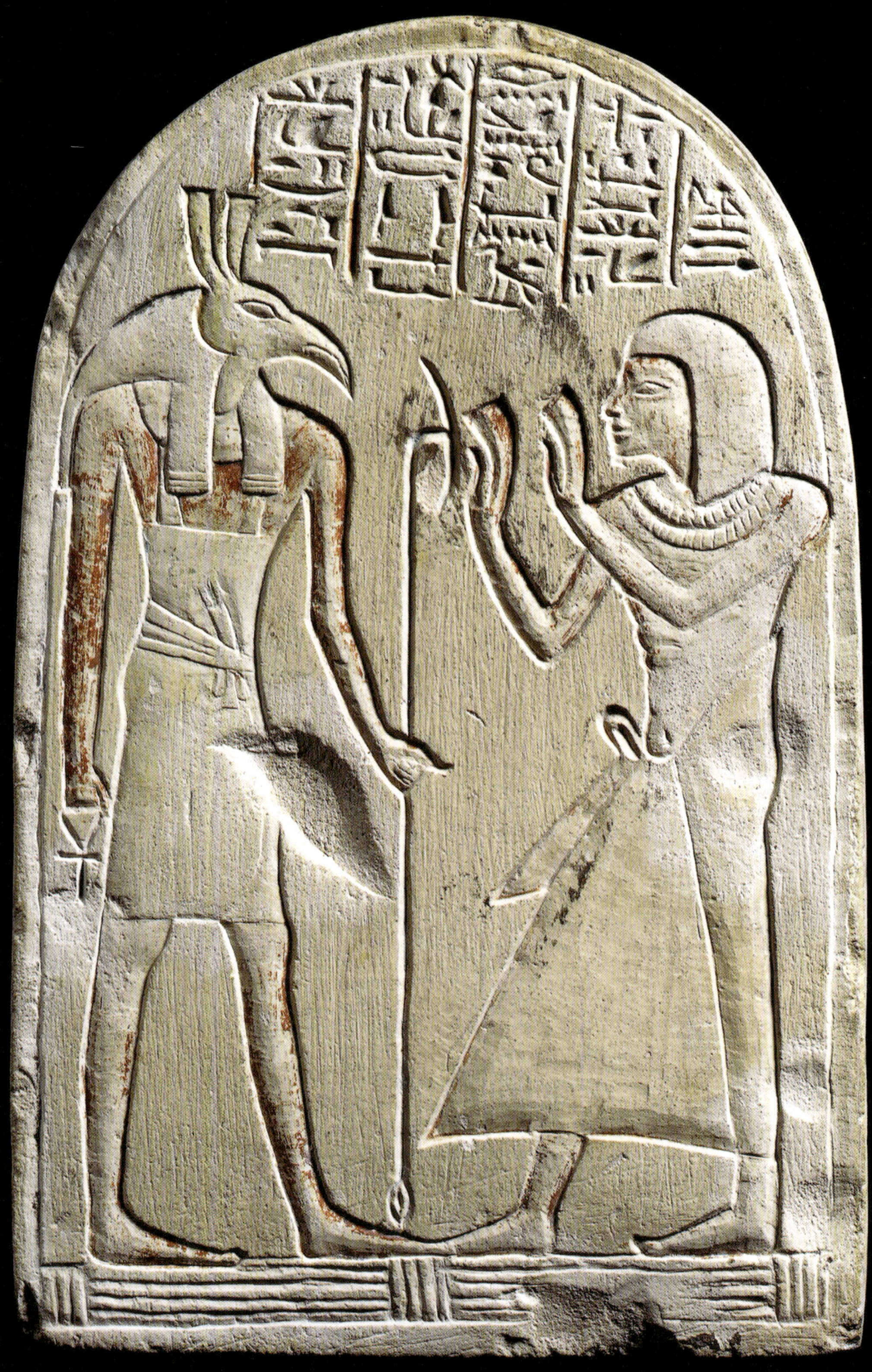

His fate is unknown, but in his contempt for traditional values he was at the vanguard of a rising trend.[14]

The tomb's purpose was to safeguard the pharaoh's mummy (whose wrappings enclosed magical amulets of gold and precious gems) and a palace's-worth of burial goods, all of which were held sacred and necessary to ensure his reanimation and comfort in the afterlife. The grave was not a final resting place so much as a combination launchpad and shipping container for that longest of journeys. Entire households were interred with their mummified owners: furniture, linens and utensils, food and drink, board games, cosmetics, jewelry, musical instruments, even mummified pets. The ancients literally placed stock in eternity, blurring the lines between metaphysics and materialism. Not only the pharaoh and his family, but anyone who could afford mummification and a properly equipped tomb did not spare the expense. Like a fruitful retirement, death required a lifetime of planning and was doubtless the topic of many a dinner conversation. Nor were such investments taken lightly. The penalty for rifling mummies and robbing tombs was impalement on a wooden stake.

The growing momentum of tomb and temple theft signaled the end of the so-called New Kingdom (Eighteenth to Twentieth Dynasties). It lasted some 480 years (ca. 1550–1069 BC), a time of imperialist expansion under clever, ruthless leadership with Thebes as its religious capital. Between plunder and tribute from conquered lands, the palace coffers swelled and the pharaoh's favorites prospered. The kings and their courtiers launched building sprees to thank the gods and commemorate themselves, equipping their tombs and monuments more sumptuously than ever before. It was a golden era, especially for civil servants. Humbly born men could rise to prominence, but only within the state's institutions and only by demonstrating fealty to the king. Corruption grew alongside cronyism; power struggles among high officials led to factional hostilities akin to civil war. A floundering administration failed to pay its tomb builders, inspiring history's first recorded strikes (1148 BC) and treasures were disappearing from tombs and temples like towels from a five-star hotel.[15]

Motivated by need and greed but also disillusionment, theft flourished as a subversive means of redistributing the wealth. Tomb robbing not only helped redress the imbalance between rich and poor; it theoretically spoiled the tomb-owner's chances for immortality and effectively undermined a system geared toward the accumulation of literally dead capital. Little wonder that the theft of sacred property became a *cause célèbre* in the most sensational court case of antiquity. Papyri containing court transcripts of two investigative proceedings that took place in the late Twentieth Dynasty (1124–1123 and 1084 BC) describe a stolen goods distribution network extending north to Memphis, a virtual underground economy. In addition to tomb builders, scribes, and priests, the gang members included a beekeeper, a sailor, a jeweler, a gardener, a water carrier, farmers, several citizenesses, and a trumpet player. In depositions obtained with the help of the bastinado ("he was examined with the stick"), the defendants often refer to their loot using the startlingly familiar term "bread."[16]

Whether or not all tomb robbers considered themselves followers of Seth, they were outlaws and transgressors, the terrorists of their day.[17] And just as national security is prominent among today's concerns, so tomb security absorbed the ancients. Constant theft shaped the Egyptian art of tomb building, forcing architects to move deeper beneath the desert and devise a variety of deterrents and booby traps. While early royal tombs consisted of a mud-brick building under which lay a passage of several meters leading to the burial chamber, later rock-cut tombs have shafts up to thirty meters deep. Using copper or bronze spikes struck with a wooden mallet, tomb builders split and quarried living rock. With heavy wooden-handled bronze hoes, they tunneled like gophers, displacing countless tons of rock and sand. The most basic security technique was to fill the finished shafts with rubble. When that didn't work, architects tried portcullises, rock slabs, or plugs placed at intervals along the tomb entry passage. Thieves simply tunneled around the obstacles. The architects got trickier, using dummy doors, secret chambers, decoy passages, and forty-ton stone trapdoors, but the raiders were motivated and relentless. If they hit the wrong chamber or a dead-end passage, they backed up and started again.

Opposite: Limestone stela of Aapehty, eldest son of Paneb, the foreman of a crew of tomb builders, late Nineteenth Dynasty (ca. 1295–1186 BC). Aapehty, who served as his father's deputy, is seen worshipping the god Seth. Courtesy British Museum.

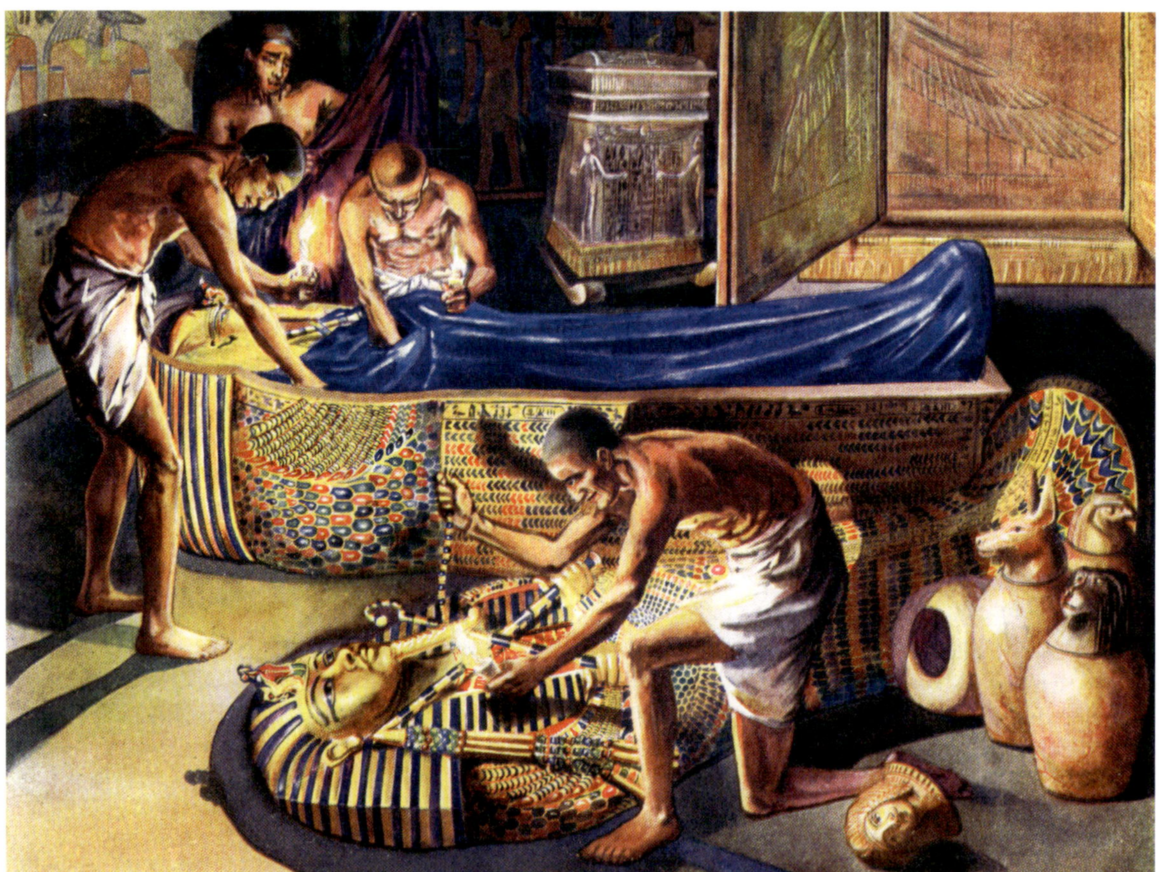

The Egyptians were intimate with the properties of sand. Heavy and unwieldy, it doesn't stay where you put it, is susceptible to wind and gravity, and follows the path of least resistance, like water. As early as the Thirteenth Dynasty (ca. 1773–1650 BC), tomb builders put sand to work for them, lowering massive stone slabs into place using sand released from adjacent shafts.[18] Sand hydraulics were later adapted as a security device, "the ultimate achievement in tomb protection" evidenced in a Twenty-Sixth Dynasty (ca. 664–525 BC) burial belonging to a wealthy individual.

The burial chamber with its stone sarcophagus was placed at the bottom of a giant pit, around ten meters wide and thirty meters deep. Beside the pit was a shaft leading from the surface to the burial chamber, just wide enough for a man to crawl through. The roof of the burial chamber was fitted with a series of clay pots and the pit above it filled with sand. The last workman out broke the pots that allowed the sand to flow from the pit above to engulf the burial chamber below. The workers exited with the help of ropes up the narrow adjacent shaft, which was likewise filled with sand. Anyone who tried tunneling into this tomb would encounter an overwhelming sand flood, either from the shaft or the pit itself. The only way to gain access would be to clear the entire pit, "a lengthy process as archeologists know to their cost."[19] This burial was in fact found intact, but without a single object of value in the chamber or on the person of its occupant. This was a proudly pious man, one supposes, insofar as he trusted that his journey could be made with only his embalmed body, but also one who wished to spite any thieves brazen enough to disturb his tomb.

Archeologists often remark how much of our knowledge of ancient Egyptian life has been derived from tombs and their contents, coincidentally preserved through the ages by a climate that is kinder to the dead than the living. Their decorated walls are biographies of the people who built them, depicting

---

Above: Plate from 1920s book depicting Theban tomb robbers plundering a pharaonic tomb.

their activities and accomplishments in the most flattering of lights. But not everyone could afford a richly decorated tomb or the requisite funerary accessories that over time grew more numerous—inscribed coffins, books of the dead, statuary, amulets; it all added up. The majority of individuals who wished for an afterlife had to work hard to get by in this one and simply disappeared, leaving barely a trace. The processions of glamorous, scantily clad lotus sniffers that adorn tomb and temple walls describe ancient Egyptian society no more than *Fortune* 500 CEOs exemplify ours. Knowledge of the motives and methods behind tomb and temple theft is essential to an understanding of ancient Egypt. Like Seth, the god of confusion, the perpetrators were both society's antagonists and a revelatory expression of its weaknesses and conceits.

The contrasting realities of life and death are etched in Egypt's topography and iterated in the dualities that informed the ancient ideology (divine and mortal, fertile and barren, order and chaos), but these were recognized as aspects of a greater whole. In parts of Egypt, a pair of falcons was worshipped as a dual god, Horus-Seth, order and confusion united.[20] Civilization may be described as the act of reconciling contradictions; Egyptian culture at its best was characterized by its dedication to maintaining equilibrium and the continuity this implied. Survival depended on close observation of nature's manifest order, with all its pros and cons. To the ancient Egyptians, the desert was a vast and tangible *memento mori* whose presence instilled the awareness of vulnerability that is a requisite for real strength. In more ways than one, they were way ahead of us.

1 Milad Hanna, *Acceptance of the Other*, trans. Ahmed A. El-Sherif Hammad (Cairo: Al Ahram Center for Political and Strategic Studies, 2001), p. 26.

2 Herman te Velde, "The Egyptian God Seth as a Trickster," *Journal of the American Research Center in Egypt*, vol. 7 (1968), p. 37. Available at <jacobusvandijk.nl/docs/Trickster.pdf>. See also Herman te Velde, *Seth, God of Confusion: A Study of His Role in Egyptian Mythology and Religion*, trans. G. E. van Baaren-Pape (Leiden: E. J. Brill, 1977), pp. 23–24.

3 Herman te Velde, *Seth, God of Confusion*, p. 56.

4 Ibid., p. 54. Seth was sometimes equated with Baba, god of the erect phallus, as noted in the Coffin Texts: "My phallus is Baba. I am Seth." The impotent man can turn to Seth for help, as can whoever hopes for sexual gratification both in this life and the next.

5 Herman te Velde, *God of Confusion*, p. 59. In retaliation for his lost eye, Horus stole Seth's testicles during the "battle of Horus and Seth." The "eye of Horus," victor and protector of order, was and remains a popular good-luck amulet in Egypt.

6 Ibid., pp. 66, 116.

7 Ibid., pp. 150–151. The Nineteenth and Twentieth Dynasties (ca. 1298–1069 BC) are considered the height of Seth's popularity, which declined in the Third Intermediate Period (after the Twentieth Dynasty).

8 Herman te Velde, "The Egyptian God Seth as a Trickster," p. 37.

9 John Romer, *Ancient Lives: The Story of the Pharaohs' Tombmakers* (London: Weidenfeld and Nicolson, 1984) p. 66.

10 I am grateful to Ray Johnson, director of Chicago House, Luxor, for providing this reference and link: Alan H. Gardiner, *Hieratic Papyri in the British Museum*, Third Series, Chester Beatty Gift (London: The British Museum, 1935), vol. 1, p. 20. Available at <academia.edu/8175912/hieratic_papyri_i_inthe_british_museum_i_i_i_a_i_v_i>.

11 Ibid., p. 9. Papyrus No. III of the Chester Beatty Collection in the British Museum, which bears the "followers of Seth" text, is part of a larger "Dream Book," a list of dream interpretations classified into good and bad (the word "bad" appears in red ink) and organized into two categories: the dreams of the followers of Horus, which account for the bulk of the list, and those of Seth's followers, of which only several are attested. Gardiner dated the text to the Twelfth Dynasty (2000–1790 BC). The years of Qenherkhopshef's birth and death are uncertain but those given here reflect his appearances in the available record.

12 The source for my description of the village and its workmen is Morris Bierbrier, *The Tomb-Builders of the Pharaohs* (Cairo: The American University in Cairo Press, 1982), pp. 18, 22–25, 27–30. There were several words for "bribe" in ancient Egyptian, including "a little something" and "bonus." See Pascal Vernus, *Affairs and Scandals in Ancient Egypt*, trans. David Lorton (Ithaca, NY: Cornell University Press, 2003), pp. 151–154.

13 For Paneb's exploits as described in the papyrus documents recovered from Deir el-Medina, see Pascal Vernus, *Affairs and Scandals*, pp. 70–86. Paneb was one of two foremen overseeing two tomb-building crews that varied in size at different times from 32 to 120 men. Paneb, who did not get on well with his colleague Hay, is on record as telling him, "I'll attack you on the mountain, and I'll kill you." See Vernus, p. 75.

14 Tombs were robbed throughout antiquity, but never as systematically as during the Twentieth Dynasty.

15 For the strikes, see Pascal Vernus, *Affairs and Scandals*, pp. 50–69.

16 T. Eric Peet, *The Great Tomb Robberies of the Twentieth Egyptian Dynasty* (Oxford: Clarendon Press, 1930), reissued in 2005 by Martino Publishing, based in Mansfield Center, Connecticut. The thieves' professions are mentioned in the translations of papyri depositions on pp. 107–109; lady raiders appear on pp. 132–133, 143; and raider slang for "loot," pp. 143, 149.

17 The cult of Seth was held in high regard in the Nineteenth and earlier Twentieth Dynasties (when Paneb operated and when tomb raiding became endemic). Herman te Velde, *Seth, God of Confusion*, p. 66.

18 A. J. Spencer, *Death in Ancient Egypt* (Harmondsworth, UK: Penguin, 1982), p. 88.

19 Ibid., pp. 106–108.

20 Herman te Velde, *Seth, God of Confusion*, p. 69.

ARTIST PROJECT / PARTICULATE PAPER RECORDS OF TIME

Chris Domenick

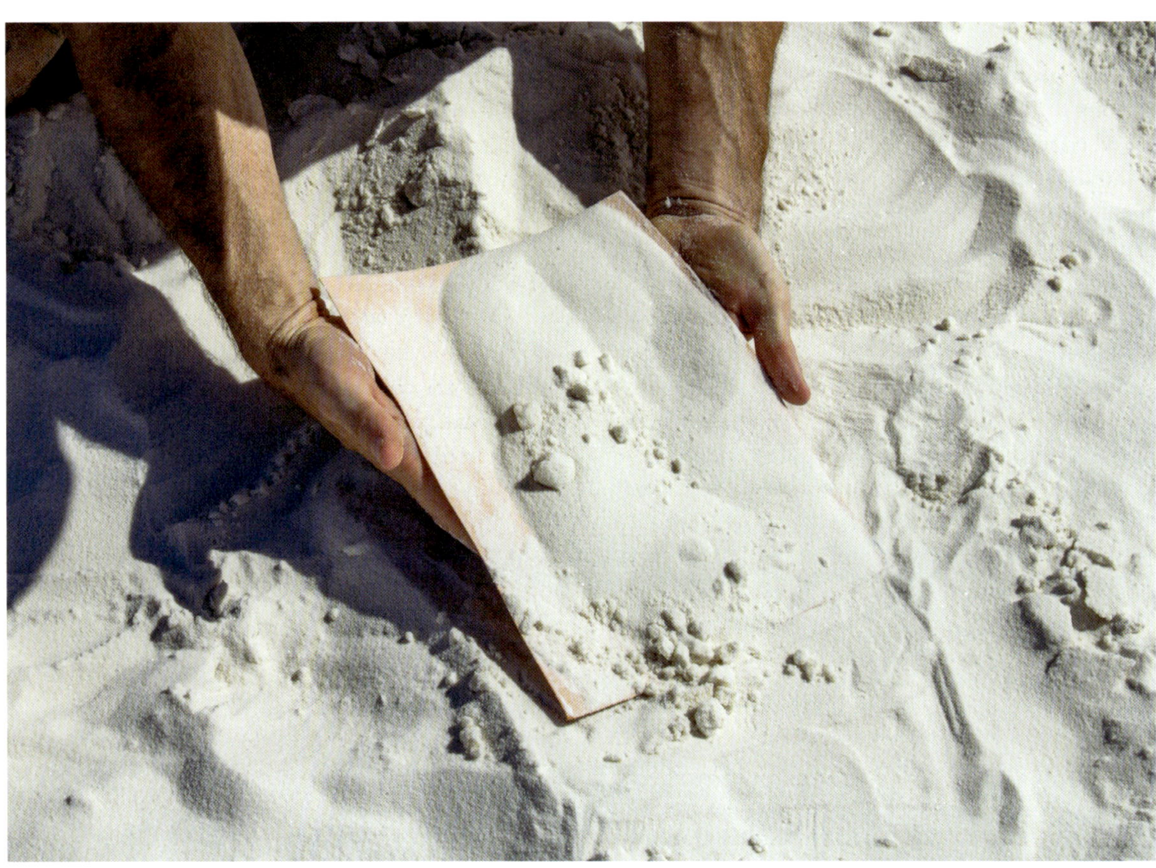

In the opening scene of Michelangelo Antonioni's 1975 film *The Passenger*, Jack Nicholson, a well-known journalist making a documentary on Chad's civil war, is in the Sahara. After a botched shoot, he returns to his hotel room and discovers that the Englishman with whom he had a brief friendship has died. Attempting to escape his marriage, career, and unfulfilled life, he steals the Englishman's identity and departs into what makes up the rest of the film. Best known for its penultimate scene in a different and yet similarly evocative desert landscape, *The Passenger* is a beautiful, lush, and desperate excavation of the existential implications of the loss of identity—at least as experienced by an American man wandering around Europe. Just three years earlier, Nicholson had appeared on a different sandy landscape, the beaches of Atlantic City, as the depressive brother of Bruce Dern, a con man with flawed real estate prospects, in *The King of Marvin Gardens*. In both films, the characters are perpetually on the brink of collapse, aided by, and in collaboration with, the landscape they inhabit. Beaches and deserts, albeit quite different in the social imagination, are linked by their physical makeup. Both are comprised of sand.

Sand is infinite, and miniscule. This is well known by members of the International Sand Collectors Society, who devote their time to sampling, sorting, and classifying their acquired collections. As their microscopy advisor Thomas J. Hopen writes, "A sand sample can be described in terms of grain size, color, composition, morphology (angularity and shape), and surface texture. Grain size is a result of several factors, including composition, durability, severity of

Above: Collecting sand at White Sands, New Mexico. Photo Chris Domenick.

weathering conditions, transport distance from its site of origin, and physical sorting by wind and/or water currents." These arenophiles, or sand lovers, point out that sand is a microcosm of geological transformation over time—a remnant of thousands of years of erosion and of the earth's perpetual changeability. Sand offers evidence of prehistoric volcanic explosions and points of meteoric impact, as well as traces of military conflict; it tells a prehistorical story and of a recent past. The sand on the beaches of Normandy now contains tiny, corroding fragments of shrapnel as well as glass and iron beads created by the heat from mortar explosions. The Allies' assault on D-Day is literally inscribed in its earth. Then there are the milk jugs, water bottles, diaper liners, toys, and Tupperware that not only litter our oceans and wash up on its beaches, but also have transformed into microscopic morsels now indistinguishable from the grains of sand we call "natural." Sand bears witness to the transformation of plastic utensils into coastline.

But think of the discomfort it may cause at a seaside resort on an aggressively windy day. On a recent trip with friends to the beach at Jacob Riis Park in Brooklyn, violent gusts of wind carried sand into every crevice of my bag, sandwich, and body. We had to leave the beach early, after only an hour. I wondered what effect the queerness of the beach might have on the physical makeup of the sand I rinsed out from between my butt cheeks later that day— perhaps on the straight beach, just south of Riis, you might encounter (unbeknownst to you) diaper or fecal particulate, while here at Riis beach your skin is more likely to come into contact with latex or a dislodged piece of body jewelry. But as is the case with all landscapes, the boundaries that differentiated these minerals from any others are ephemeral at best. Sand travels indiscriminately, and lines that get drawn in it are lost with the water or the wind. While on this journey, it may become ruinous; populating bike chains, iPhones, camera shutters, and eyeballs. It is, after all, its quality of perpetual mobility from which its symbolic power derives.

"The sands of time," the hourglass, a footprint: each evokes the passage of time and suggests that we are only brief insignificant events in an infinite expanse (though these metaphoric associations seem remote when chewing an unwashed piece of lettuce). The desert, as told by Antonioni and Nicholson, is equally complex. Depicted in films as a lawless space—and as the setting for, and spur to, psychological unraveling or psychedelic experience—the desert is off the grid, where one goes to get outside of oneself, voluntarily or not. It has been primarily white men, driven by an insatiable wanderlust, inexplicable necessity, or pre-existing social and economic conditions—Lawrence of Arabia, John Wayne, Clint Eastwood, Werner Herzog, Mad Max, Ralph Fiennes, and Daniel Day Lewis—who have perpetuated this understanding of the desert landscape through the lens of the West. Its tacit danger is an existential device.

Undisciplined as it is, sand also disciplines. It is a useful tool; manipulated with the utmost control, it shapes the objects that populate our surroundings. It smooths facades, polishes surfaces, finishes furniture, removes rough edges, and otherwise helps to disguise the unruliness and irregularity of other materials. On a job recently, I noticed an unusual scar on my coworker's arm. When I inquired about it, he explained that, with the guidance of a YouTube tutorial, he had spent forty-five minutes sanding off the skin that bore the marks of his first tattoo. For him, sandpaper was used to erase what would otherwise be a clear and possibly painful marker of the past.

Appropriately, sandpaper emerged at the moment that mass production, and the regularization that it entails, arose as an organizing social force. Despite recorded cases from as early as the first century AD of sharkskin, Coelacanth skin, and crushed shells and seeds glued with natural gum to parchment being used as abrasives, sandpaper is largely a product of the Industrial Revolution. It was in 1834 in Springfield, Vermont, that Isaac Fisher Jr. patented the first process for the mass manufacture of sandpaper. It is now made in jumbo rolls by a standardized process that supplies countless industries with the product.

Despite the name, most coated abrasive products are made from neither sand nor paper. Rather it is comprised of three parts: the abrasive, the adhesive, and the backing. Modern abrasive materials, although they share some of the characteristics of those found on the windy beach, vary depending on their application and include garnet, emery, aluminum oxide, silicon carbide, chromium oxide, and diamond grit, among others. Such material is industrially attached with resin-based adhesives; in some cases, the material is electrostatically charged so that all the abrasive particles line up in the same orientation. The backings are a variety of cloth, fiber, Mylar, and rubber, and are characterized by their flexibility, strength, and durability. As technologies continue to specialize, new customized approaches to production are used for burgeoning industries. As a result, sandpaper gets increasingly remote from its semantic origins.

The conventional narrative that industrialization follows a simple trajectory from the natural toward the artificial is complicated by the production of sandpaper. Though approximately 99 percent of abrasives used in the industry are industrially manufactured, the remaining 1 percent is mined from the earth. And synthetic abrasives are produced through processes that have been designed to simulate the chemistry of geological activity, specifically those processes that occur over extremely long periods of time. Despite the names that these minerals share with their real cousins, their origins and the economies through which they pass are very different. While African diamond mining operations exploit child laborers, General Electric employs chemists to experiment with nanotechnology and high-powered kilns to produce synthetic diamonds. In addition to its value as a rarefied commodity, diamond is the hardest material in the world and comes in handy in the abrasive industry. Today, used as a starter, a penny-sized natural diamond can be infinitely multiplied by simply adding methane and carbon dioxide within a hydrogen plasma reactor. This insane machine replicates the process that powers the sun.

Like the nomadic tendencies of sand, industrial materials travel (although we have yet to create universal metaphors that trace their paths). Instead of the wind or geological movement, sheet abrasives move through the world according to the logic of the global economy. Producing a standard abrasive requires several stages: extraction, production, distribution, consumption, and disposal. Take, for example, the mineral emery. Historically mined on the Greek island of Naxos, it is now often produced in a sintering furnace that can be purchased and transported globally. Once produced, it is sent to the German company Festool and manufactured into pristine sanding discs with materials and products (plastic, rubber, metal, etc.) originating from different parts of the world. These are then purchased by a construction company in Los Angeles. After the discs have been unpacked, assembled, and employed, they are used for a few days and discarded, moving on to either a waste-to-energy facility or a landfill for disposal. Maybe they will contribute to the famous island of trash in our Pacific Ocean, decomposing through their exposure to saltwater, or to the digestive enzymes of fish after being ingested. Like the formation of sand through the breakdown of mineral deposits within rocks, the harder aspects of these products remain intact after separating from their softer counterparts. By chance, the miniscule synthetic minerals will find their way to the beaches of Howland Island in the center of the Pacific, the site of Amelia Earhart's disappearance. Or maybe our emery particulates travel to a place without a name, sinking to the bottom of the ocean, later to appear on the surface of a desert in a spaghetti Western ten thousand years from now.

In the economy and in culture, real minerals continue to reign superior over their artificial counterparts. This is not only because of their scarcity and the laborious process of their extraction, but precisely because their origins can be traced to the inside of the earth itself—they are the geological miracles of mineral metamorphosis absent human intervention. Exemplified by the likes of Queen Victoria's Koh-i-Noor diamond, in culture, exchange value is not always determined by use value. In industry, that is not the case; it's good if it "gets the job done." This ideological hierarchy has particular relevance when we look closely at what actually composes the real in our material world. The more we use the environment, the more it is transformed into a by-product of that which once stood for its very opposite. The nature-culture dichotomy is no longer applicable. Rather, the picturesque pastoral becomes the fiction that hides the scars of industrialization, a seductive attempt to alleviate the cultural guilt that accompanies the violence of progress. Furthermore, that same bygone aesthetic admiration of landscape is what enabled Jack Nicholson to indulge in his untethered self in the remote Sahara. Our onscreen arbiters of individualized liberation embody the Western fetishization of the nomad. Historically mythologized by and in the figures of the pioneer and the lone explorer, these archetypes are characterized by a rejection of modern identities defined by global connectivity. And yet their real is equally mired in a misrepresentation of the spaces they inhabit. These places have names, political climates, social dynamics, and histories, most of which are eclipsed by the image of the white man alone on a dune.

This ideological manifestation of colonial enterprise does not stop on Earth. One of the most commonly applied abrasives is silicon carbide. Moissanite is the name given to this mineral in its naturally occurring state, named after the inventor Henri Moissan, who discovered it in the 1890s while examining rock samples from a meteor crater located in Canyon Diablo, Arizona. (He also designed the very first electric arc furnace to produce synthetic diamonds.) Despite its common use, moissanite is rarely found on earth. Yet it is incredibly abundant in space, found in meteorites and in the stardust surrounding carbon-rich stars. Recently, scientists have discovered that this free-floating cosmic dust contains remnants of complex organic compounds produced by stars. Like sand, stardust is inscribed with the events of its formation; once a part of a comet or meteorite or earth's ancient atmosphere, this stuff meanders across the universe and contributes to the creation of new stars. To explore this matter, the NASA mission Stardust sent a spacecraft to Comet Wild 2 on a seven-year journey that ended in 2006. Its goal was to trail behind Wild 2 and, using an ultralight substance called aerogel, gather the material that the comet left behind. The mission yielded a sample of comet dust stored in aerogel that can fit in the palm of your hand. These intergalactic arenophiles hope to learn something about the origins of the universe. Meanwhile, on Earth, using industrial furnaces and small atomic explosions in isolated chambers, we are recreating this cosmic sand in order to polish the surfaces of our furniture and automobiles. Inscribed in its surface lie the unwieldy stories that we are constantly generating as writers and actors of Western mythologies. Like Jack Nicholson in *The Passenger*, we're on the run, flanked by the guilt of our privilege, dogged by an existential drive to wander, driven to do more, and see more, changing, degrading, and regenerating ourselves all the while. The camera slow pans across the empty desert landscape.

• • •

Since 2011, I have been collecting sand from beaches and deserts. Using jade glue (a pH-neutral glue often used in bookbinding processes) as the adhesive, this sand is flocked to the surface of individual sheets of paper that are painted the beige color of sandpaper. On the verso is a simulated screen-printed image of the back of a manufactured sheet of sandpaper produced by 3M, including company logo, trademark, place of origin (often, Made in Canada), and grit size. Each sheet is labeled in pencil with the date and location of the sand's acquisition. The project began as a re-creation of this utilitarian object, a play on the semantics of its constituent materials (a true semantic equivalent, you might say), as well as a way of documenting a given site. It has become an ongoing personal travelogue of sand-based landscapes. The sheets live in a box reminiscent of the sandpaper storage bin of a craftsman, with each slot labeled by year (rather than grit number). The box speaks to my own history; a full 2013 slot is evidence of the extensive traveling I did that year. The empty slot has recorded the fact that I visited not one beach or desert in 2015, a blank entry in this sculptural diary. One noteworthy piece of sandpaper was made on the beaches of the Salton Sea and is covered in sand made up of thousands of ground-up fish bones, the remnants of a deadly man-made environmental disaster. I often wonder how many plastic bits might have blended into the sands and are now stored in the box. This project will continue indefinitely, with new boxes built for new decades, documenting the physical transformation of our landscape.

The project would surely offend the committed arenophile; the details of the sand have been stripped of their physical and geological qualities and contextualized as utilitarian bits. The record of the site remains, imported into the form of this industrial object whose tacit wanderlust is inscribed in its identity as a global *flâneur*. The labeled names of these sites are but a microcosmic representation of the places from which the sand is collected. They replace the complex identity of the site—its politics, geography, sociological attributes, etc.—with a flattened version of itself, one that reflects the collector's projected desire; albeit metaphorically, this collection underlies a colonialist ideology of spatial expansion and domination. One day I may be a proud owner of the sand of a Bermuda beach! Insofar as this project documents the loss, substitution, and change in identities that are occurring in the world at large, the poetic pessimism of this transformation is written in the sand in the shape of an Adidas footprint. How long will it take for me to recognize that the footprint is my own?

Sandy Beach, Acadia, Maine, 2013 (recto and verso).

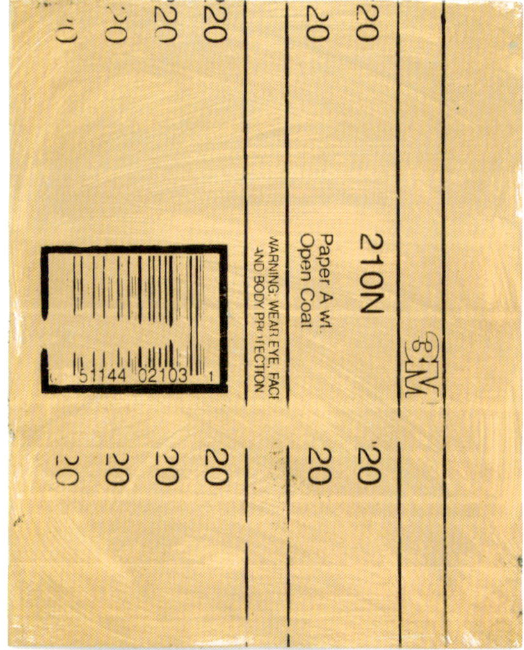

Avalon, New Jersey, 2014 (recto and verso).

White Sands, New Mexico, 2016 (recto and verso).

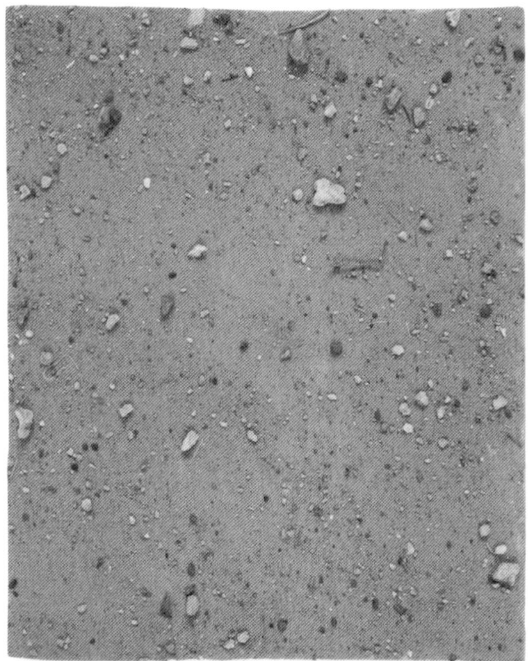

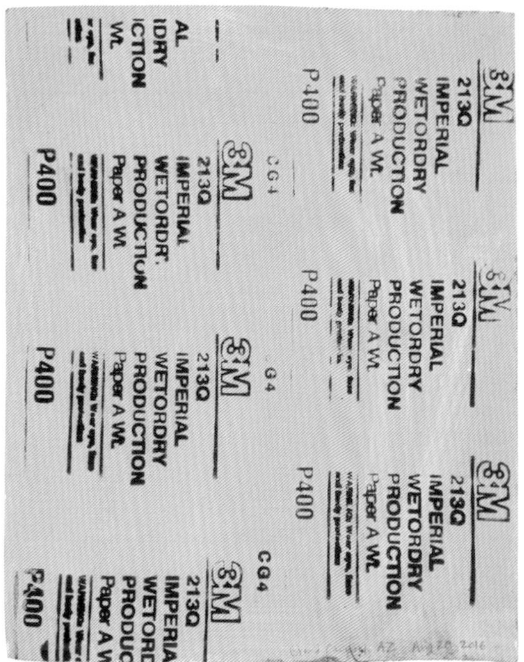

Grand Canyon, Arizona, 2016 (recto and verso).

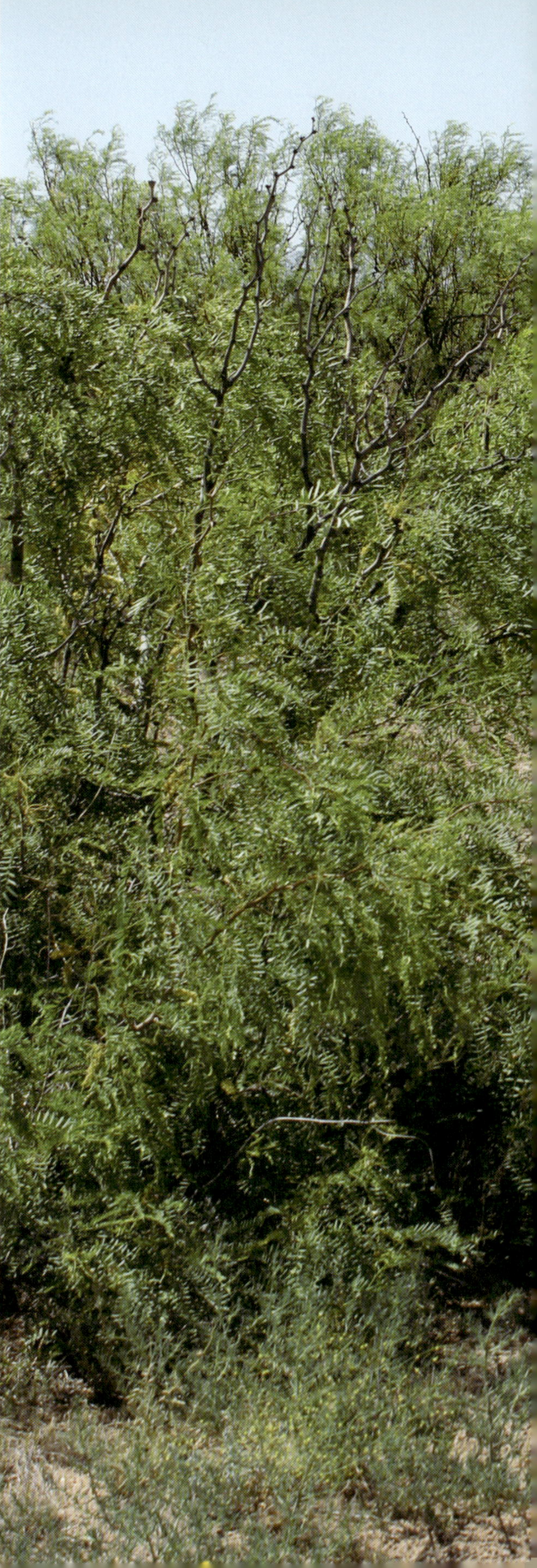

The desert always wins. This mailbox, proudly installed in 2003 on Cabinetlandia—a half-acre of scrubland purchased by the magazine the previous year outside Deming, New Mexico—had already been humbled by the desert by June 2010, when *Cabinet* contributors Melissa Dubbin and Aaron Davidson visited the site and documented the ruin. But the desert was not content to mock our postal fantasies; according to a recent report from subscriber Bob Dorsey, the entire site is currently inaccessible. Updates to follow.

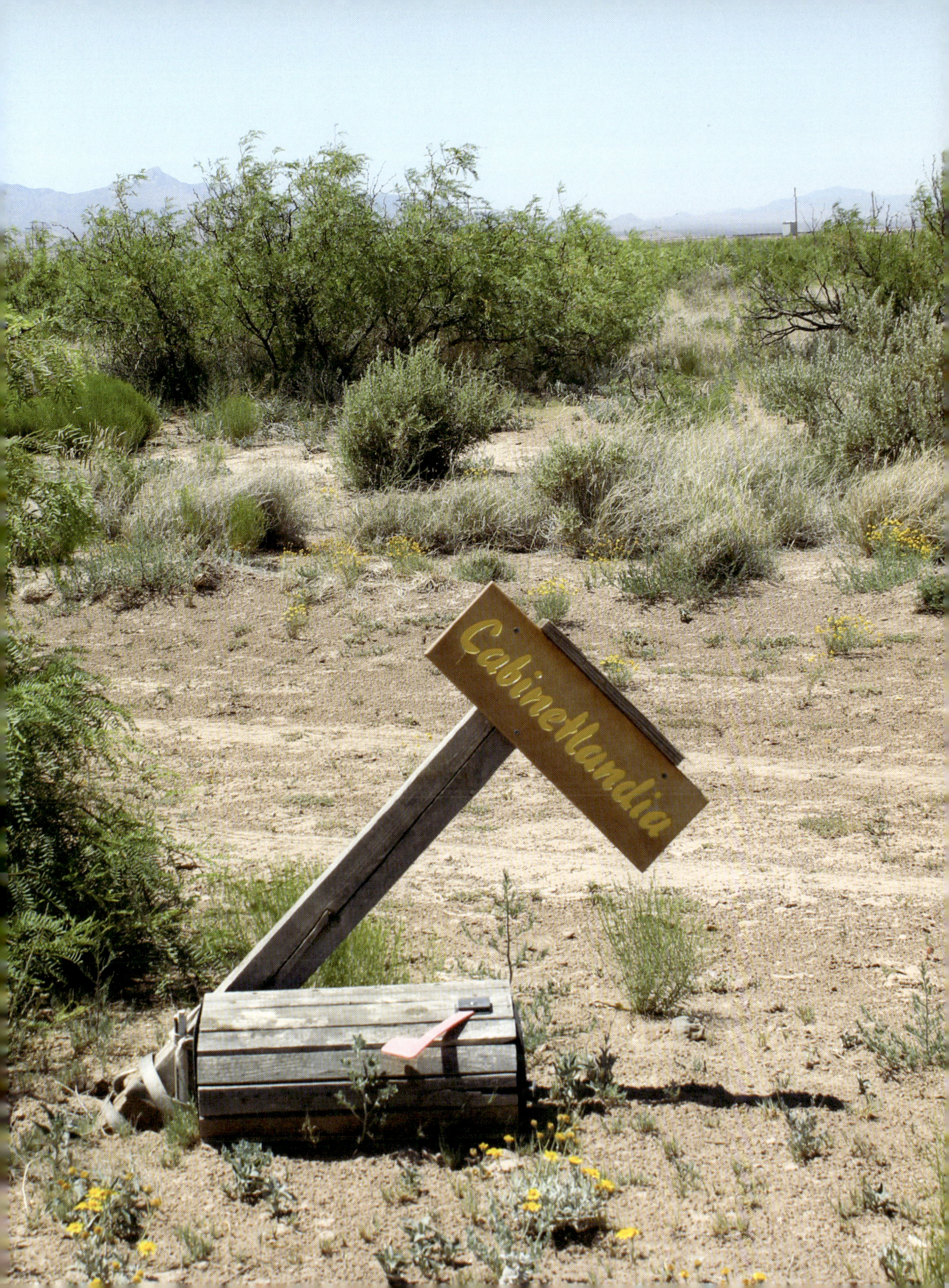
Cabinetlandia

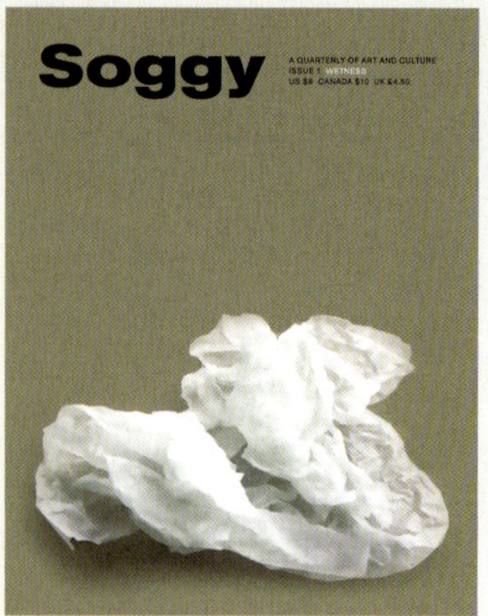

Imagine your name is Ralph. One day, when you are seventeen years old, your mother tells you that you had almost been named Alger. You are crushed, but then, to your surprise, you slowly recover by imagining what life would have been like as an Alger. A similarly introspective mood has pervaded the *Cabinet* office since a recent bout of spring cleaning unearthed a long-forgotten list of the names that were under consideration for this magazine as it was being conceived in 1999. (See this issue's "Inventory" column.) What would life have been like as *Soggy*? Would you have subscribed to *The Wedge*? The most uncanny thought experiments, however, were the result of seeing titles that recalled those of other publications. One of the names we came up with wasn't just close to that used by another magazine; unbeknownst to us, it was identical. *Might* had in fact been a little magazine published in San Francisco between 1994 and 1997. But by far the most transporting names were those that predicted, entirely inadvertently, the titles of magazines-to-be. If we'd plumped for *n*, would we have ended up more like the peerless *n+1*? Would naming ourselves *And...* have destined us to be more like the excellent, and now sadly defunct, *Dot Dot Dot*? *The Friend*–stolen from Coleridge, who ran a magazine of the same name–would probably have fated us to be more genial like *The Believer*. Had we chosen *Omnivore*, we would surely have become like the lamentably short-lived journal of the same name. And *Mixer*? Its proximity to the music magazine *Blender* suggests.... Enough! *Ralph* we have been for seventeen years, and *Ralph* we will remain.

You will have noticed in the above fantasy that magazine titles are always italicized. As are books, films, plays, artworks, and albums. But not poems, short stories, songs, or essays, which only get to be comforted by double quotes. The worst novel is italicized, but Flaubert's story "A Simple Heart" is not. So, italicization is not a gauge of the quality of an individual artifact, but a marker of the category to which it belongs. But this simple formatting decision does seem to drag in with it a certain amount of gravitas, to privilege certain forms of cultural expression. We've recently been pulling our hair out over the question of whether or not to italicize video games. Some publications, for example, *London Review of Books*, do; others, such as *The New Yorker*, do not. One way to think about this question is to ask: Are video games more like films, or more like games? No game–even one as intellectually complex as chess or Go–is italicized. But perhaps making a video game is more akin to making a movie. This would be a value-neutral judgment, one centered on the mode of production rather than any intrinsic artistic value. But it remains the case that video games have users, not spectators; they are meant to be played, rather than watched. And so, drum roll, for the purposes of our own stylesheet, we have decided to leave video games unitalicized, where they can hang out in the same pasture as such classics as Monopoly, backgammon, poker, and Gas Crisis.

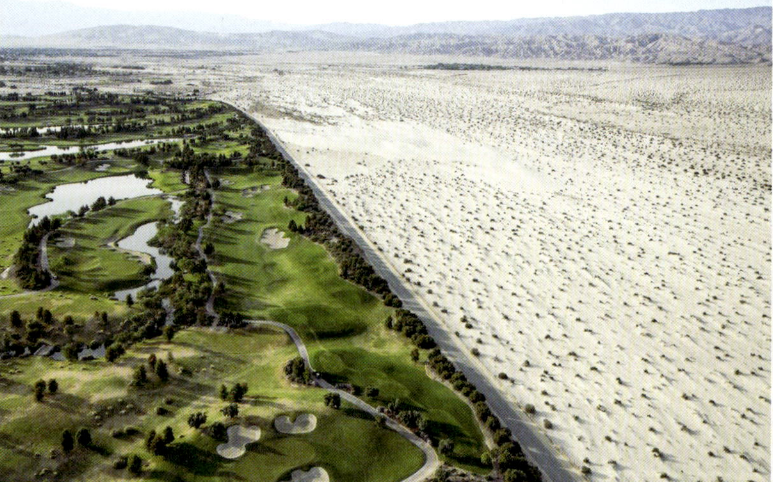

Speaking of petroleum products, we all know that America's worst enemies congregate in arid, oil-soaked wastelands close to the equator. At least that's the opinion of one Randy Voepel, a *homo "sapiens"* who is a legislator in the California State Assembly. While running last fall for the seat he currently occupies, Voepel hailed accelerating climate change for its potentially deleterious effect on Muslim-majority nations he deems unfriendly to US interests. "Most of the Muslim nations are in the hot areas of the world," he told reporters, an "observation" he elaborated upon in a later interview: "It will probably have a negative effect on their environment." Given that the American desert is inexorably creeping into Voepel's district in Southern California, it's likely that the climate change he is cheering on will soon bring the sand dunes he imagines are a signifier of Muslim backwardness to his own front door.

As the parching of the area under Assemblymember Voepel's "stewardship" ramps up over the coming years, he will need to offer his constituency alternative options for transportation better suited to the approaching dunescape. One place to start would be with the story of George H. Crosman and Henry C. Wayne. (See "Tales of Desert Nomads" in *Cabinet* no. 21.) Crosman and Wayne were a pair of American military officers who in 1855—in the aftermath of the Mexican-American War, much of which was fought in harsh desert conditions—convinced then-Secretary of War Jefferson Davis to found the so-called Camel Corps. Using an allocation of thirty thousand dollars, the army imported over the following years more than seventy camels from North Africa and installed them at a place they had built to house them in south-central Texas called Camp Verde (memorialized recently in the above mural painted on the side of a lumber company in the nearby town of Ingram). The army had the intention of using the animals for both troop and supply transport in the Southwest, and by many reports the animals performed ably, but the experiment was short-lived. Camp Verde was taken over by the Confederate Army at the beginning of the Civil War in 1861 and the bulk of the camels were eventually sold to zoos and carnivals, although a number were simply abandoned or escaped into the surrounding wilderness.

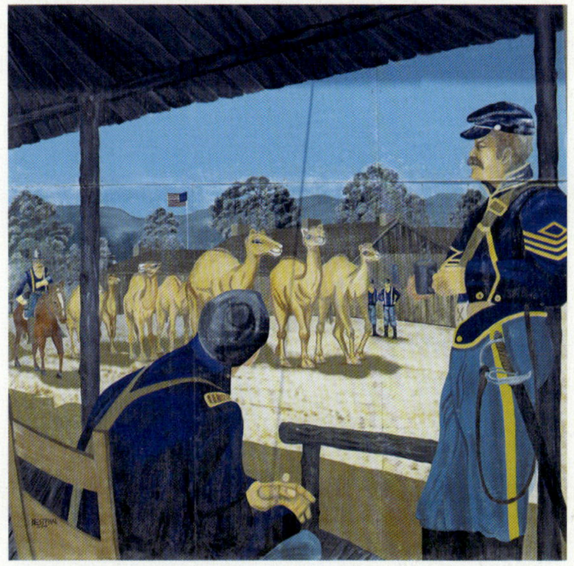

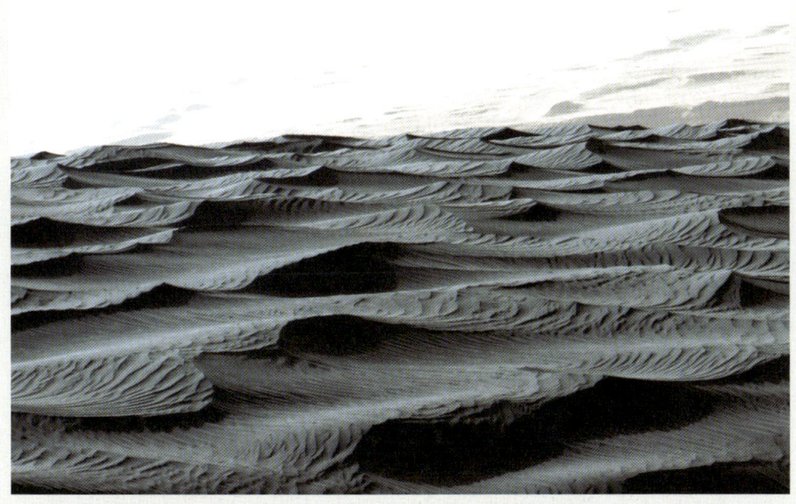

While rummaging around in the sand for ideas for this issue, one of our colleagues alerted us to the fascinating figure of Brigadier Ralph Alger Bagnold, the founder of the British Army's Long Range Desert Group, a unit that played an important role in the Allied effort in North Africa during World War II. (That wrecked Chevy truck on pages 58–59 of this issue was one of his.) But years before the war, Bagnold had already begun a life of deep engagement with the desert sands. Taking a degree in engineering from Cambridge after serving in the Great War, Bagnold returned to active duty in 1921, serving in India and then Egypt, where he explored the surrounding deserts with an eye to determining what sorts of vehicles and maneuvers were most effective for negotiating dunes. It was not, however, just vehicular transportation in the desert that fascinated Bagnold, but also the transportation of its most familiar element: sand. His investigations of dune structures–so influential on later scientific work that Mars boasts a Bagnold Dune Field, shown here–were based on close studies of the three ways in which wind moves sand in the desert: saltation, suspension, and creep. Oh, hi Randy!

e-flux

HOW TO ORDER

1. Mail a check to Cabinet, 300 Nevins Street, Brooklyn, NY 11217, USA.
2. Shop online at <cabinetmagazine.org/shop>.
3. Call +1 718 222 8434.
4. Fax +1 718 222 3700.

Checks, made out to "Cabinet," must be in USD and drawn on a US bank. We also accept Visa, MC, AmEx, Discover, and Paypal (paypal@cabinetmagazine.org). Prices valid till 1 December 2017. Visit <cabinetmagazine.org> to view our limited and unlimited editions, posters, and other tchotchkes.

A SELECTION OF OUR BOOKS.
VISIT OUR ONLINE SHOP FOR MORE.
Prices include postage.

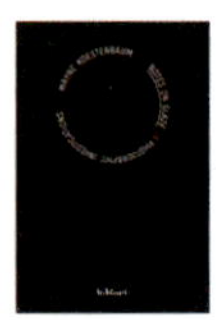

Notes on Glaze
A collection featuring all 18 of Wayne Koestenbaum's "Legend" columns, as well as an introduction by the author.

US $25
Elsewhere $28
(Subscriber discount: -$7)

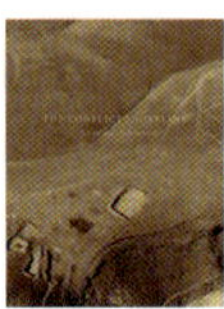

The Conflict Shoreline: Colonialism as Climate Change
Eyal Weizman's analysis of climate change as a political tool used to displace the Bedouins in the Negev Desert.

US $33
Elsewhere $40
(Subscriber discount: -$7)

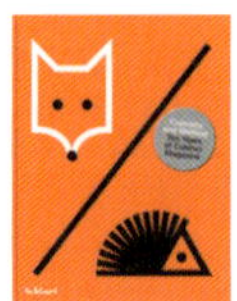

Curiosity and Method: Ten Years of Cabinet Magazine
An encyclopedia with entries culled from the first 10 years of *Cabinet*.

US $41
Canada & Europe $57
Elsewhere $63
(Subscriber discount: -$5)

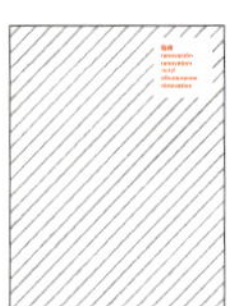

Renovation
Photographer Nancy Davenport's visual meditation on the recent overhaul of the United Nations' headquarters.

US $32
Elsewhere $48
(Subscriber discount: -$7)

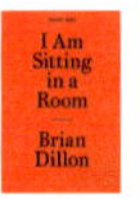

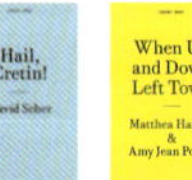

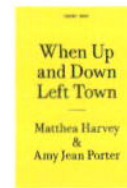

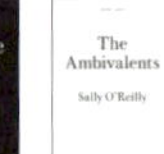

The first 5 volumes in our "24-Hour Book" series: *I Am Sitting in a Room* by Brian Dillon; *Hail, Cretin!* by David Scher; *When Up and Down Left Town* by Matthea Harvey & Amy Jean Porter; *Take Care* by Jeff Dolven; and *The Ambivalents* by Sally O'Reilly.

US $15 (Harvey & Porter: $12)
Canada $16 (Harvey & Porter: $14)
Elsewhere $20 (Harvey & Porter: $17)
(Subscriber discount: -$2)

A SELECTION OF OUR BACK ISSUES.
VISIT OUR ONLINE SHOP FOR MORE.
Available back issues are $10 each plus postage. Postage rates: US $2 per issue; Elsewhere $7 per issue, $17 for 3 issues.

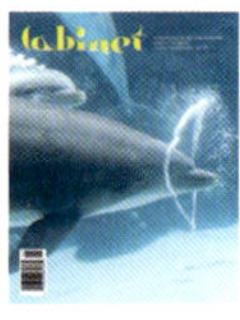
Issue 37
Bubbles

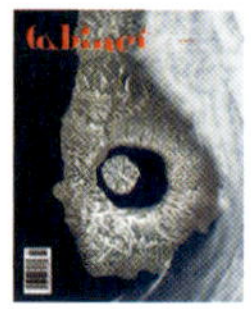
Issue 38
Islands

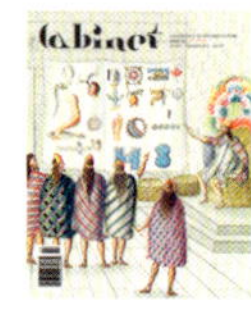
Issue 39
Learning

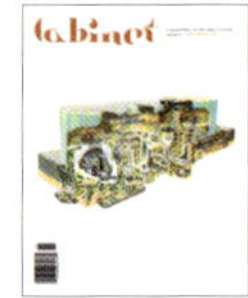
Issue 41
Infrastructure

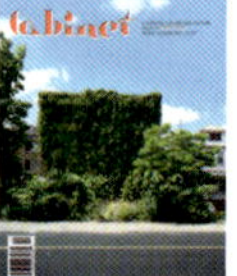
Issue 42
Forgetting

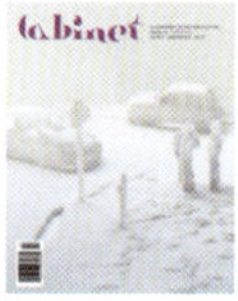
Issue 43
Forensics

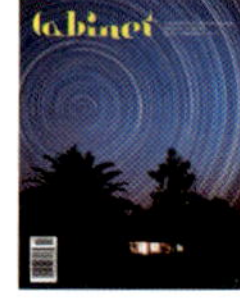
Issue 44
24 Hours

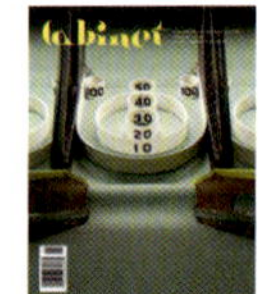
Issue 45
Games

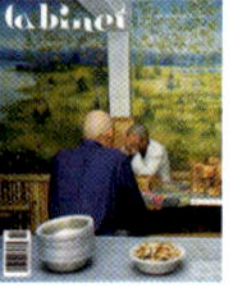
Issue 46
Punishment

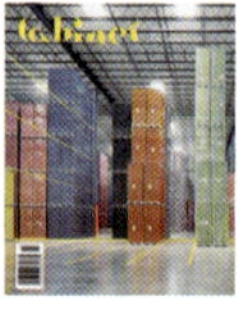
Issue 47
Logistics

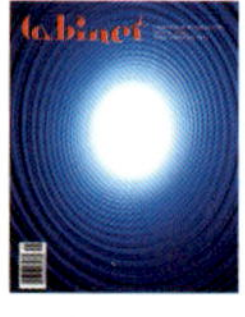
Issue 49
Death

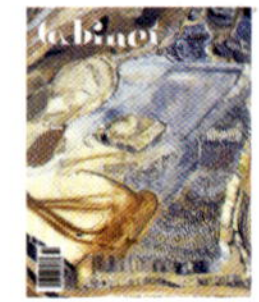
Issue 50
Money

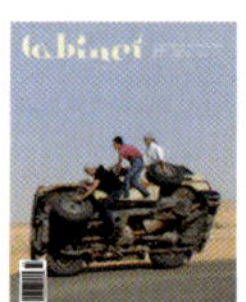
Issue 51
Wheels

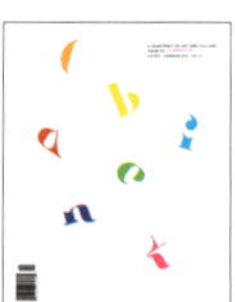
Issue 52
Celebration

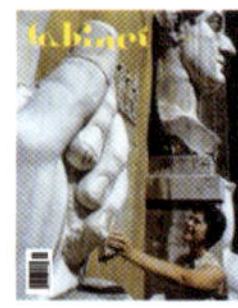
Issue 53
Stones

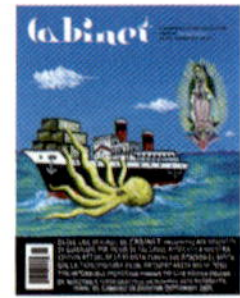
Issue 54
The Accident

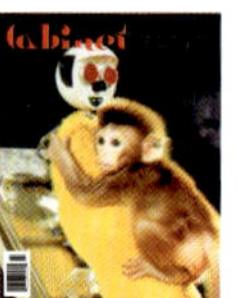
Issue 55
Love

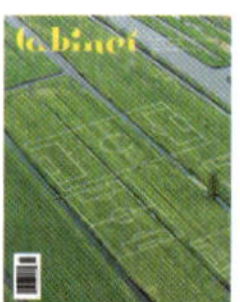
Issue 56
Sports

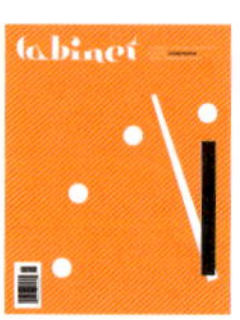
Issue 57
Catastrophe

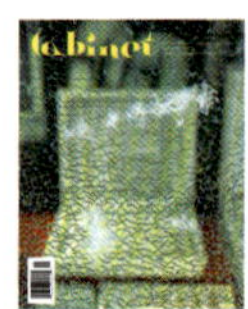
Issue 58
Theft

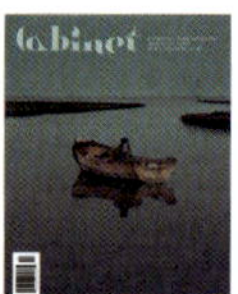
Issue 59
The North

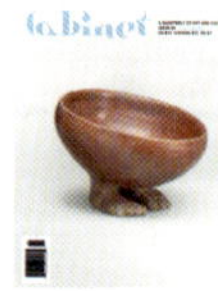
Issue 60
Containers

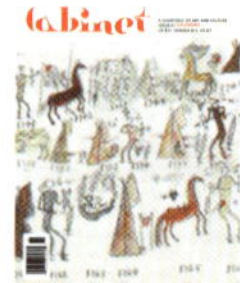
Issue 61
Calendars

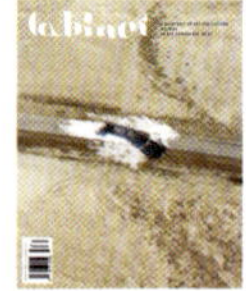
Issue 62
Milk